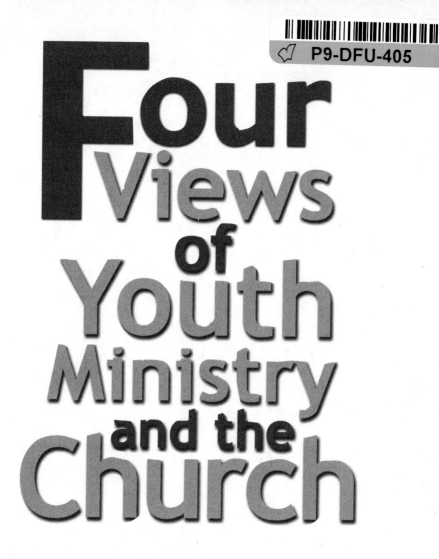

Four Views of Youth Ministry and the Church

Inclusive congregational

Preparatory

Missional

Strategic

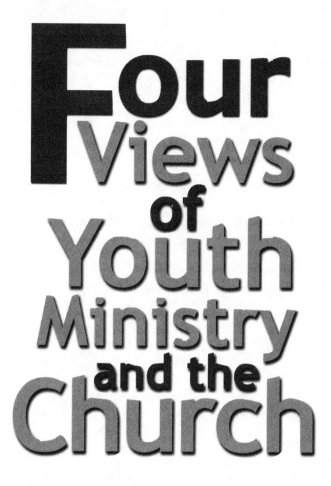

Four Views of Youth Ministry and the Church

Inclusive congregational

Preparatory

Missional

Strategic

Mark H. Senter III

Wesley Black

Chap Clark

Malan Nel

YOUTH
SPECIALTIES

ACADEMIC

ZondervanPublishingHouse
Grand Rapids, Michigan

A Division of HarperCollins*Publishers*

Four Views of Youth Ministry and the Church: Inclusive congregational, preparatory, missional, strategic

Copyright © 2001 by Mark H. Senter III

Youth Specialties Books, 300 S. Pierce St., El Cajon, CA 92020, are published by Zondervan Publishing House, 5300 Patterson Ave. S.E., Grand Rapids, MI 49530.

Library of Congress Cataloging-In-Publication Data

Four views of youth ministry and the church : inclusive congregational, preparatory, missional, strategic / Mark Senter III ... [et al.]
    p. cm.
    Includes bibliographical references and index.
    ISBN 0-310-23405-0
    1. Church work with youth. I. Senter, Mark.

BV4447 .F68 2001
259'.23—dc21

00-043937

Unless otherwise indicated, all Scripture quotations are taken from the *Holy Bible: New International Version* (North American Edition). Copyright © 1973, 1978, 1984 by International Bible Society. Used by permission of Zondervan Publishing House.

Edited by Tim McLaughlin
Cover and interior design by Razdezignz

Printed in the United States of America

01 02 03 04 05 06 07 / / 10 9 8 7 6 5 4 3 2

To my father, Mark H. Senter, whose ministry shaped my understanding of youth ministry and the church.

—M. H. S. III

About the Authors

Mark Senter (Ph.D., Loyola University Chicago) is associate professor of educational ministries at Trinity Evangelical Divinity School. Prior to Trinity he served in the field of Christian education and youth ministries for 18 years. Senter is author of several books—*Recruiting Volunteers in the Church, The Complete Book of Youth Ministry* (coeditor), *The Coming Revolution in Youth Ministry,* and *Reaching a Generation for Christ* (coeditor)—and a frequent contributor to youth ministry journals and magazines.

Wesley Black (Ph.D., Southwestern Baptist Theological Seminary) has been in youth ministry for more than three decades and has taught at Southwestern Baptist Theological Seminary since 1983, where he serves as professor of youth/student ministry and departmental chair. He is the author of *An Introduction to Youth Ministry.* He has also contributed to numerous books, journals, and magazines, including *Living with Teenagers, Youth Ministry Update, Group, DiscipleNow Manual,* and *Evangelical Dictionary of Christian Education.*

A 25-year youth ministry veteran, **Chap Clark** (Ph.D., University of Denver) teaches at Fuller Theological Seminary, where he is associate professor of youth and family ministries as well as director of youth ministry programs. Clark is also executive administrator at Glendale Presbyterian Church. His books include *The Youth Worker's Handbook to Family Ministry, Daughters and Dads,* and the youth curriculum *Creative Bible Lessons in Romans.*

Since 1964 **Malan Nel** (D.D., University of Pretoria) has been involved in the youth ministry of South Africa, as youth director for the Synod of Natal and for the Dutch Reformed Church of South Africa. For the last two decades, he has been professor in youth ministry and Christian education at Vista University; he is currently the head of the division for contextual ministry there. Malan is an executive member of the International Association for the Study of Youth Ministry, editor of the planned journal of that association, and editor of *Journal: Practical Theology in South Africa.* Nel's publishing credits include nearly 70 professional articles and books—among them an English translation of an Afrikaans volume, under the title *Youth Ministry: An Inclusive Congregational Approach.*

Contents

Acknowledgments

For years I have been concerned that we in the field of youth ministry are talking to ourselves without paying attention to what we are saying. To make matters worse, no one else in related academic and ministry fields seems to be listening either. Perhaps one reason for the mute conversation has to do with the quality of youth ministry literature. Most of it is designed for college sophomores or youth ministers in the early stages of their ministries.

As the field of youth ministry matures, we have a need for thoughtful books that engage deeper issues and connect with other academic disciplines. Students in master's degree programs and thoughtful practitioners need and deserve literature that stretches their minds and questions their basic assumptions about the field.

When I approached Youth Specialties about creating a line of issue-oriented books, they took a risk. Assuming the proposed books would not be as popular as *Purpose-Driven Youth Ministry* or *Student Ministry for the 21st Century*, the publisher nevertheless expressed a willingness to serve the field of youth ministry by publishing *Four Views of Youth Ministry and the Church*. Hopefully other publishers—and books—will follow.

I am profoundly grateful to Wesley Black, Chap Clark, and Malan Nel for their sacrificial cooperation in meeting the deadlines that made this book possible. Our cyberspace collaboration spanned four continents at times, yet deadlines were rarely missed. Each person responded promptly and creatively.

I appreciate Trinity Evangelical Divinity School and its generous sabbatical policy for allowing me to use part of my sabbatical to complete this book.

Thanks go to Nicola Hollis, Yoshito Noguchi, Dale Rakebrandt, Brian Schwammlein, and Anita Traum, my initial focus group (also called a class) who read and critiqued the early manuscripts. They threw the writing behind schedule with their insightful comments.

Of course I must express my appreciation to my wife, Ruth, for sharing office space without seeking to read my writings, thus keeping our marriage in proper perspective.

Mark H. Senter III
November 2000

Of Churches, Youth Groups, and Spiritual Readiness: The Context of the Debate

High school football games were wonderful venues to do relational youth ministry. Half the kids there had absolutely no interest in football. "Just here to see my friends," they often said. Even though I would have preferred to watch the game, I could hang out by the concession stand and talk to a cross section of high school students as they drifted by me. It was also a natural place to meet parents, faculty, and school administrators.

The Saturday afternoon gathering at Ost Field was a ministry opportunity made to order. Kids expected adults to show up in this part of their world. Because they were comfortable with us, introductions to their friends seemed natural. Contacts that started near the concession stand led to conversations in the halls of Palatine High School, at McDonalds, on the phone, at a Young Life club, and occasionally while standing in the narthex at Arlington Heights Evangelical Free Church.

As the stadium emptied, two youth ministers stood on the torn sod of the gridiron, reflecting on their conversations of the afternoon. Cliff Anderson, the former math teacher, had found his niche as a Young Life staffer at the high school where he used to teach. I served as youth pastor in a nearby church. Two distinctly different starting points, one common passion.

"My problem," I confessed, "is that I cannot find enough football-game-type situations for me and my staff to establish significant relationships with non-Christian kids."

"And my problem," responded Cliff without missing a beat, "is that I cannot find churches where my club kids feel welcome enough to attend on a regular basis, even after they return from camp." For my Young Life colleague, camp was frequently a spiritual watershed which should have resulted in new believers flowing into churches in their home communities.

Meanwhile back at the church

A few years later a large church in the Sun Belt asked me to serve as their minister to youth. Professionally it looked like a great opportunity. Ruth and I were treated royally when we candidated there. The ministry opportunities appeared endless. Resources were plentiful. Their tradition of youth ministry was well established.

But there was something missing.

I returned home and agonized over a decision for weeks. I could not put my finger on the missing piece, but it wasn't fair to either my church or the Sun Belt church to drag my decision out any longer. And it was during a mile-and-a-half walk one Sunday evening, in quiet and in prayer, that the missing piece became brilliantly clear. This nationally known church did not see young people as a vital part of the church. Unless, of course, I could condition some very bright young people to sit passively and be entertained by professionally crafted worship services. What they were looking for was an in-house parachurch agency. Their invitation was based on a flawed doctrine of the church.

Youth culture and church culture

The Ost Field discourse and that Sunday night walk framed two tensions in the discussion of youth ministry and the church. Both involve a clash of cultures. How can youth ministry respond both to the youth culture and culture of the church? How can young people be vitally connected to the church both now and in the future?

For many church members the first issue revolves around lifestyle. Young believers bring with them the baggage of their prefaith lives. Language, dress, tastes in entertainment, humor, relationships between the sexes, possible use of tobacco and drugs—all these wave red flags to the godly people of the church who are convinced that the faith community must strive for biblical norms in every aspect of life.

By contrast, adolescent believers—especially recent converts—find the church culture to be a foreign land. Language, customs, rites, heritage, musical styles—even intergenerational awkwardness—create barriers that discourage all but occasional forays into the foreignness of the adult church.

Issues related to maturity and life stages define the second question. At what age should young people be considered ready for baptism? For full membership? For leadership positions? What criteria should be used to determine the readiness of a young person to teach or preach? To evangelize? To make decisions that will affect age groups other than their own?

But are the questions of the relationship between youth ministry and the church based in sociology and developmentalism? Yes, partly. Yet the issues are far more complex. Solving the sociological problem may be possible only when more complicated missiological and theological questions about the nature of the church are resolved

What is the church?

An architectural structure or a group of worshipers? A denomination or a local fellowship of Christian believers? Is its focus primarily on community, mission, or worship? Does the church require people in leadership to be ordained by prescribed formal procedures, or does it informally recognize believers whose Christian lives have been shaped in the course of ministry? Is there such a thing as a parachurch ministry or are all ministries an expression of the church? Must the church be intergenerational or could it be age-group specific?

Unlike the development of most Christian teachings, the doctrine of the church has never received the kind of attention and debate that could result in a clear definition and explanation of the nature of the church. Millard Erickson comments:

> **At the first assembly of the World Council of Churches in Amsterdam in 1948, Father George Florovsky claimed that the doctrine of the church had hardly passed its pre-theological phase. By contrast, Christology and the doctrine of the Trinity had been given special attention in the fourth and fifth centuries, as had the atoning work of Christ in the Middle Ages, and the doctrine of salvation in the sixteenth century. But such concerted attention has never been turned to the church.[1]**

Youth ministry is filled with pretheological ecclesiology. From its beginning in the late eighteenth and early nineteenth centuries, youth ministry has had an inside-out and outside-in relationship to the church. Usually nonordained Christians went out to the young people in an effort to bring them to faith in Jesus Christ. The Sunday school, YMCA, Youth for Christ, and Young Life movements were all inside-out ministries, at least in their beginning stages. Where Christian faith was closely associated with church attendance, the outside-in progression was assumed, and oftentimes freshly converted adolescent believers found a home in the church. De facto sociology linked with a pretheology of the church allowed youth movements to flourish while simultaneously sowing seeds of confusion as to where mission ended and church began.

Local or universal?

One reason youth ministers find it difficult to forge an ecclesiology of youth ministry is because in the New Testament the word *church* is applied to situations ranging from small groups or house churches (Romans 16:5; 1 Corinthians 16:19), to all of the believers in an entire city (1 Corinthians 1:2; 1 Thessalonians 1:1), to the Christians throughout an entire region (Acts 9:31), and beyond that to the universal church, all followers of Christ from all nations and all generations (Hebrews 12:23).

This is further complicated by nonbelievers' attendance. While Roman Catholic, Orthodox, and Protestant understandings of the nature of the church differ, all would agree that not everyone who is physically present at a worship service is considered to be a true member of the church. There are sheep and there are goats (Matthew 25:31-46). There is wheat and there are weeds (Matthew 13:24-30). While the Heavenly Father knows the difference between the faith community and the world, pastors and youth ministers have a difficult time distinguishing between them and in the end they must rely on their Spirit-led perceptions as to which is which.

In some cases unbelief is found among adult participants, leaving the believing youths of the church to serve as witnesses of faith. Of course the opposite is true as well, where the adults must pass the faith to the younger generation.

What is worship?

Most church leaders will agree to a threefold to sixfold purpose of the church. For the purposes of this book, the authors have followed Wayne Grudem's description of purposes: ministry to God, ministry to believers, and ministry to the world.[2]

Ultimately the church is a worshiping community. The chief end of man, says the Westminster Shorter Catechism, is to "glorify God and enjoy him forever." While participation in church will satisfy many human needs, the ultimate purpose of the faith community is to lift people's eyes from their human condition and fix them on the Creator-Redeemer.

In order to be a healthy part of the church, youth ministry needs to facilitate all three purposes among the adolescents of the body of Christ. Teaching and fellowship have traditionally taken precedence in church-based ministries, while evangelism and fellowship activities dominated parachurch youth ministries. In recent years, however, more time has been designated for worship in both contexts, where worship has become synonymous with praise songs and prayer. Yet the question must be raised: is this what God intended worship to be?

A century of resistance

Unfortunately, church leaders throughout the 20th century resisted allowing their young people to become full participants in accomplishing the purposes of the church. Writing in 1917, Frank Otis Erb cites criticism of the Christian Endeavor movement, stating that its denominational counterparts were "without scriptural authority and usurping the place of the church, which alone had divine authority."

> **It was greatly feared that [youth work] would divide the church on the basis of age, and supplant the church in the affection of the young. It was declared by many that it interfered seriously with other church meetings, particularly the Sunday evening preaching service, usually evangelistic, and the midweek prayer meeting. Many feared that [Christian Endeavor] would divert the young people's money from denominational channels and**

would lead to haphazard giving and a lack of interest in the causes to which the church and denomination were pledged.[3]

What fearful church leaders failed to realize was that an age-related division had already taken place in the church. Attempts by Francis Clark, founder of Christian Endeavor, and his denominational counterparts were simply a rearguard action. An 1875 Supreme Court decision to allow public tax dollars to fund high school education laid the groundwork for what would become known as the youth culture. By 1920 a third of the population between the ages of 14 and 17 gathered daily in the high schools of America.[4] The church had no choice but to respond to this dramatic social change.

Churches should have seen the explosive potential that young people brought to the body of Christ. During the previous 26 years (1886-1912), college students involved in the student volunteer movement provided a dramatic corrective to the spiritual apathy of church leaders in America and the United Kingdom, sending 7,265 volunteers into foreign missionary service and profoundly influencing American church life.[5]

Church leaders viewed youth ministry as mere preparation for future leadership. Youth societies became holding tanks where youthful zeal could be channeled into harmless activities. Developing skills in churchmanship overshadowed the professed desires of pastors for evangelism, character development, and Christian service. The explosive power of youthful Christian idealism wasted away in a series of youth society meetings and related committee assignments. Churches, both liberal and conservative, settled into an uneasy slide toward religion defined by a social agenda rather than by the power of God. If young people were to become full participants in local churches, then the young people would have to change.

Twice during the middle of the 20th century, youths led concerted efforts to break free of the stranglehold of church polity and tradition. The Youth for Christ movement, peaking in the mid-1940s, introduced musical and preaching styles reflective of the popular culture as heard on the radio. Evangelism of youths and soon adults catalyzed many churches to embrace innovations in worship services. Yet local church youth ministries remained muted in their harmless renditions of "Christ for Me."

The Jesus movement provided a similar effect toward the end of the 1960s. Christian music adapted from the protests of an alienated generation and forms of communication shaped by television temporarily jolted congregations out of their systems of doing church. Youthful congregations shaped new church movements, leaving the existing churches to maintain a liturgy and style of evangelism relevant only to older generations, while their youth groups sang "Kumbaya."

Assumptions made by church leaders about the two mid-century youth ministry explosions mimicked the presumptions of church fathers at the beginning of the century. Youth ministry was a force to be contained, not an energy to be released. What God did in the lives of young people resembled a developmental stage rather than a flowing of the Spirit. Youth pastors were free to do anything they wished as long as the real church remained unaffected. Discipleship was good for young people but a bit much to expect from the older generation. Evangelism, for the most part, remained safely contained within cultural and architectural walls.

Addressing the problem

Youth workers' frustration with the absence of spiritual vitality and ministry flexibility in the church surfaced more frequently as the century progressed. Youth ministers found themselves confronted with a problem that would seem ridiculous if it were not so universally true. The church was simply not prepared to handle young people who were committed to evangelism, discipleship, and worship—at least not in a manner that would express the diversity of the body of Christ.

Former Young Life personnel became so baffled by the inability of local churches to reach politicians and world leaders with the gospel that a group of them formed a nonchurch called "the fellowship" in order to reach and disciple people for whom identification with a local church was a barrier to becoming a follower of Jesus Christ. A former presidential aide came to faith in Christ through the incarnational witness of people associated with the fellowship. Then after years of significant ministry with Prison Fellowship, which he founded, Charles Colson wrote *The Body*, a book calling for the church to move people to commitment and sacrifice in the name of Jesus Christ.[6] Though Colson was never in youth ministry, his book identifies many of the obstacles youth ministers face in dealing with the church.

Larry Richards and Dann Spader attacked the "church problem" from a context of youth ministry. Richards, whose *Youth Ministry* was a basic text for college and seminary programs in the 1970s, also wrote *A New Face for the Church* as a means of expressing what church should be like after one graduated from high school.[7] More recently, Spader found pastors and church leaders so receptive to his Sonlife principles of youth ministry that he wrote *Growing a Healthy Church* and shortly thereafter began offering training that, in effect, helps churches become as biblically grounded as their youth ministries.[8]

In *The Coming Revolution in Youth Ministry,* I identified 10 megatrends of the coming revolution.[9] To date, most appear to be on target. "Resistance from the church" was the one negative trend I projected; unfortunately, like the others, it is coming true, yet in a far more subtle way than I envisioned. The resistance is not to youth ministry outside of the church—in youth centers and recreation rooms, at camps, concerts, and retreats. The opposition focuses on young people who expect to bring their idealistic, faith-driven, feeling-responsive, obedience-oriented Christian walk into the homes and churches of professed followers of Jesus Christ.

Fellowship or mission?

One core issue in the discussion of youth ministry and the church is an examination of the relationship between fellowship and missiology. The relationships of community to evangelism, of intergenerational to age-group-specific ministries, and of heterogeneous to homogeneous groupings of young people all create challenges in our understanding of youth ministry and the church.

The conversation is not new. Missiologist George W. Peters framed the discussion as centrifugal versus centripetal approaches to mission. *Centripetal* efforts draw momentum towards a central point (in other words, the church), while *centrifugal* strategies spin energy toward the periphery (or the nonchurch). Traditionally, church-based youth ministry has paid attention primarily to building leaders in community (centrifugal), while parachurch youth ministry concentrated on evangelism (centripetal). Ministry models reflect "come" (centripetal) or "go" (centrifugal) postures.[10]

In recent years the seeker-focused, purpose-driven youth ministries of local churches have taken on a parachurch character. Driven by a desire to attract and evangelize adolescents, these youth ministries appear to have combined both "come" and "go" approaches. This has been accomplished by sending these young disciples into their respective high schools with the specific intent of bringing their peers to youth gatherings for the explicit purpose of communicating the gospel and bringing them into a community of believers.

The fact that the "go" strategy has been housed within a Willow Creek or Saddleback church has not, however, produced an effective way to integrate youths into the church. For some reason young people remain isolated in an age-specific ghetto. Before graduation, very few teens find spiritual nurturing outside the youth ministry ghetto. And after graduation, only a minority integrate into the larger body of believers. The invitation to "come" has not resulted in an intergenerational expression of the faith community, but a gathering of peers.

The fellowship versus mission issue might be plotted on a continuum that suggests a variety of responses but where a majority of youth ministries find themselves clustered at one end or the other. The continuum would look like the following:

Fellowship ←————————————————————→ Mission
(come)   (go)

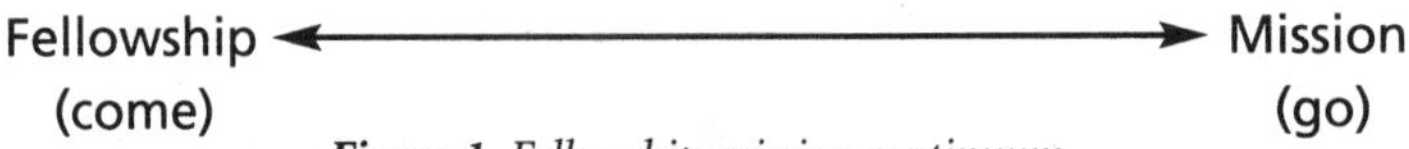

Figure 1. Fellowship-mission continuum

Developmental issues

Another set of issues at the core of our discussion cluster around developmental issues. At what stage of a young person's life is it possible for evidences of spiritual maturity to appear so that the young person can be a full participant in the life of the faith community? Are there theological issues that prevent adolescents from full participation in the life of the church?

Traditionally these questions have been understood as questions regarding baptism, confirmation, and church membership. In churches with a strong confessional or traditional heritage, church polity provides an answer. While people coming from Anglican, Catholic, Lutheran, Methodist, and reform (Presbyterians, Reform churches) traditions have historically defined and limited the role of youths in the faith community, in recent years these same traditions have shown an increased openness to including youths in most aspects of congregational life.

By contrast, the most recent church movements have a much more flexible response to young people in the church. Respect for the leading of the Holy Spirit in the lives of even the youngest individuals has allowed children, frequently with the encouragement of their parents, to choose baptism, church membership, and in some movements even ordination. Ironically, within traditions that place a heavy emphasis on personal experience (such as Baptist, free church, Pentecostal, and charismatic denominations), as well as in emerging church movements like Calvary Chapel, Vineyard, or Willow Creek, youthful leadership and full participation in the leadership of the church are generally viewed with suspicion.

Simply put, the question boils down to whether young people are the church of the future or of the present. Nearly all youth ministers in the West will insist that young people are the church of the present, yet the very isolation of youths within their own classrooms and activities suggest a de facto concession to church of the future assumptions.

The developmental issue might be plotted on a continuum contrasting the manner in which the senior pastor and church leadership view young people. The continuum would look like the following:

Church of the present
(now)

|

(later)
Church of the future

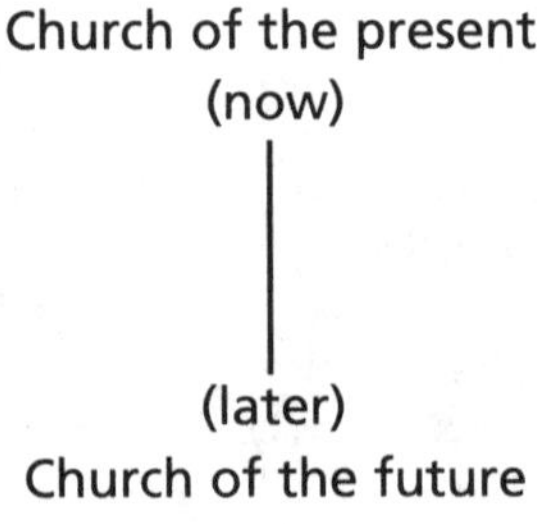

Figure 2. Developmental continuum

When we consider the fellowship/mission and developmental issues simultaneously, a pattern begins to form, which shapes the structure for this book. The following figure places the two issues in relation to each other.

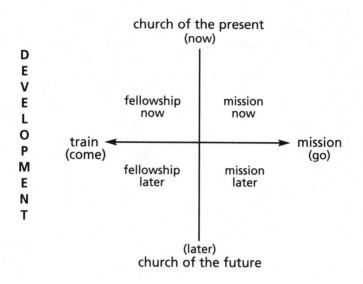

FELLOWSHIP/MISSION

Figure 3. Relationship between fellowship/mission and development

From the four quarters of this grid emerge four approaches to youth ministry and the church. The lines are clearer on paper than they are in practice. Postmodern thinkers may find the following diagrams irrelevantly modern. Generation X youth ministers and millennial youths may feel discomfort with the seemingly mechanical analysis of youth ministry. Yet the lines become clearer to those who can step back and observe what is actually happening.

Four views

The four understandings of youth ministry and the church to be presented in this book are—

- **The Inclusive Congregational approach** integrates youths into congregational life. Characterized by friendly relations between youths, children, and adults, this approach sees youths as full partners in every aspect of God's coming to the faith community.

- **The Missional approach** views youth ministry as a mission. Using responsible evangelism to disciple young people into established churches, youths and youth ministers are considered to be missionaries. By functioning semiautonomously as church-, school-, or community-based, their responsibility is to communicate the kerugma, or the gospel, with their generation.

- **The Preparatory approach** is a specialized ministry to adolescents that prepares them to participate in the life of existing churches as leaders, disciples or evangelists. Students are viewed as disciples in training with opportunities for service both in the present and the future. Developmental dynamics suggest the youth ministry be viewed as a laboratory in which disciples are permitted to grow in a culture guided by spiritual coaches.

• **The Strategic approach** prepares the youth group to become a new church (in other words, a church plant). Using continuity in discipleship between the youth minister and teens, potential leadership members are nurtured to assume responsibility for roles in evangelism and fellowship. The youth pastor then becomes the pastor, and a new church is formed with the blessing of the mother church.

These four approaches can best be understood as they relate to each other (see figure 4).

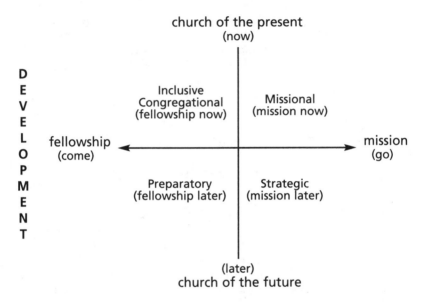

Figure 4. *Relationships among the four approaches to youth ministry*

As neat and clean as these approaches may seem, they are mere theory unless the young people involved are God-seekers. Programs have never produced spirituality or created churches. For that matter, neither have relationships, Bible studies, retreats, cross-cultural projects, prayer meetings or evangelistic events. Instead it is the Spirit of God working in the lives of young people that creates a hunger for discovering God through Jesus Christ.

Spiritual readiness

This brings into focus a third set of issues clustered around questions of spiritual readiness. In that the Spirit of God is the One who draws people to Christ, the best place to look for readiness is in the visible working of the Spirit. What evidences of the fruit of the Spirit, spiritual giftedness, fullness of the Spirit, and qualities for church leadership exist in the lives of young people and should be expected of those who lead the ministries to youth? By examining an individual's readiness we are attempting to weave together a tapestry ranging from tight to loose compliance with the expectations of Scripture. A tight weave means abundant fruit of the Spirit, spiritual gifts being used effectively to build up the body of Christ, fullness of the Spirit shown by responsiveness to doing God's will, and qualities of church leadership evidenced in age appropriate means. A loose weave would be weak or minimal responses in each of these areas.

The spiritual-readiness issue is a bit harder to diagram, but for the sake of the discussion in this book we will look at the tight weave of spiritual readiness as represented by a four on a scale of one to four, while a loose weave would be represented by a one. In order to get a better picture of how spiritual readiness relates to the two prior continua that were diagrammed in figures 3 and 4, and to provide a means of connecting them, the spiritual readiness scale will be represented as follows:

Figure 5: Spiritual-readiness scale

Spiritual readiness, when applied to any of the understandings of youth ministry and the church, can suggest a level of effectiveness in a given situation. Another way to view spiritual readiness is as a passion for God. When young people have a passion for God, any approach to youth ministry will result in the church functioning in a biblical manner. Unfortunately, there are times when the passion of young people grows cold because they have not experienced the church in a manner that will sustain them either in the present or in the years after they leave a youth ministry.

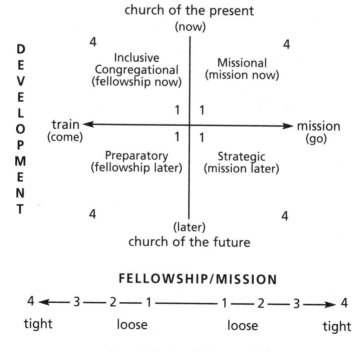

Figure 6: Passion-effectiveness scale

In the chapters that follow, Wesley Black (Southwestern Baptist Theological Seminary), Chap Clark (Fuller Theological Seminary), Malan Nel (Vista University, South Africa) and I (Trinity Evangelical Divinity School) will present arguments in favor of four approaches to youth ministry and the church. We will then interact regarding the other perspectives and allow each writer a rejoinder.

While it would have been great to spend a week together in an Aspen ski lodge and discuss our ideas face to face, distance and schedules made this impossible. Consequently, our virtual gathering came by means of the Internet. You will find that while we approached our chapters in different ways, our responses and rejoinders simulate a face-to-face discussion. Our virtual fellowship has provided stimulation as we have grown to know and respect each other. Editorial changes were generally made only to create a unified writing style.

As writers we wish to present theologically responsible views of youth ministry and the church. Because of the diversity of our church traditions and church polity, our approaches and conclusions will differ. The reader is asked not to pit one author against another, but to build a theology of youth ministry and the church based upon the collective insights gained from our discussion.

Readers can use this book in any number of ways. Some will want to read the book straight through the four approaches. Others may want to skim the responses to an approach before reading about the approach itself (this method allows readers to flag weaknesses in the main argument before reading it). Others may want to start with the rejoinders, and work their ways backwards through the arguments. In any case, this is a book to be used more than it is a text to be read.

Or readers may want to interact with this book in this manner: they can write down questions they think the authors should answer, then judge how well those issues are explored. For such readers, here are some sample questions to get them started:

1. **What is the church to which youth ministry must relate?** *(Universal church? Regional church? Local church? House church? Worship service?)*

2. **In what way does youth ministry connect with the church?** *(Through the students? Through leaders? Through the building? Through their beliefs?)*

3. **What roles do older adults play as youth ministry connects with the church?** *(Authority figures/permission givers? Models of godliness? Spiritual mentors? Teachers of biblical truth?)*

4. **What roles do young people play as youth ministry connects with the church?** *(Submissive followers? Mentorees? Prophetic voices? Active workers? Partners in ministry?)*

5. **How do youth worship as a part of the church?** *(Separate from older worshipers? Learning worship forms from older people? Teaching new worship forms to older people? Experimenting with various forms of worship?)*

6. **How does youth ministry relate to evangelism and missions in the church?** *(Recruiting pool for missions? Peer evangelists? Leaders in evangelism? Innovators in evangelism?)*

As you read *Four Views of Youth Ministry and the Church*, remember, the church is God's ordained agency for accomplishing his purposes in the world. With all its flaws, the church is still the focal point for God's work in the world.

Notes

1. Millard J. Erickson, *Christian Theology* (Grand Rapids: Baker Book House, 1985), 1026.

2. Wayne Grudem, *Systematic Theology* (Grand Rapids: Zondervan Publishing House, 1994), 867-868.

3. Frank Otis Erb, *The Development of the Young People's Movement* (University of Chicago Press, 1917), 59.

4. Edward A. Krug, *The Shaping of the American High School* (Harper & Row, 1964), 170.

5. Erb, 94.

6. Charles W. Colson and Ellen S. Vaughn, *The Body* (Word, 1994).

7. Lawrence O. Richards, *Youth Ministry: Its Renewal in the Local Church* (Zondervan, 1972), and *A New Face for the Church* (Zondervan, 1970).

8. Dann Spader and Gary Mayes, *Growing a Healthy Church* (Chicago: Moody Press, 1991).

9. Mark H. Senter III, *The Coming Revolution in Youth Ministry* (Wheaton: Victor, 1992), 181.

10. George W. Peters, *A Biblical Theology of Missions* (Chicago: Moody Press, 1972), 21-22; 52.

The Inclusive Congregational Approach to Youth Ministry
by Malan Nel

Responses
Black: from a Preparatory perspective
Clark: from a Missional perspective
Senter: from a Strategic perspective

Rejoinder
Nel

The Inclusive Congregational Approach to Youth Ministry
by Malan Nel

Scenario: Giving teens both roots and wings

"The problem is not our youth ministry," Pastor Guda heard himself saying. "The problem is our church."

Silence thick as smoke from a Dutchman's cigar filled the boardroom. For over two hours the session had struggled with issues related to the youth ministry, and this was not the first time. On at least four other occasions during his seven-year pastorate, church leaders had wrestled with nagging questions related to the Christian commitment and involvement of the youths of the church. The answer was always the same: If we get the right people to work with the young people, they would solve the problems.

"This is not the first time we have discussed the problems we are having with our young people," continued the pastor. "Remember when we realized that young people quit attending church services as soon as they were confirmed? What was our solution? New youth workers and better curriculum for catechesis. Did it change anything? Not really.

"Then there was the problem related to methamphetamines at the youth group retreat at Camp Hebron. It nearly split the church. What did we decide to do? Hire a youth minister and implement a drug awareness program. Did it work? Well, we haven't had any more drug-related crises, but I'm not sure we got to the root of what our youths need to grow in their Christian faith."

Pastor Guda was on a roll. Instead of interrupting with their standard objections, the session members appeared willing to allow their pastor to reframe their youth ministry problem.

"Then there were the complaints that came after the *Family-Based Youth Ministry* book circulated among the parents. So what did we do? Remember the mentors we assigned to the young people? It seemed to work for a year or so before it ran out of gas.

"And the discipleship approach that resulted in six or eight young people committing themselves to minister to unreached people groups. Remember the crises our session experienced when we realized the financial implications of the discipleship emphasis on our missionary budget and how relieved we were when several of them changed majors and career directions a couple years later?"

"Now, Pastor," interrupted a senior member of the session, "that is a bit harsh. We all know the Lord would have provided."

"You're probably right, Ernie," replied Pastor Guda. "Maybe it was my faith that was too small. But what would have happened if a half dozen young people *did* go into mission work every year? Would we be prepared to support them? More importantly, would the parents of the church be thrilled with a youth ministry that produced *that* kind of disciple? I'm not sure they would.

"So what *do* we want to have happen in our youth ministry? Honestly, as a church we have treated the young people like foster care, not family. They've become problems to deal with, rather than flesh and blood to love. We keep thinking *they* have to change to fit into our church family. Instead we should be adapting the family to include them, just like we all did as children were born into our own families."

"No offense, Pastor," objected Henri, "but our young people don't respond like babies. They have a will of their own. They want independence."

"Independence, yes; but isolation, no. Our youth ministry, I fear, has isolated our young people in their own little ghetto. The best families allow young people to have both roots and wings. I think that what we haven't done well so far relates to the students' roots. Pardon my analogy if you think I'm pushing it too far, but we have set up a little garden plot in the back of our property and asked a tenant farmer to make sure the plants have good roots. It can't be done that way if we want them to grow and become a part of our olive tree."

"You're sounding rather biblical, Pastor, with the olive tree and all," responded Henri. "But where are we going with all this? You caught our attention when you said the problem is not the youth ministry but the church. How is the church supposed to change in order for young people—to use your analogy—to grow deep roots in the church?"

Henri's question placed the issue into clear focus. If young people are to be completely included in the life of the congregation, the church must be prepared to change. But how?

A comprehensive, inclusive approach

Although Pastor Guda and his church are fictitious, their dilemma is faced by actual churches large and small. Responding to the youth ministry needs of his church provides more than enough reasons to see youth ministry as a comprehensive, inclusive congregational ministry, with catechesis (that is, Christian education of youths) as a vital component.

Historically speaking, the church and organized youth work were typically autonomous, and often still are—probably because youth ministry did not really exist before the Industrial Revolution of the mid-19th century. In the rural context of the world, up to and during the

> "Remember when we realized that young people quit attending church services as soon as they were confirmed?" the pastor asked. "What was our solution? New youth workers and better curriculum for catechesis. Did it change anything?"

Industrial Revolution, children and young people were perceived as part of the family.[1] Yet studies of catechesis (or Christian education) have been done since the time of the New Testament and probably were the sum total of church involvement with youth for many centuries. Catechesis has been viewed as part of the church's task without any reference to the rest of what we now know as youth ministry.

This historical explanation for the dichotomy between catechesis and youth ministry, however, does not mean that one should accept matters as they stand.

For some time now, attempts have been made to give youth ministry a theological grounding. For over a century, theology and society have been calling for a radical change from the pattern of the autonomous church/autonomous youth ministry. The Industrial Revolution that put youth ministry on the agenda was no flash in the pan. It drew the attention of individuals and eventually the church to youths inside—but especially outside—their parental homes. This revolution continues daily.

Some societies—such as my own in South Africa—are now experiencing something of the Industrial Revolution felt by other countries in the 19th century, and something of the youth revolution felt by other countries in the 20th century. In all of society, and for varying reasons, youths are the center of attention. Sometimes it's because of their numbers, their rebellion, their poverty, or their criminal involvement. Other times it is a result of their academic or democratic frustrations. In any case, churches are being challenged to notice the youths, to know them, to sense their needs, and to serve them.

Before I supply the necessary theological justification for this ministry, I will first explain how an inclusive congregational approach needs to be understood.

No more traditional distinction

To my mind there is no argument that holds water for the preservation of the traditional dichotomy between youth ministry as a duty of the local church and youth ministry as an organized form of working with youths separate from catechesis, or Christian education. Young people are not just *partly* the congregation's responsibility, they are wholly so. The essence of God's dealings and relationship with people—and especially with those in the community of believers—makes such a distinction indefensible.

Put simply, youth ministry is part of a comprehensive ministry of the congregation. It includes more than the organized efforts of this or that institution that, possibly in association with the congregation, organizes the youths. Youth ministry (*Jugendarbeit*) and youths themselves are part of the total congregational ministry and not a separate entity.[2] It is an integral part of the congregational whole, in that the whole is never complete without youth ministry.

Results of including youths as full participants

Even before a case for a comprehensive and inclusive approach to youth ministry is argued, a summary of the consequences of the theological justification given below is necessary here. The church must realize the implications of including youths as full participants in the church.

- *The congregation will never think of the faith life of youths separately from the faith life of adult members.* People do not need to reach a certain age before God becomes interested in them and starts working with and through them. Youths are part of the congregation's service to God because they share in God's relationship with his people and are incorporated into the congregation.

- *Youths will not become a separate group within the congregation.* Even though they are unique and have distinct characteristics, they are not apart from the rest. The relationship of God with the believers and their children, as well as the nature of the congregation as something created by God, makes this impossible. So although the youths, because of their distinct nature, require and need to receive specific attention, they should still be approached and ministered to as essential members of the congregation.

- *Youths will not be neglected or ignored.* The congregation does not consist only of adults or only of youths. The youths have to be incorporated in every line of thought and received into every part of the ministry. They have to be taken into account, regardless of the type of ministry on the agenda.

- *Youths will be the congregation's responsibility, not merely the responsibility of the "youth workers."* Children and adolescents are not simply the charge of a few people who particularly love and understand them and want to help them—however well-meaning these people might be. Youths are the responsibility of parents, Sunday school teachers, elders, deacons, the membership as such, as well as one another (in other words the youths themselves). This responsibility is inalienable and not transferable.

These sentiments have been stated over many years by a number of theologians—among them, Dietrich Bonhoeffer. In his eight theses on youth work, he rejected the existence of anything resembling a church youth league because its very existence discredits the cause of the church as such.[3] Beyer also thinks the idea of young people *and* the congregation should change to young people *within* the congregation.[4] Sara Little is of the same opinion, writing that they are a part of the ministering body of Christ *now*.[5]

In spite of such stellar advocates, the typical congregation does not readily accept this comprehensive approach—possibly because theological faculties still teach youth ministry as a kind of supplement to catechesis (and in Anglo circles, to Christian education). As long as the whole is reduced to a part, even the part—in this case, education/catechesis—will not come into its own.

How Should a Comprehensive Approach Be Understood?

God approaches people

A fundamental question of theology is *How does God approach us?* Theology's answer is *God approaches people and his creation in many ways—by means of his Spirit and of his Word, but also by means of other people.* (Ultimately, of course, God can come to us in any way he pleases.) In fact, the Bible is quite clear that God approaches people by means of people—which is the essence of ministry. Our attempts to understand ministry are attempts to explain God's coming, yet human insight and expression are severely limited trying to articulate these things.

One such attempt is to investigate biblical accounts of how God approached people. Practical theology generally asserts that the gospel is primarily about the kingdom of God that has come and is yet to come. God comes to people by means of the gospel; furthermore, God includes the people to whom he has come and is yet to come in the very act of bringing the kingdom to us. In short, practical theology attempts to put words and descriptions to just *how* this coming takes place.

> Historically speaking, the church and organized youth work were typically autonomous, and often still are—probably because youth ministry did not really exist before the Industrial Revolution of the mid-19th century.

Giving names

In a sense, in fact, the Lord Christ himself is the first Witness of his own person and work. Then the church became the witness about Jesus Christ (and his life, work, crucifixion, resurrection, and ascent), first through the apostles and the first congregation, and primarily by means of the New Testament. Their witness about the Witness is the witness of the early church. And the church remains as the witness of Jesus. In fact, the church's primary ministry is the witness— in Greek, the *marturia*—of Jesus Christ. Whatever names are given to the ways in which God comes to people, these ways of coming are a participation in the *marturia* of Jesus Christ.

God's ways of coming by means of his Word and by means of people's service have traditionally been listed under seven headings; I have added an eighth. In all eight ministries it's about serving God, serving one another, and serving the world—in all cases, as a community of the faithful. In this way every designated mode of God's coming is founded on God's communicative involvement in the church and the world.

Figure 7. *The integration and coordination of ministries in building up the local church*

Notice that there is a unique dimension to God's coming in each kind of ministry—a dimension that asks to be distinguished. It is this unique dimension of each kind of ministry that must be discovered again and again in the context of Scripture wherever this ministry is referred to. And just as significantly, God comes in these ministries to youths as he does to the church at large (and in ways as yet undiscovered and unnamed in theology).

Definition of the Inclusive Congregational Approach

The Inclusive Congregational approach asserts that youth ministry is not a separate or additional mode of God's coming to the youths—which is why there is not a ninth ministry listed in the above diagram. Youth ministry is not about finding an extra place for yet another ministry, but about finding a place for youths within every ministry and among the people that the ministries are designed to reach and serve—the people to whom God comes by means of the ministries.

The Inclusive Congregational approach, therefore, is more about *finding a place* for children and adolescents than about dreaming up new modes of ministry. The modes of ministry are largely fixed, and as such they should be studied and developed as far as possible. The point is, whatever is described and discovered in these modes of ministries is relevant to the youths as well as to the adult congregation. Every ministry in the church is relevant to the youths. Every ministry contains rich potential for youth ministry.

The task in youth ministry, as is the case in building up the local church, is not to study and describe the ministries as such. Rather, the task is twofold—to sensitize every discipline of ministry for its relevancy to the youths (as part of the whole) and to rediscover and define the place of the youths as part of the congregation. The question then becomes, How can theology and the congregation (in which theology functions) become more sensitive to and aware of the youths? How can the youths become more sensitive to and aware of theology and the congregation as a whole?

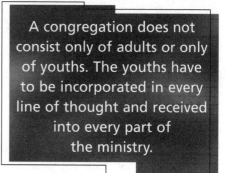

A congregation does not consist only of adults or only of youths. The youths have to be incorporated in every line of thought and received into every part of the ministry.

In short, how can youths *find a place* in their church?

Description of Inclusive Congregational Ministry

Comprehensive first

There is no theological reason why what is valid for adults is not valid for the youths. The comprehensive ministry is meant for them as part of the congregation. Yes, there should be differentiation for youths—but once and for all, it is time for us to stop missing this comprehensive and inclusive perspective.

There is quite enough proof that the traditional idea of youth work grew out of and was fed by congregations, parents, Sunday school teachers (catechists), ministers, elders, and deacons. Yet it failed in taking the youths into account in, and as part of, the congregation. Merton Strommen shows how the impersonal approach in the Lutheran church, reacting to historical events, led to a formal, impersonal, and intellectualized approach to young people by the 1860s—at about the time when many youth leagues came into being. In 1908 a youth committee wrote, "We look forward to the day when we have only the devil and not also our church fathers to fight."[6] Such an approach is counterproductive to a comprehensive, inclusive congregational ministry and its differentiation.

The absence of such a comprehensive congregational approach has often led to a negative evaluation of the congregation by children and adolescents. In such a case the youths often seek to meet their spiritual needs and worship elsewhere—historically in the youth organizations. The matter of identification with the congregation, which is so crucial to teaching, is important here. It can be said with a great deal of confidence that traditional youth work was fed not only by the Industrial Revolution and the consequent cultural changes, but also by the inability of adult members of congregations who could not (or would not) change or adapt old traditional forms and thought patterns in order to meaningfully integrate the youths into the local church and minister to them as part of the whole. In a sense the church culture, on the one hand, was too paternalistic and legalistic to open up. On the other hand, it was also too evangelically indi-

Youth ministry is not about finding an extra place for yet another ministry, but about finding a place for youths within every ministry.

vidualistic to appreciate the whole. Some would call it the legacy of the individualistic spirituality of pietism. But it is not that simple either.

Within reformed theology the question remains whether the traditional attitudes, which separated youth ministry from the larger life of the church, were not, at least in part, the result of the encyclopedic categorization of theology by Abraham Kuyper. In his work some functions belong to the duties of the "institute," while others, like evangelization, are the duties of the "organism." In any case, with or without Kuyper's help, reformed theology contributed to this worldwide loss of the youths (especially of adolescents) in churches. All communities, countries, and denominations were affected by it, some only sooner than others. During the American youth revolution, Louis Cassels wrote, on the basis of what young people were saying, that the church was losing them because of cold worship services, lack of involvement, and phoniness.[7]

In my own country, South Africa, the question is whether we are not, for the first time in our history, involved in a similar kind of revolution.[8] Until 1994 cultural groups were stabilized in an artificial way under the government; still, however, the disappointment of young people in the adult section of the church seldom led to a large-scale withdrawal from catechesis. And this disappointment frequently resulted in youths who, however active they had been in youth ministry and church, became mere spectators. They did what their religious commu-

> When Christian youths have no reason to value their congregations, they often meet their spiritual needs and worship elsewhere—historically in youth organizations outside the church.

nity expected of them—confirmation—and then departed. It was almost like what had occurred in Germany, where the sacrament was often referred to as being "confirmed *out* of the church."

After 1994, however, everything changed in South Africa. Disillusioned white young people find it more and more difficult to see the past through the eyes of those who shaped it. Poverty, frustration, and unrealistic expectations of youths are still serious tests for the churches. Ministry to the youths has probably just begun.

Even well-intentioned churches, in South Africa or anywhere, can be disloyal to the nature of Christ's congregation, and this unfaithfulness is rationalized in all kinds of ways—as in expecting children and adolescents to grow up (to an age determined by adults) before they can share in what Christ is and has done for his congregation and participate in the comprehensive ministry entrusted by Christ to his congregation.

This kind of church, firstly, loses the youths and shoves them into the arms of any person or organization that cares and treats them like they're important. Secondly, such a church rears a generation—even generations—of adults with whom the youths don't want to identify or associate. And this can be fatal to the identity formation of the youths and their faith development.

Comprehensive, but differentiated and focused

Differentiation in youth ministry refers to at least two levels:

- Youths need all that adults need, but there is a difference between how to feed a need in a 10-year-old and how to feed that same need in a 50-year-old. One has to differentiate within the ministry.
- Characteristics of youths at different ages or at different development levels must be taken into account.

Youth ministry is not a separate or different ministry. It does, however, take into account that which is typical of a specific ministry and what is typical of the specific age group at whom the ministry is directed. For example, in youth ministry, preaching is still preaching, but it is focused on and directed at the youths. This focus is determined by the youths' phase of life and the needs peculiar to that phase.

In an inclusive congregational approach, then, youth ministry is at the very least *the mediation of the coming of God to the youths as integral and vital parts of the congregation, through his Word and through the service of people, by means of all modes of ministry, in a differentiated and focused way.*

Modes of Youth Ministry

Kerugma—preaching

Through *kerugma*, God comes to the congregation and, in a differentiated and focused way, to the youths. The youths must be considered in the preaching ministry of a church—they must figure into the preacher's agenda or text. Preachers who "think youth" and routinely take them into account on an everyday basis will do the same when they step into the pulpit to preach. The *kerugma* has to enter the here and now of the youths and proclaim the new

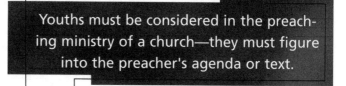

Youths must be considered in the preaching ministry of a church—they must figure into the preacher's agenda or text.

reality that has arrived with Christ's coming. The youths (children and adolescents) should also be summoned by the *kerugma* to a new existence.

Of course, the better the preacher's textbook delivery and dynamics, the more relevant the message will be for the youths. Modern insights in homiletics—insights that emphasize the dialogical character of the sermon—all these make the sermon that much more meaningful for youths. Almost by definition children and adolescents are people for dialogue, because they are relational in nature.

Leitourgia—worship service

The gathered congregation is the basic form of the functioning of the congregation and its ministries.[9] Where people, on the basis of the *leitourgia* of Christ, enter into the presence of God, there is a dynamic that no one should deny the youths. They should never miss out on it. They should be an integral and a vital part of it. If this mode has stagnated as a result of unchanging liturgical agendas, the fault is not in the *leitourgia* mode itself; the fault should be identified and corrected in a practical theological way in the subdiscipline of liturgy.

It is important to state here that liturgy is the corporate encounter between God and his people—including the youths. Like anywhere else in the life of the congregation, the young and the old need each other in worship, too. For worship is rich in potential for the youths. The use of symbols, for example, is no less beneficial for youths than it is for the rest of the congregation.

A congregation's willingness to be relevant to the youths during worship services may have more far-reaching consequences than any other mode of ministry. To be contemporary as well as traditional is no easy matter.

Didache—teaching

Youth ministry is about those who have just joined the (relatively) older people on the road of *Yahweh*. Initiation into, guidance along, and wise choices for living on the way are part of the congregational ministry to, with, and through the youths. This is the central aspect of the *didache*. It is about a lifelong commitment to be a disciple, or pupil, of Christ.

Like other modes of ministry, *didache* seldom if ever occurs in isolation. It emphasizes that the congregational *didache* become part of the edification (*oikodomein*) and training (*katartizein*) of the people of God to ably represent him as his people in this world. Thus the inclusive congregational approach once again gives integrity to the differentiated focus.

Paraklesis—pastoral care

When it comes to children and adolescents, pastoral care may be the most neglected ministry. The youths are at a time in their lives when they especially need all the facets of pastoral care in a congregational context. They need to know that this mode says that God is with us in all circumstances and situations—in anxiety, pain, sin, doubt, error, weakness, loneliness, and success.

God is with us to free us from the constraints of brokenness that threaten us. *Paraklesis* wants to lead us out of a life of imperfection and into a life of wholeness in spite of and in the midst of all the brokenness within and around us. Few other modes of ministry explain as well as *paraklesis* that children and adolescents need all that other believers need, only to a greater extent and in a differentiated, yet focused way.

Koinonia—mutuality

Closely related to *paraklesis*, the mode of God's coming to people through others is built on this truth: God is with people by means of each other, because in Jesus he came to us in flesh. Through the indwelling of the Spirit, people can live and discover their humanity through one another.

About the mode itself there is little doubt: Christians are people *for* one another and are the people of God in their togetherness. This mutuality should be intensely focused on the youths in the congregation. Children and adolescents need more community than that provided by one's immediate family, as important as family is.[10] Young lives can mature fully within a climate of *koinonia*. Much has been written on this subject; it is enough to say that the youths need *koinonia* as part of the whole, and in a focused way.

Diakonia—service

The term *diakonia* underwent its own development throughout history.[11] *Diakonia* was a comprehensive term that denoted everything in which humans were involved in the name of God. In Scripture, for instance, the term is used to show that individuals find the fulfillment of their calling in service. *Diakonia*, therefore, is the umbrella term for all that the congregation does, for all its ministries. What we today call modes of ministry was, in the first century, simply the *diakonia* of the congregation. The term refers to an activity performed out of love for God for the sake of one's fellow man—so much so that it is called a service of love. It is easy to understand how the term changed to refer mainly to the ministry of care: in acts of caring and deeds of mercy the *diakonia* finds special expression.

Children and adolescents need more community than that provided by one's immediate family, as important as family is.

Among the youths there is a striking, characteristic selfishness that is almost antiserving—yet at the same time, there is a paradoxical readiness to serve in a way that befits their phase of life. Strommen has determined in his empirical studies, in fact, that the youths have a specific inclination to a service-oriented life.[12] This mode is therefore about involving the youths, at their level of maturity for certain kinds of service, in the comprehensive service of the congregation in this world. They are, after all, part of the ministering body of Christ—even now. Congregations should therefore continually discover, cultivate, and live their identity as the serving people of God, and at the same time involve the youths in service suitable to their age. In this way the *diakonia* becomes the central mode of the serving ministries of the congregation—including its ministries that serve children and adolescents.

Marturia—witness

The church is to be understood in missionary perspective, not because it is the primary activity of the church, but because we know that God is constantly involved in bringing wholeness—that is, salvation—to his creation. The *missio Dei* includes the *missio ecclesia*. The congregation participates in and is involved in the *missio Dei*, and in this way: the church is not the one who sends, but rather the one who is sent.[13] This *sentness* is therefore not one of the results of being a church, but a prerequisite. It is a characteristic of the true church. To understand that youths are an integral and a vital part of the church is to understand that they are also an integral and a vital part of the congregation's mission. And this congregational *raison d'être* can only be understood as missionary in nature.

This essential *sentness* of the entire church, youths included, carries many implications. Sermons cannot urge congregations to let themselves be sent; sermons must address people who *are being* sent. The local church should not minister as if some of their number may be called to be witnesses, but as if all are already witnesses.

All that has to be understood is that this *marturia* also has to be relevant to the peculiar needs and characteristics of each age group. One witnesses to a 10-year-old differently than to an adult. Furthermore, a 10-year-old witnesses to others differently than an adult does. This mode of God's coming to and through the congregation includes the youths and should be differentiated with an eye to their missionary involvement.

Kubernesis—administration

The ministry of the management and administration of the congregation is usually explained with a helmsman term, *cybernesis* (1 Corinthians 12:28). The early church was often contemporarily described as a ship with Christ himself as the helmsman. This *cybernesis* ministry is related to a strongly pastoral term for leadership, used in Romans 12. It connotes a pastoral ministry of care and empathy, which was the duty of the leading members of the early church.[14] This ministry is about caring guidance in the name of the Helmsman, and implies an orderly and appropriate journey toward a destination (1 Corinthians 14). The unity and the edification of the congregation should be served in this way.

What reason is there that a congregation's youths should not be part of this? Granted, their interest in complicated regulations is weak, and they are typically unconcerned about dogma and administration. Still, an inclusive congregational approach asserts that youths should not, even for these reasons, be excluded from this aspect of church life. They need it for healthy growth and development as part of the whole. When administration makes sense and is handled in a pastoral manner, the youths often surprise the older generation with their abilities and insights into this ministry.

A special focus on parents

In the theological justification below (see Hermeneutic Perspective, page 16), the family is referred to as the basic hermeneutic *lebensraum*, in which God comes to the youths (both children and adolescents). Parents are primary mediators in the relationship (or covenant) between God and families, and as such are key in the roles that humans play in the coming of God to children. Not that families are exclusively important or that people outside of caring biological or custodial families are at a spiritual disadvantage. My point is only that youth ministry should be evangelically realistic and open to pivotal roles that parents can play in the lives of youths.

Yet even families require intensive and focused attention. Where natural family ties are lacking, youth ministry once again requires intensive attention to the founding of other relationships that can facilitate growth and development. Each child that is ministered to, is ministered to with an eye to the founding of a future family. Not that procreation is the goal of youth ministry, but that reinforcing relationships *is* part of the goal—and for this the family remains the ideal *lebensraum* and structure.

Youth ministry, therefore, is differentiated also in the way it focuses on parents. This insight, fortunately, is generally acknowledged in youth ministry.

A theological definition

In light of the above modes, then, the definition of youth ministry can be further refined to this: *Youth ministry is a comprehensive congregational ministry in which God comes, through all forms of ministry and with especial regard to parents (or their substitutes), with a differentiated focus to youths (as an integral part of the congregation), and also with and through the youths in the congregation to the world.*

It's as if God thinks ecclesiologically. He makes it clear that the person who belongs to him is part of his people. This principle is absolutely conclusive in youth ministry.

Theological Justification

The Bible, children, and other young people

As the Bible is no manual for liturgy, it is likewise no manual for youth ministry. On the other hand, as the Bible offers direction to liturgy, so it points the way for youth ministry. My purpose in this section is not so much to prove that an Inclusive Congregational ministry is biblical (I attempt to answer that elsewhere in this chapter), but that Scripture does indeed contain theological insights about children and adolescents.

- God is involved in a special way in the giving of children. Children are "a reward from him" (Psalm 127:3; cf. Psalm 128; Psalm 139:14-16). Children are no surprise to God—though their conception may be a surprise to their parents.

- Not only is God involved in conception, but also with the born. He is the God of their parents, and he wants to be their God as well (cf. Genesis 17). Even the outcast's cry is heard by him (Genesis 21:17) though the promised one has just been born (Genesis 21:2). When the poet sings about the power of God, it is part of his prayer that sons should grow high, like plants, and that daughters should stand firm and beautiful, like pillars (Psalm 144:12; Psalm 115:14-15).

- God involves children and young people in his coming to his people. It pleases him to use children when approaching people, for they are a special part of religious ceremonies. The Passover meal and the instruction in the Deuteronomist (Deuteronomy 6), for example, are strong evidence of this. They are conversationally involved in these events and are not mere receivers of information. They are also present at the sacrifice (1 Samuel 1:4).

- Youths are included when God deals with people outside the community of his covenant people. A young girl tells Naaman's wife of the prophet in her own country (2 Kings 5:2-3). David is probably in his mid-teens when he becomes involved in God's dealings with Israel, and at this age he is anointed to become king of Israel (1 Samuel 16-17). According to some, Daniel is an early adolescent when he refuses, at the table of the king himself, to eat and drink what is set before him (Daniel 1:8). There are many instances of children and young people being included by God in his dealings with people.

- A hallmark of Jesus' ministry on earth was how he manifested both existing and ancient views of God—and he did no less when it came to youths. God loves children, and Jesus confirmed this in his care for them. He maintained their rights over and against anyone who caused them to stumble (Matthew 18:1-14; 19:13-15). Only here and now in Christ is God's love for children fully recognized.

- The New Testament also emphasizes the importance of the youths in the acts of God. Young men are involved in the first tragic and disciplinary act in the early church (Acts 5). Children knelt together with their parents during a prayer meeting for a departing apostle (Acts 21:5), and unmarried daughters are said to have the gift of prophecy (Acts 21:9).

These examples are not mandates and directives, but merely instances of God's dealings with and through children and other young people. Again, the Bible is not a book about youths, but about God and his dealings with people—and the youths are essentially a part of these people. What God did and still does, he also does for, with, and through the youths (as a part of his people). That is why the Bible is as rich in principles for youth ministry as it is in principles for any other ministry.

And what are some of these principles?

Covenantal/Relational Perspective

It is clear from the Bible that God created humankind, binding himself forever to people as his creation. Although man often rebelled and pushed away the Creator's hand, God remains true to his creation. According to the Bible, this relationship was seriously damaged—broken off by humans themselves, one could say. One could also say that the relationship was reinstated from God's side. The Bible is clear about this: God was and is always a saving God, healing those with whom he deals. God is involved with creation and humankind by means of grace that repairs and restores what is broken. And this restoration can be understood only in a covenantal way, for at the root of restoration are relationships—relationships with God, with one's fellow beings, and with creation itself.

These things become clear in the reading of God's dealings with Abraham. First, there is God's initiative—he begins, he maintains, and he completes what he has started in and through Abraham. The story and its every detail is fitted into this scheme. God binds himself to a human being, to a stranger from a foreign land. *It is this binding—this bond or covenant—that is so important for the theological grounding of youth ministry.* God wants to make himself

> The most natural form of relationship is the biological or custodial family. God is indeed the God of households; in a unique way he is known within the hermeneutic sphere of the family.

known to persons and their descendants, not just for their sake, but by means of them (Genesis 12:7; 22:18; Galatians 4). In this we again see God's devotion as Creator to his creation (cf. Genesis 9).

The nations—that it, those who do not (yet) know, love, and serve God—are his goal. God never discards what he has made. His plan to take creation toward its fulfillment is on the agenda. Through a human being—here, Abraham—and his descendants, God's uniqueness as Creator-God is again acknowledged and confessed before the nations.

All of which places youth ministry not only in a relational perspective, but also in a missional and ecological one.

Within this relationship (or covenant, or contract) God commits himself to be a God for *people*, and he wants humankind to commit their humanity to him. The nature of this contract is that God has a covenantal right to humankind—but the covenant also stipulates that humankind has the right to address God.

The biblical account of the Abrahamic covenant is not merely an intriguing pattern for youth ministry. Youth ministry is veritably rooted in these truths. God founded the relationship between Christ and humans through his Spirit—a relationship for children and young people as well as adults. To be active in youth ministry is nothing less than working with youths in the name of this God.

After all, God has always been dealing with youths. He has kept them in mind from the very beginning. Parents and others need merely get into line with what he has been doing all along. Youth ministry is to be taken up into and involved in the covenantal dealings of God with children and young people—borne by the certain knowledge that God has covenantally attached himself to dealings with and through them.

> In a congregation both the 15-year-old and the 60-year-old observe change in each other—and both note that some changes are painful.

Ecclesiological/Somatic Perspective

How does God deal with his people?

From the inception of the covenant and all that followed in its wake, it is clear that God begins with *one* person, but his aim is the *many*. From the One comes the sand of the sea and the stars of heaven. Out of the One the whole is born. When the whole is established, the one is part of the whole. The one is not absorbed by the whole, but is taken up into it. The importance of the one is related to the whole, and it does not stand detached from and independent of the whole.

In Pauline terms the individual members of a body are what make the body function as an entity. Independent of the church and alone, however, the *one* loses its importance. As part of the whole, the *one* is irreplaceable. One could therefore say that God thinks somatically, or corporately. He takes pleasure in the wonder of the unity of his people. Their unity is a witness to his glory. In this way the restoration to wholeness attains its peak. God restores to relatedness. The covenant, relational in its essence, leads to further relatedness—relatedness to God and others.

This corporate thinking of the Bible is striking. Families, groups, and nations all play a significant role. It's as if God thinks ecclesiologically, thinks in terms of his gathered people, his assembly. He makes it clear that the person who belongs to him is part of his people.

This principle is absolutely conclusive in youth ministry; furthermore, it provides the ministry with integrity. Youth ministry is often threatened by individualism—which is to say, by a lack of insight into the corporate purpose and dealings of God. Maintaining this theological principle in youth ministry is not always easy. Yet it must not be compromised. Even where the corporate character of this ministry is understood, it often leads to yet another form of individualism—denominationalism—which deprives youth ministry of a necessary ecumenical perspective and respect for the larger corpus.

> Many so-called parachurch and interdenominational youth organizations would never have been necessary if congregations had been willing to change and fulfill their calling.

This theological departure point is admitted by more and more leaders in youth ministry. Wesley Black calls this a building block: "the church as the basic unit for ministry."[15] This is hardly new, only forgotten and neglected. In answering why youth ministry is necessary, G. E. Ludwig states twice (almost as if it were self-evident) that the congregation is important and that young people should be integrated into the life of the church.[16]

There is no space here to explain why and how youth ministry evolved into something apart from or appended to the congregation. Suffice to say that there are no theological grounds for this false dichotomy. Children and adolescents are an indispensable part of the congregation. Like all other members, they are part of the congregation, and as such they are a congregational responsibility. W. R. Myers writes that the—

> ...key to a church's faithful youth ministry is the presence of *faithing* adults who incarnate God's love in genuine, appropriate ways. Faithing describes the intentional and appropriate activities of those who embody God's love.... While the presence of such individuals (the faithing individuals) is critical, no less important is...*Collective Incarnation*, i.e., the presence of the gathered body of Christ, the congregation, the community of the faithful.[17]

Hermeneutic Perspective:
The Family as Hermeneutic Sphere

Within this ecclesiological sphere (*lebensraum*), there is a smaller unit to which God grants, in a special way, the hermeneutic function: the family. One could say that the child needs parents in order to gain understanding. The Passover meal is a unique example (cf. Exodus 12; see also the well-known reference to families and faith education in Deuteronomy 6). Children must understand who God is and how he deals with people. When the story of God's dealings with his people comes from the people whom youths are supposed to listen to first and can trust, a story makes more sense.

Children ask questions and parents answer—this pattern is so children can learn that "the Lord brought us out of Egypt with a mighty hand" (Deuteronomy 6:20). What today's parents once heard as children from *their* parents, they recount to their own children, telling the upcoming generation of "the praiseworthy deeds of the Lord, his power and the wonders he has done" (Psalm 78:3, 4).

Within this hermeneutic sphere of family life, one learns and gradually understands in a relatively spontaneous and natural way. Certainly, God is not restricted to a domestic context, and insight is available in countless other contexts. God is not limited to the family when he wants to enlighten someone. Yet he has offered the family as primary hermeneutic sphere, and it pleases him to grant an understanding of who he is and how he acts within the security and intimacy of a family.

Our era requires a special sensitivity to the crisis of families. Thousands of children are born into single-parent or blended families. Thousands are born each year with scarcely any kind of family connections. Youth ministry must take these facts into account. The emphasis on the family as a hermeneutic principle should in no way be used to cause hurting people to hurt even more, nor to create the idea that one who is born into a family has a head start on grace.

When I say that the family is a hermeneutic sphere, I mean only that God in his wisdom works in the realm of relationships (as biblical accounts of his covenantal dealings with people underscore), and the parent-child relationship is the most natural relationship. Where ties between fathers, mothers, and children are deficient for whatever reasons, God still works within primary relationships; relationships other than parent-child ones can take up the slack. In many cultures the extended family often plays this role. Many African churches often function on this basis. In industrialized societies the congregation as extended family is typically an unnoticed and underused support system; yet there are other ways of making up for the deficiency—as in daycare centers and preschools. The integrating approach to relational groups in local churches holds great promise for the development of the congregation as an extended family.

Relationship is the password to understanding, and the most natural form of relationship is the biological or custodial family. God is indeed the God of households. In a unique way he is known within the hermeneutic sphere of the family. Here a lived and shared faith in God plays a crucial role in the understanding of him by the next generation.

Lifestyle Perspective:
The Congregation as the Sphere for Change

Nobody is ever finished in the sense of being changed into perfection. Yet every adolescent is a total person and must be accepted and respected as such. The development of a person into someone who can represent God anew, as the Creator originally visualized him, is in continual process. As people in Christ, we are new creations—an irrefutable fact. We are becoming what we already are in him. God created the end in the beginning and he has already begun to realize this end for which he created everything. In fact, in a sense he starts with the end. In another sense he ends at the beginning. Perhaps it is for this reason that he has never tired of starting anew with people.

Theology perceives change in lifestyle as a work of the Holy Spirit. And in a congregation, God has created a sphere in which change ought to be normal, where growth ought to be axiomatic. Those who don't change, who remain the same, ought to feel uncomfortable and out of step. Conversion (in its catechetic sense, at least) ought to be a normal, daily thing for all members of a faith community. Among those who have been longer in the faith, it may be

> Leadership and parents must return to the drawing board—this time, with the youths. Together, an Inclusive Congregational approach and its consequences must be thought through and worked out.

no longer a *fundamental* change—the change may instead be a process of increasing awareness, of insight, of choice. Myers uses the verb *faithing* to underline his belief that the concept is more than a noun—"more of a total lifestyle than a commodity to be possessed, more of a process than a product."[18]

The congregation motivates and facilitates growth and change. Here the 15-year-old and the 60-year-old observe change in each other—and both note that some changes are painful. People do not become who they are in Christ without a struggle. Sometimes the struggle against sin is a bloody one. Myers writes of the older members, whom he calls "guarantors," as those who are "appropriately anchored in adulthood but who will walk with youths on their journey. Guarantors share the burden of the journey, help read the road maps and offer encouragement." As W. H. Hebbard says: "For this the congregation and also the pastors should be willing often to confess: 'I don't know all the answers, but I am here to cry with you' and…a new definition of valid, God-blessed ministry awaits."[19] The congregation is in many ways a mediating structure.

To change, one needs others. Of course one needs God, the Complete Other, but one also needs others who have been changed by God. For one of the reasons God changed them was in order to change others through them. This is the missional aspect: the congregation grows so that, through them, others and creation can become what God meant them to be. The Holy Spirit binds the congregation to Christ so that the congregation can demonstrate a Christ-existence. In this way it becomes a change motivated by the love of Christ (cf. 2 Corinthians 5:11-21). And love is always partial: it defends the voiceless and the deprived, the sick and the poor, slaves and exiles, orphans and strangers.

The dynamics of rapidly changing young people raise two questions for the rest of the congregation: Will the congregation also be willing to change, and will its changes be encouraged and facilitated? A changing congregation naturally invites the youths who are changing and who seek change to "[be] transformed into his likeness with ever-increasing glory, which comes from the Lord, who is in the Spirit" (2 Corinthians 3:18).

When youth ministry takes this basic theory as a departure point, it will "create a context in which faith can be awakened, supported, and challenged."[20]

At this point, the creation of change-friendly situations within the congregation becomes crucial.

Changes Required in the Church

Being built as a part of the whole

In a sentence, youth ministry is all about building Christ's congregation to the glory of God. Those who confess that glory care for each other, and are cared for. Those who do not as yet confess faith in Christ, are cared for on behalf of God and are ministered to with a view toward becoming whole. Within the congregation each age group is incorporated into this building process. And in this multifunctioning body, youth in itself disqualifies no one from contributing to the building up of the church. The only qualification is the confession that Jesus Christ is Lord.

The youths should therefore be built up as a part of the whole. They are in no way a group whose equipping should take place apart from the center of the congregation. A church's youth ministry is not a mere supplement to the whole, but as much of the essence of the congregation as any other age group.

The congregation plays a pivotal part in youth ministry. I am convinced that many so-called parachurch and interdenominational youth organizations would never have been necessary if the congregations had been willing to change and fulfill their calling. In part the congregation provides continuity for youth and provides a spiritual home in which to seek shelter.

"The youths, time after time, have responded to genuine warmth and care evidenced by adults in the faith community."[21]

Critical changes required

What we need in order to become fully functioning local church families again is nothing less than a change of mind and heart. This should start with a church's leadership—ideally, with the senior pastor, for this is nothing less than ecclesiological reformation. As history has taught us, no reformation is without a price—and most reformers were considered heretics, at least for some time. The reformation I am suggesting is against the grain of individualistic Western culture, where materialism and comfort—to the point of narcissism—are inclined to determine our understanding of God's will for his people.

The challenge for leadership and parents is to return to the drawing board—this time, *with* the youths. Together, an Inclusive Congregational approach and its consequences must be thought through and worked out. Many churches are doing just this. As they listen and search together, something begins to happen.

Though not quickly. In my own church it took a decade before the firstfruits were enjoyed. It started with the conviction of a few members of the youth committee. Many long discussions took place over several years. "We know our youths are an integral part of this local body of believers, but where are they?" we kept asking. When changes finally started, they happened fast and often simultaneously: a realization of who we are in principle (including youths as an integral part), and the empirical fact that they are obviously absent and apathetic. So our first practical step was to instill in our Sunday school teachers and parents the concept that young people are an integral part of our church. Soon, almost at the demand of the parents, a family worship service was started in the church hall—at the same time as the traditional Sunday morning service. "Why is this family worship service not in the sanctuary?" I asked. "The youths need the symbols of worship even more than the adults who are meeting in the sanctuary do." The family worship service is now held in the sanctuary.

Then their Sunday school classes moved to meet on Sunday afternoons, and the adolescents developed under the leadership of two of the local pastors at their own vibrant, but very traditional, worship service in the evening. And many parents attend.

Meanwhile, the congregation at large kept thawing, too. Small groups sprouted in the church: youth groups, target groups, family clusters. The church restructured its ministry to the world. Because of a now-well-established basic philosophy to youth ministry, the youths are part of these ministries. Sometimes youths go out by themselves to visit and help the urban poor; other times they join the efforts of the whole church.

We have a long way to go, but I can see it happen before my eyes: children and adolescents are developing a sense of belonging and awareness of being an integral part of their body of believers. Almost spontaneously, they are cared for, and they in turn care for each other. They are being respected for who they are, not how old they are.

The inclusive congregational approach is not for the faint of heart. It takes a lot of courage and faith. After all, you will have to deal with long-established myths in the minds of many of the congregation. It is, however, a challenge of hope and of faithfulness to the gospel.

Notes

1. I deliberately distinguish between *children, adolescents,* and *youths* (by which term I mean both children and adolescents).

2. It should be mentioned that several terms have been used in the course of history for this ministry. Of the most familiar are *youth work, youth care, Jugendpastoral,* and *shaping young people.* In this book I have

chosen the term *youth ministry*, which I deem most comprehensive. It is most commonly used in the Anglo-Saxon world to describe this ministry. From time to time the English term *youth work* has also been used to describe what is here called youth ministry.

3. Dietrich Bonhoeffer, *Gesammelte Schriften.* Vol. 3. (Munich: Kaiser, 1960), 292-293.

4. K. Beyer, *Gemeinde Jugendarbeit* (Wuppertal: Brockhaus, 1978), 7.

5. Sara Little, *Youth, World, and the Church* (Richmond: John Knox, 1968), 11.

6. M. P. Strommen, *Profiles of Youth* (Saint Louis, Missouri: Concordia, 1963), 3.

7. L. Cassels, *Forbid Them Not* (Independence, Missouri: Independence, 1973), 8-9.

8. B. B. Haldenwang, "South African Youths in Crisis: Facing the Future," *Occasional Paper 24* (1994); F. van Z. Slabbert, *Youths in the New South Africa: Towards Policy Formulation* (Pretoria: HSRC, 1994).

9. J. Firet, *Dynamics in Pastoring* (Grand Rapids: Eerdmans, 1986), 82.

10. See M. P. Strommen, *Five Cries of Youth* (1974, reprint. San Francisco: Harper & Row, 1979), 33. (For his "cry of psychological orphans.")

11. See Collins (1990).

12. Strommen, xi.

13. D. J. Bosch, *Transforming Mission* (Maryknoll: Orbis, 1991), 389ff.

14. B. Reicke and G. W. Bromiley, trans., "Proisteimi," *Theological Dictionary of the New Testament*, G. Friedrich (Grand Rapids: Eerdmans, 1968), 6:700-703.

15. Wesley Black, *An Introduction to Youth Ministry* (Nashville: Broadman, 1991), 15.

16. G. E. Ludwig (1979:37). See also 1988:18-37.

17. W. R. Myers (1987:xviii).

18. Myers, xviii.

19. D. W. Hebbard, *The Complete Handbook for Family Life Ministry in the Church* (Nashville: Thomas Nelson, 1995), 15.

20. R. R. Osmer, *Teaching for Faith* (Louisville: Westminster John Knox, 1992), 15.

21. M. Marshall, "A Rich Heritage," *Affirmation* 2, no. 1 (1989), 37-48.

REFERENCES

Beyer, K. *Gemeinde Jugendarbeit.* Wuppertal: Brockhaus, 1978.

Black, W. *An Introduction to Youth Ministry.* Nashville: Broadman, 1991.

Bonhoeffer, D. *Gesammelte Schriften.* Dritter Band. München: Kaiser, 1960.

Bosch, D. J. *Transforming Mission.* Maryknoll: Orbis, 1991.

Brierley, P. *Reaching and Keeping Teenagers.* Tunbridge Wells: MARC, 1993.

Cassels, L. *Forbid Them Not.* Independence, Missouri: Independence, 1973.

De Vries, M. *Family-based Youth Ministry.* Downers Grove, Illinois: InterVarsity Press, 1994.

Firet, J. *Het agogisch moment in het pastoraal optreden.* Kampen: Kok, 1977.

————. *Dynamics in Pastoring.* Grand Rapids: Eerdmans, 1986.

Foley, G. *Family-Centered Church.* Kansas City: Sheed & Ward, 1995.

Gilbert, W. K., ed. *Confirmation and Education.* Philadelphia: Fortress, 1969.

Haldenwang, B. B. "South African Youths in Crisis: Facing the Future." *Occasional paper 24.* Stellenbosch Institute for Future Research, 1994.

Hebbard, D. W. *The Complete Handbook for Family Life Ministry in the Church.* Nashville: Thomas Nelson, 1995.

Little, Sara. *Youth, World, and the Church.* Richmond: John Knox, 1968.

Marshall, M. "A Rich Heritage." *Affirmation* 2, no. 1 (1989): 37-48.

Nel, M. *Jeug en evangelie.* Pretoria: NGKB, 1982.

————. *Die Jeugbeleid.* Bloemfontein: AJK, 1983.

————. "Kerklike bediening aan die jongmens." *Kerkjeug Antwoord,* ed. M. Nel. Pretoria: NGKB, 1985.

————. "Die kind en die Bybel 2. 'n Benaderde oplossing." *NGTT* 32, no. 4 (1991): 631-643.

————. *Gemeentebou.* Halfway House: Orion, 1994.

Osmer, R. R. *Teaching for Faith.* Louisville: Westminster John Knox, 1992.

Procksch, O. "The Word of God in the Old Testament." *Theological Dictionary of the New Testament,* Vol. 2, 90ff, ed. G. Kittel. Grand Rapids: Eerdmans, 1967.

Reicke, B. and G. W. Bromiley, trans. "Proisteimi." *Theological Dictionary of the New Testament*, by G. Friedrich. Grand Rapids: Eerdmans, 1968. 6:700-703.

Richards, L. O. *Youth Ministry: Its Renewal in the Local Church*. Grand Rapids: Zondervan, 1978.

———. *A Theology of Children's Ministry*. Grand Rapids: Zondervan, 1983.

Sell, C. M. *Family Ministry*. Revised Edition. Grand Rapids: Zondervan, 1995.

Senter III, M. H. "Axioms of Youth Ministry." *The Complete Book of Youth Ministry*. W. S. Benson and M. H. Senter, III. Chicago: Moody, 1987.

Slabbert, F. van Z. *Youths in the New South Africa: Towards Policy Formulation*. Pretoria: HSRC, 1994.

Strommen, M. P. *Profiles of Youth*. Saint Louis, Missouri: Concordia, 1963.

———. *Five Cries of Youth*. 1974. Reprint. San Francisco: Harper & Row, 1979.

——— and A. I. Strommen *Five Cries of Parents*. San Francisco: Harper & Row, 1985.

Trimmer, E. A. *Youth Ministry Handbook*. Nashville: Abingdon, 1994.

Van der Ven, J. A. and W. J. Berger. "Analysen van gesprekken met jongeren." *Graven naar geloof*. Assen:Van Gorcum, 1976.

Response to the Inclusive Congregational Approach from a Preparatory Perspective
by Wesley Black

It seems to me that the opening scenario of your chapter hints at the problems addressed in this approach: a group of church leaders struggles with the best approaches to dealing with youths and how to shape the congregation's youth ministry. Yet there are no youths present for this discussion (at least none are mentioned, or are reported to have said anything). It is a group of adults in a discussion about youths.

Perhaps this is one reason the congregation is in a predicament. There is low youth attendance and participation, drug abuse among some of the young people, and inadequate funding for some youth programs. The pastor, however, feels urgently that the proper response is not yet another program *for* youths, but an inclusive congregation approach *with* youths to involve them at every level of congregational life.

The pastor's comments apparently get a mixed reaction from his congregation. There is some doubt and even some cynicism in the congregation's comments: "You're sounding rather biblical, Pastor, with the olive tree and all...But where are we going with all this?" The pastor's conclusion is that the church must be prepared to change—a radical suggestion for this church, as it would be in many churches.

I find your views of the church and the inclusive role that youth ministry plays in the life of the congregation very similar to the Preparatory approach in many ways. There are critical differences, however. Nevertheless, the Inclusive Congregational approach has a number of positive points. For the purpose of this response, I would like to mention two positive reactions and two negative reactions to the Inclusive approach.

Theological arguments and view of the church

You state the case in a solid theological argument. This chapter spells out the basis for youth ministry as an expression of the whole congregation, on the argument that the work of the people of God includes what we traditionally call "youth work" (among other names and descriptions). You state unequivocally that you reject "the traditional dichotomy between youth ministry as a duty of the local church and youth ministry as an organized form of working with youths" apart from the ministry of the church.

In this case, first and foremost, you couched the argument admirably in theological terms. It is biblically well-grounded and based. You proceed with a short but comprehensive description of the functions of the church and the various modes of ministry, including the threefold formula of serving God, serving one another as a community of the faithful, and serving the world. This is expressed in eight ministries drawn from solid biblical references.

You remind us that the congregational body is incomplete without children and adolescents, and that youth ministry comes up short without the relationships that come from inclusion in the congregation.

All this grows out of the overall purpose of communicating the gospel of Jesus Christ.

I believe you rightly emphasize that youth ministry is not another mode of God's coming to children and adolescents, but is instead "about finding a place for youths within every ministry and among the people that the ministries are designed to reach and serve—the people to whom God comes by means of the ministries." You said it well.

Furthermore, I appreciate how you unwrap the several modes of youth ministry. In worship, for example, you underline the benefits to intergenerational experiences. While there are ample arguments for age-specific worship times, those adolescents who spend time worshiping with only their peer group risk shallow, one-dimensional experiences before God.

You remind us, too, that the congregational body is incomplete without children and adolescents, and that youth ministry comes up short without the relationships that come from inclusion in the congregation.

Youth ministry tasks of the church

You and I also agree about the functional areas of youth ministry within the scope of the congregation's work. Youths, you write, cannot be franchised out to someone else for their spiritual nurture and growth, but are the *congregation's* responsibility—a responsibility that is "inalienable and not transferable."

This tenet, by the way, is echoed by the Search Institute's Peter Benson in his book *All Kids Are Our Kids*, in which he reminds us that it takes many voices, with similar values and life examples, speaking with intentional redundancy, to provide the assets that youths need in today's secular world.[1] Youth ministry calls for all Christians to be witnesses to the life-changing message of Christ, not just a few specialized youth workers who can relate well to youths.

In addition, you emphasize that youth ministry is a task of the whole church—despite the fact that seminaries typically and unfortunately teach youth ministry as a kind of supplement to other, seemingly more important, forms of pastoral ministry. You conclude rightly that "as long as the whole is reduced to a part, even the part—in this case, education/catechesis—will not come into its own."

This leads to the conclusion that the pastor and congregation have a responsibility to include youths in the priorities and functions of the congregation. This is easier stated than done—though you seemed to recognize the difficulty in this approach when you wrote that "the challenge for leadership and parents is to go to the drawing board with the youths. *Together* this new approach and its consequences must be thought through and worked out." (Which, in fact, is a good argument for the Preparatory approach to youth ministry: adults working with youths to train them to assume leadership for their ministry now and in the future. But more about this in my chapter on the Preparatory approach.

There is much to commend in the Inclusive Congregational approach. Yet there are two areas that I believe are weak: a poorly defined description of youth ministry, and a weak view of the developmental needs of adolescents.

Just what is youth ministry?

You write that your definition of youth ministry is comprehensive yet "differentiated and focused." What exactly do you mean by this? There are strong arguments for comprehension and inclusion, but little to explain how to express youth ministry in tangible ways. "Youths need all that adults need," you rightly state, "but there is a difference between how to feed that need in a 10-year-old and how to feed that same need in a 50-year-old." But you do not clearly describe *how* those two experiences are different.

Again, you write that "preaching is still preaching, but it is focused on and directed at the youths. This focus is determined by the youths' phase of life and the needs peculiar to that phase." Yet how is that to be done? Will it happen in the course of congregational worship times? If so, how is it focused? Will it happen in occasional sermon examples and illustrations, or through customized sermons written especially for youth? You recognize the difficulty for pastors to pull this off in a congregational that spans several generations ("To be contemporary as well as traditional is no easy matter"). But isn't there a need for *separate* times of preaching, teaching, ministry, and interaction with other youths? Don't they need their own time as well as meeting corporately with the congregation? And does the Inclusive Congregational approach even permit this?

You seem to hint at the answer when you say, "Then their Sunday school classes moved to meet on Sunday afternoons, and the adolescents developed under the leadership of two of the local pastors at their own vibrant, but very traditional, worship service in the evening." However, isn't this something different from an inclusive approach? You seem to be moving toward separating the youths from the larger body in order to focus on their worship needs.

Programs similar to your Inclusive Congregational approach have historically proven faulty, at least when American mainline denominations adopted them particularly during the 1970s: several denominational offices dismissed their youth staffs and officially encouraged congregations to approach youth ministry from an inclusive perspective, as you recommend in your argument. Youths were to be considered full members of the congregation. Yet churches that followed this approach suffered setbacks in their youth ministries from which many congregations and even some denominations have never fully recovered.

I believe that too often churches attempt the Inclusive Congregational approach only to have their efforts reduced to tokenism, in which a youth is placed on each standing committee in the church. Or they structure all programs and educational groupings so that everyone is experiencing a similar type of ministry (normally something decided by adults). Or youths are invited to be a part of all discussions and decisions of the congregation, with little regard for the limited attention span or interest level of adolescents.

Just what are the developmental needs of youths?

It strikes me that your view of adolescents' developmental needs is weak. "Few other modes of ministry," you write about pastoral care, for example, "explain as well… that children and adolescents need all that other believers need, only to a greater extent and in a differentiated, yet focused way." What does this mean if not that, at times, youths need to be set apart for specialized forms of ministry?

In discussing *diakonia* or service, after pointing out that Strommen determined in empirical studies that youths have a specific inclination to a service-oriented life, you write, "This mode is therefore about involving the youths, at their level of maturity for certain kinds of service, in the comprehensive service of the congregation in this world…and at the same time involv[ing] the youths in service suitable to their age." The problem here is that too often congregations want youths to participate as *adults* participate, rather than as *youths* participate. Youths need developmentally specific ways to channel their energies and idealism; they need their own ways to put into practice the movement of God in their lives. They need to be able to serve in ways that are different from adults. The entire congregation will benefit from this youthful inclination to serve unselfishly (even though they may act quite selfishly at times.)

Churches that do not recognize the need for youths to invest themselves in something meaningful and worthwhile *to them* miss out on contributing to the proper nurture of youths and fail to benefit from the fruits of their students' youthful idealism and energy. You seem to recognize that "this kind of church," as you put it— accurately I believe—"loses the youths and shoves them into the arms of any person or organization that cares and treats them like they're important."

There may be yet another developmental blind spot, this one in your discussion of *marturia*, or witness. You got it right when you wrote, "One witnesses to a 10-year-old differently than to an adult. Furthermore, a 10-year-old witnesses to others differently than an adult does." This is especially true among adolescents. Who better to witness to a teenager than another teenager? Your concession underscores the need for preparation and focus on youths witnessing to their peers. But how is this accomplished? More importantly, how is it done with specific focus and within an Inclusive Congregational approach? Your chapter is fuzzy on answers to questions like these.

> Approaches like yours have historically proven faulty, at least when American mainline denominations adopted them particularly during the 1970s. Many congregations and even some denominations have never fully recovered.

Finally, I am troubled by how apparently little regard the Inclusive Congregational approach has for unchurched adolescents. This approach seems to deal mainly with those who grew up in church or those who attend with their families. While I appreciate the emphasis on family ministry, there are huge numbers of adolescents outside the family of God—adolescents who can often be reached by the witness of a peer and so brought into the family.

Notes

1. Peter Benson, *All Kids Are Our Kids* (San Francisco: Jossey-Bass, 1997).

Response to the Inclusive Congregational Approach from a Missional Perspective
by Chap Clark

Malan, I found your article to be an insightful critique of one of the most important aspects of parish youth ministry—the congregation's commitment to their young.

There are several points about the Inclusive Congregational approach to youth ministry with which I agree.

Unwillingness to include youth

Your piercing appraisal of the state of youth ministry in the church—specifically, that local churches are typically unable or unwilling to include or even care about the young of the congregation—is more than justified, at least in those societies in which an adolescent subculture has developed. When you claim that young people have been treated like "foster care, not family" in the church, there is significant cause for alarm. The most recent history of youth ministry reveals that this is indeed the case in the vast majority of parish youth ministries: youths have indeed been segregated from the community of the church at large, relegated instead to a programmatic holding tank until they are ready to be included in the life of the church.

Youth ministry should not and cannot be reduced to a programmatic sideshow of a local congregation. Ministry toward and care of young people at all levels is a central responsibility of every member of a congregation. Your assertion that the youths are part of the congregation cannot be shouted too loudly, and I was grateful to hear it.

Banished to catechesis

I also share your disappointment how youth ministry has historically been banished to the narrow focus of the church's educational program, or catechesis. Your chapter disputes the claim of those committed to a catechesic philosophy, asserting again and again that the integration of youth and adult congregation is complex, systemic, and highly relational.

Individualism as opposed to community

You touched lightly but significantly upon the tug that modern Christianity feels (at least in industrialized societies) from individualism on one hand, and community on the other. Theologically there is no question that the basic mode of experiencing biblical Christianity—including youth ministry—is within the context of the Christian community. Youth ministry that segments and divides the body, even if for the sake of winning the lost or similarly noble reasons, does a disservice to the youths it seeks to attract and disciple.

I do, however, take issue with four aspects of the Inclusive Congregational approach as you described it:

- The idea that youths need to be included in every ministry.
- The lack of acknowledgement that adolescence is a transitional phase that needs specific and focused attention.
- The lack of acknowledgement that adolescence has changed dramatically over the past few decades.

• The idea that a healthy youth ministry is the result of a church that is simply willing to change and programmatically adapt to the tastes of the young.

Adolescence as a transitional phase

It appears that you never do reconcile an apparent conflict between a youth ministry's need for age-specific, programmed discipleship options (where youths "require and need to receive specific attention")—between that and immersion in the life of the church like any adult (the church, you write, must find "a place for youths within every ministry"). You seem to favor, at least in statements like these, some sort of focused youth ministry—yet the remainder of your article appears to deny even that concession. That is, until your examples at the end, which you intended as evidence of your chapter's premise—but which seemed to me to be instances of how most churches attempt to merely placate an uninterested adolescent population.

> To what extent should youths be allowed to experience age-specific training, fellowship, and worship? Yet to what extent should that be balanced with intergenerational relationships?

Granted, this is a difficult and delicate theological balance. To what extent should youths be allowed and even encouraged to experience age-specific training, fellowship, and worship? To what extent should that be balanced with intergenerational relationships? This is not easily resolved, nor should it be, at least on a macro scale. Each church must determine for itself what is appropriate for its history, traditions, and polity in terms of deciding on programmatic responses to the needs of adolescents. Consider a church, for example, with a sizable elderly population that requires sensitivity in its style of worship—there may be other ways to connect this church's young with the elderly than forcing them into the same worship services or mission projects. Although I fully endorse what you write about the theological bases of the Inclusive Congregational approach, the application of that theology, I believe, needs to be context specific.

Denial of the adolescent task

Your chapter seems to pass over and ignore the essence of the adolescent task. "There is no theological reason," you write, "why what is valid for adults is not valid for youth." This assumption pervades your article and is especially prevalent in your categories of mission and administration. The implication, at least as I read your argument, is that adolescents are herein considered to be a *different kind* of adult, rather than individuals who have not yet achieved the status and maturity of adulthood.

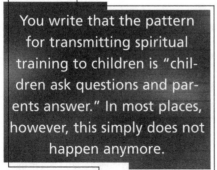

> You write that the pattern for transmitting spiritual training to children is "children ask questions and parents answer." In most places, however, this simply does not happen anymore.

By its very nature and design, adolescence is a time when one tries out different "selves," when one is inconsistent (even in matters of faith), and when one is often more concerned about how the self emerges from a social setting or environment than about others in general. When given too much authority, too loud a voice, and too much autonomy, the adolescent stage can be more harmful than healthy for a young person. Yes, I believe that leadership options and seasons of significant responsibility are a vital component of the youth ministry task, but only when contained within the protective embrace of adults (or congregations) who watch out for the young person's growth and development. Adolescents are not another type of adult needing to be included in every ministry of the church so much as they are trainees in life who need a congregation that is committed to their spiritual and personal development.

Young people's world has changed

Not mentioned in your chapter is the fact that the world affecting young people has dramatically changed over the past few decades. Yet the adolescent's world must be considered when discussing the pragmatics of youth ministry. Again, I agree with the theological assumptions of an Inclusive Congregational approach as you spell out those assumptions—what I question is the sociological and programmatic response to this theological stance.

Yes, the congregation is called to the youth ministry task. And yes, parents (and family) provide the "primary hermeneutic sphere" in the discipleship of the young. Yet the cultural gap between the young and those in power has shifted dramatically. You write, for example, that the pattern for transmitting spiritual training to children is "children ask questions and parents answer." In most places, however, this simply does not happen anymore. Of course, in more stable societies, in which knowledge was passed to younger generations through traditional modes of education, children certainly sat with their parents and asked them questions. But for the past few decades, this kind of willingness and teachability has been all but jettisoned by adolescents.

It is generally accepted by cultural observers that we live in a society with a postmodern worldview. There is also strong evidence that young people, as a population if not as individuals, have sensed for some time that adults have generally withdrawn from their traditional nurturing role to adolescents. This has caused a sense of cultural abandonment, adding fuel to what is already smoldering. If this is correct, then your article is an important voice in calling youth ministry practitioners to strategically incorporate families and the congregation in our work with adolescents. But the answers provided here—to simply include youths at all levels of ministry without the slightest nod given to embracing the developmental needs of a disenfranchised subculture—could backfire badly. Teenagers today simply do not want, at least on the surface, what you claim they need. The church must find a way to bridge that cultural gap.

If we change, they will come

It is true, of course, that churches must be willing to adapt to a new subculture and must see the ministry to adolescents as the entire congregation's responsibility. But I am also firmly convinced that the church's primary function is to be a witness of salt, light, and proclamation to a world that needs to encounter the living God (as I discuss in some detail in my chapter on the Missional approach). In general, the Inclusive Congregational approach is a wonderful and appropriate first step to caring for the young of a given congregation. But this approach will have virtually no impact on the missional calling of the church to disenfranchised, uninterested, and antagonistic young people. Most of these adolescents simply will not be drawn to a church congregation, even if it is a loving, caring, and inclusive family. There is simply insufficient incentive for such youths to take that first step and explore the possibilities of involvement in (not to mention commitment to) a religious community—unless they have the assurance that the church will in turn invest in their lives.

Today's young people are aware that adult institutions have abandoned them and left them on their own to discover life. They also know that most adults are willing to help them, but usually only if the youth show up for a program. But that is risky, especially for an unchurched adolescent. Yes, the church must be inclusive for its own—but it must be willing to reach out beyond its doors to bring the gospel to the lost, the broken, and the lonely. And as you've made clear in your chapter, all in the congregation are sent—adults, youth, everyone. For this is the ultimate mandate of the youth ministry task.

Response to the Inclusive Congregational Approach from a Strategic Perspective
by Mark H. Senter III

I appreciate how you dealt holistically, biblically, and theologically with the issues related to youth ministry, Malan. In the youth ministry fraternity we have a tendency to cluster ourselves around the pragmatic questions that grow out of developmental psychology (What is his level of moral reasoning?), sociology (What influence does the peer group have upon her daily decisions?), communication theory (What impact does MTV have upon their understanding of my message?), and even cultural anthropology (How can I understand the youth culture?). As important as these questions are to youth ministry, they are really secondary questions that arise from theological disciplines—which is where your argument was rooted, I was pleased to see.

God approaches people

You have placed the entire discussion of youth ministry and the church in the context of God approaching people. What an insightful way to frame youth ministry—so obvious from a theological perspective, but so absent in most of the youth ministry literature, music, conferences, and even seminary training. Seldom do we take that necessary step backwards to see the big picture of how God comes to young people. You are correct when you write that

> Seldom do we take that necessary step backwards to see the big picture of how God comes to young people, relentlessly, just as he always has: through the church and through his Word.

"youth ministry is not a separate or additional mode of God's coming to the youths." It is part of something profoundly larger. Suddenly, I don't feel as alone in youth ministry. God is relentlessly coming to young people just as he always has—through the church and through his Word.

In your definition of the Inclusive Congregational approach, I hear you in effect saying, "Do not marginalize youths. Do not rob them of the full richness of God's coming by segregating them either physically or through a failure to pay equal attention to the language in which God's coming is communicated." You lift a tremendous load off the shoulders of youth ministers and place it squarely where it belongs—on the broad shoulders of the church leadership and entire congregations.

And even from the beginning of your chapter, you certainly do not downplay the consequences of adopting an Inclusive Congregational approach. It's as if you say, "If you don't want this, read no further." If only these consequences were a normal part of the everyday community life of the church. There would be no second-class citizens in the faith community. The church would honor the contribution of every child and adolescent, realizing that the congregation is impoverished without what young people bring to fellowship.

Malan, your approach turns youth ministry on its ear, at least in this way: years ago the counseling profession began moving from an individualized intervention towards a family-systems approach to therapy, in the belief that most problems faced by children and adolescents were best solved by dealing with the dynamic web of family relationships, which had often fallen into disrepair. Your theological perspectives introduce a similar perspective to youth ministry and the church. (I wonder if you consider the church to be dysfunctional and in need of healing. If so, how can the church and its youths find that healing?)

> The problem is not that theology is irrelevant to youth ministry, but that 19th-century theological categories are inadequate for addressing either modern youths in the 20th century (your point) or postmodern youths in the 21st century.

Historian's perspective

As a historian I appreciate your use of the historical development of both theology and youth ministry to advance your case. The impact of Abraham Kuyper on the categorization of theology, for example, with the resulting loss of youths from churches, does suggest a closer tie between theology and youth ministry than most people might imagine. In fact, many in youth ministry might argue for a *greater* distance between formal theology and youth ministry for the sake of saving those you describe as "lost to the church."

The problem, as I see it, is not that theology is irrelevant to youth ministry, but that 19th century theological categories are inadequate for addressing either modern youths in the 20th century (your point) or postmodern youths in the 21st century. Like you, I feel a theological understanding of the church must drive the church's ministry to youths. Your chapter suggests a framework that, if applied to almost any other approach, would dramatically weave youth ministry back into the fabric of the church tapestry.

I agree that most of the critical theological issues that face youth ministry are related to ecclesiology. The recent attempts to address a theology of youth ministry by Dean Borgman and Rick Dunn have found their focus elsewhere. The last person in this field that I can remember addressing the ecclesiologal aspects of youth ministry is Larry Richards in the 1970s.[1]

The pragmatic question

I took an early draft of your chapter to a focus group at my school. Their predominant response was "It won't happen." This may be more an indictment of the church than of your chapter, but it is nevertheless a bleak assessment. The greatest problem may be that churches *think* they are doing what you have proposed, but never ask the youths—the customers—for their perspective. One of my students volunteered that the reason she, and eventually her family, left their church for another was precisely *because* the church practiced an Inclusive Congregational youth ministry.

I would suggest it is far easier to talk Inclusive Congregational than to live it. This approach cannot be a passive or *laissez-faire* approach to youth ministry, but must be highly active and intentional. Even the example of your own church (page 19) is not highly encouraging: the inclusive steps were the outgrowth of the youth committee, not the church leadership. And maybe this is where all youth ministries will have to start, given the current structure of contemporary churches—but it seems to violate the inclusive principles you are describing.

Also less than encouraging in this same example from your own church is the small number of modes of God's coming that I detected: *kerugma* (preaching) and *leitourgia* (worship) are there, but the *didache* (teaching) apparently turned into another worship service, while *paraklesis* (pastoral care), *diakonia* (service), and *kubernesis* (administration) are all but missing. *Koinonia* (mutuality) seems to be a byproduct of other activities, while *marturia* (witness) was a part of the fabric of the church from earlier times. If this is a best-case scenario, it doesn't bring much hope.

Is "differentiated and focused" actually a segregated experience?

Just when I thought you were making a radical statement that in effect eliminated youth ministry as we know it and reintegrated young people into every aspect of the church, you seemed to make a switch. Introducing the modes of God's coming seemed to create a parallel track—as you put it, "Youth ministry preaching is still preaching, but it is focused on and directed at the youths." Your illustration suggests integration into the larger church family, but this statement sounds like separate tracks—youth and adult.

If you concede there must be youth ministry preaching, which of the other modes also deserve differentiated approaches? Differentiated worship and differentiated teaching, to name two, sound like a youth church to me, not an inclusive congregation. (I realize you mentioned only differentiated preaching, Malan, but you seemed to imply the others were appropriate.) In fact, your illustration of the Sunday school class that became a vibrant worship service in the evening appears to be *parallel* worship, not inclusive congregational worship.

If you are arguing that youth ministry must include the eight modes of God's coming to adolescents but would allow for meetings that are for the most part segregated, then even though some adults might attend, the Inclusive Congregational approach could be placed within either the Preparatory or Strategic approaches. The only difference might be that more attention would be paid to *some* of the modes of God's coming, modes that have been shortchanged by current youth ministry models.

Involved youths eventually graduate

In my opinion youth ministry is too often a spectator sport, with adults doing the ministering and young people passively watching. Are you advocating that young people do the preaching, worship leading, teaching, pastoral care, and administrating, while facilitating mutuality, service, and witness? If so, the Inclusive Congregational approach brings a distinctive approach to the current structures of youth ministry. (It also facilitates the Strategic approach I have proposed later in this book.)

But this raises a problem for me, Malan. As youths become effective in leading the eight modes of ministry, what happens when they graduate from high school? In the past, many churches have treated high school graduates as novice adults, in effect placing them into a holding pen until they marry and have at least their first child. Only then are they allowed to assume minor roles in church leadership. By this time years have often elapsed, and much of their passion for facilitating God's coming to his people has evaporated. Whatever integration had taken place is lost, thanks to this forced hiatus from ministry.

On the other hand, we do not want to kick out the older leaders of the church just to make room for recent high school graduates. So what should we do?

Two ideas come to mind. The one closest to my heart is to use these young Christian leaders to start a new church at the rate of about one every 10 years. New beginnings provide the greatest possibility for making the eightfold coming of God a brilliant reality in the lives of young people. This should be done, however, with the full blessing of the church leadership.

The other option might be to promote 35-to-40-year-old church leaders to a council of elders and ask them to assume the role of wise counselors, though without organizational authority over younger leaders. The implications of the idea for youth ministry seem wonderfully refreshing: younger Christians would have incentive to remain involved in the church and further shape their expression among their generation.

Large or small church?

One question that repeatedly comes to my mind: *To what extent is the Inclusive Congregational approach to youth ministry possible in larger churches?* For churches with a weekly attendance of 250 or less, the approach might be an option because churches of this size still tend to operate like extended families. In fact, for the church to be an effective ministry, youths just about have to be active participants.

As churches get larger, however, and move toward a full-service orientation with staff-led or staff-supervised ministries that respond to a wide range of human needs, the inclusive nature of your approach becomes difficult and perhaps even impossible. In effect, young people become customers to be served, rather than brothers or sisters to be embraced. Still, large churches are powerful influences in presenting a Christian presence to most cultures. I would be uncomfortable writing them off because they cannot readily include young people in the fabric of their congregational tapestry.

Two practical tests

Apart from these theoretical applications (although good theory is essential to good practice, as we all know), I would suggest that youth workers who read your chapter ask themselves one question: *How effectively has my church allowed God to come to the youths through the eight modes described by Malan?* Would this be an appropriate starting place for rethinking the relationship of youth ministry and the church?

Finally, it would be useful to those contemplating the Inclusive Congregational approach for their own ministries to contact churches with experience in this approach. Then the approach would appear to be a more viable option where the rest of us are ministering.

> If you concede there must be youth ministry preaching, which of the other modes also deserve differentiated approaches? Differentiated worship and differentiated teaching, to name two, sound like a youth church to me, not an inclusive congregation.

Notes

1. Dean Borgman, *When Kumbaya Is Not Enough* (Peabody, Massachusetts: Hendrickson, 1997); Rick Dunn, *Reaching a Generation for Christ* (Chicago: Moody Press, 1997); and Larry Richards, *Youth Ministry and a New Face for the Church.*

Rejoinder from the Inclusive Congregational Approach

by Malan Nel

As I read your responses to my chapter, it was wonderful to sense a basic agreement of the importance of the local church as home base for youth ministry. I believe we are together in our struggle to relate youth ministry to the church. Second, it was encouraging and motivating to feel your deep love for and knowledge of the general fields of research and ministry, as well as your passion for the specific field of youth ministry.

Rather than address each of your criticisms, I will organize my response here according to the theological reasoning in the Inclusive Congregational approach itself.

Ecclesiology

My personal conviction is that our understanding of the church is vital to understanding the approach. Your general agreement with encouraged me. Allow me to put two dimensions of my own ecclesiology on the table and argue a case for the approach.

An important piece of information from my own theological journey is that I wrote my doctoral dissertation on *youth evangelism*. My research led me to believe that we do not have much hope to win young people back (let alone keep and prepare them for ministry) if we do not develop local churches with a heart for the lost and a heart for equipping God's people for ministry. That whole exercise led me to research the field that the Germans, the Dutch, and we in South Africa call *Gemeindeaufbau*: revitalizing the local church, or equipping and preparing God's people for ministry, or—one may say—returning the ministry to the people.

In my research in this amazing field of study and ministry, I rediscovered over and over again that the church is by definition a missionary concept. This is our God-given identity. And since then I have devoted my life to helping local churches discover who they are in order to recover who they are. A very important part of my motivation for still doing this work is to revitalize youth ministry.

> A local church is seldom composed of only adults or of only youths. The faith community is inclusive. In principle we have no right whatsoever to marginalize children and adolescents. Any division here will probably result in a tragic loss for both adults and youths alike.

Missionary church

Back to the two ecclesiological remarks concerning this approach: Wherever and whenever I used the words *local church* or *congregation* in the chapter, I meant a missionary church where people—adults and youths alike—are being prepared for ministry in the world. It is part and parcel of my understanding of the church. Do local churches view themselves as such? Probably not, or at least not to the extent that they take their calling in this world seriously enough. My conviction therefore is that it is not so much the youths that need to change (which is of course also true), but the adults.

In this sense, Mark, I find your remark healing in itself: "Do you consider the church to be dysfunctional and in need of healing?" Yes I do, and I think it is worth putting a lot of energy into that. I feel like crying when I discover through congregational analyses that churches are dying because they just miss out on the understanding of their missionary nature. I cry even more when I discover leaders who are so disappointed in the local body of believers (and understandably so from time to time) that they give up on the church as the community of God to equip and to reach the world.

May I add that my understanding of mission is a very concrete and comprehensive one: Becoming involved in this world in any way the situation calls for. It is indeed a ministry of bringing help and giving hope as the people of God. We need to love, serve, and call them back. Chap, I think you are absolutely right—young people will not come just because we change. How will they ever know if we don't show and tell them how much we care for them because we know how much God cares for us?

My second point in understanding the church, which is a given in this approach, is the biblical inclusiveness of the church. This has two dimensions to it: a local church is seldom composed of only adults or of only youths. The faith community in this sense is inclusive. In principle we have no right whatsoever to marginalize children and adolescents. Any division here will probably result in a tragic loss for both adults and youths alike. The second dimension of inclusivity has to do with the missionary nature of the church. The letter to the Ephesians is a good example of this inclusiveness.

I believe that it is really true that our theology of the church (as informed by our understanding of the Father, Son, and Holy Spirit) informs our theology of youth ministry.

Comprehensive, differentiated, focused

Taking seriously the missionary nature of the church has caused me to plead for a youth ministry approach that is comprehensive, differentiated, and focused. My reason for pleading for comprehensivity is both theological and contextual—and I feel compelled to stress the contextual reason one more time: for many reasons Western society has nearly lost any deep awareness of the corporate nature of the faith community. Specialization has played into this and sometimes taken individualism to an un-Christian extreme. That being said, however, youth ministry is indeed about a differentiated and focused approach within the frame of comprehensiveness. Youth ministry can never be without it.

Chap and Wes, I really appreciate your remarks concerning the unique nature, needs, and potential of adolescents (and children). My understanding is that when we really take differentiation seriously, we will address more of the important issues you mentioned. There is, to my mind, even a strong theological argument for what is commonly called specialization

> Parents need help to keep open conversation with their children as natural as talking about baseball. The context of Deuteronomy 6 probably assumes something of this natural and spontaneous talking.

and special attention to age-specifics (need as well as potential): the metaphor of us as children of God (cf. John 1:12). Although God is the Father of us all in the same way (comprehensivity), he is also the Father of every individual in a unique way (differentiation). He focuses on his family and on the individual. He made us, after all—and when we discover even in a science class how wonderfully he made us in every age and phase of life, how can any faith community ignore it?

Yes, I agree with you in full. My defense? This is included and assumed in the words I used in the definition, namely *differentiated focus*. I take it that it applies to every single dimension of the ministry.

"Simply does not happen anymore"

In this regard, Chap, I need to respond to the important issue you raised in response to my reference to Deuteronomy 6 and how spiritual teaching is passed to the next generation ("children ask questions and parents answer"): the fact that "in most places, however, this simply does not happen anymore." You are probably correct, in general. Yet in Christian homes where talking about God and his involvement in our lives (the issue at stake in Deuteronomy 6:4-10) is easy, parent-child dialogue probably still takes place. Thus parents need all the help in the world to keep these conversations as natural as talking about baseball. The context of Deuteronomy 6 probably assumes something of this natural and spontaneous talking.

Secondly, I take it for granted that in many societies (maybe most) the mood is very much postmodern, so much so that Deuteronomy's asking-and-answering pattern can be interpreted only as dialogue, and often critical dialogue, on both sides. To restate my conviction: the family plays a major role in revitalizing youth ministry (as an integral congregational approach). The beauty of family (where it is still in place) is the natural, God-given, ability of parent(s) to be simultaneously comprehensive, yet differentiate.

I sincerely believe that all modes of ministry should take this principle seriously. The prerequisite is to continuously work on the inclusive understanding of the faith community. To feel accepted by the church may eventually prove to be more important than any given deed. Assuming that this is happening because it became part of the vision and mission of senior and junior leadership, differentiation is not harmful or divisive. It proves that the same faith community is serious enough to give expression to the uniqueness of the children and adolescents who are an integral part of the church as extended family. Mark, I hope that in stating this I have at least partially responded to your remark about my example of differentiation in preaching and the relevance of that for other ministries.

When they leave high school

A remark you made, Mark—and which I think is important to come back to—concerns the fact that we often lose students when they leave high school. You wrote that "whatever integration had taken place is lost by this hiatus from ministry." My response in this case is probably very contextual, but very valid, I believe: as important as a *congregational* philosophy for youth ministry may be, so is a *denominational* philosophy. I am privileged to be part of a denomination that adopted a national policy for youth ministry way back in 1966. This was the result of almost 10 years of intensive research across the board, on what was generally understood to be youth ministry. My viewpoint in teaching future pastors has always been that understanding the first two points of the policy is critical, so much so that if you understand them the other five points are almost superfluous. Youths are an integral part of the local body of believers; furthermore, youths are the responsibility of the church from birth to adulthood. That is, youths are our responsibility from the cradle to grave.

Local churches have not taken seriously many issues of the denominational philosophy. The empirical reality is even more broken than we think. But one important fruit of the policy, after so many years, is the issue you referred to—making local churches available for youths to study in after high school, local churches that will give them even more opportunity to grow and serve (also as leaders). I could see it work as a full-time student pastor in a well-integrated local church where adults, teenagers, and university students really come into their own right while maintaining the integrated nature.

Based on the results of a national survey we did, my conviction is that this is partly because the youths who are not naturally interested in academics have never really felt accepted in their home churches—which means that during late adolescence they not only venture to "try out different 'selves,'" (as Chap rightly puts it in his response), but also leave. Some never come back. We need a broader inclusive picture if we want to escape the present impasse.

> Establishing an Inclusive Congregational approach is more an issue of attitude than strategy. Planning alone will not save the day for youth ministry.

Personally I believe that getting this approach established (initially at least) is more of an attitudinal issue than a strategic one. It can never exclude strategies, but planning alone will not save the day for youth ministry. It is the same as in what I call *building up the local church*: You need to help the local body of believers understand their God-given identity in order to begin living and functioning accordingly—and enjoying their identity. To say it theologically: the indicative always precedes and informs the imperative.

Three important prepositions

I will attempt to prove this point by returning to three pivotal prepositions in my definition: youth ministry is a comprehensive congregational ministry in which God comes, through all forms of ministry and with especial regard to parents (or their substitutes), with a differentiated focus *to* youths (as an integral part of the congregation), and also *with* and *through* the youths in the congregation to the world.

To my mind youth ministry will only change from a one-sided educational approach to an inclusive congregational approach (many-faceted and multidimensional as it may be) when the faith community begins to value children and adolescents as not only being recipients but as worthy co-workers in every sense of the Word and ministry. But this is an insight or understanding far more than it is just a strategy. In many churches I know, this asks for a new birth, a hermeneutical experience of who God is and who we are because he is who he is.

Conclusion

"Your approach is not for the faint of heart," Wes wrote. I agree. I worked within the system for many years and know how difficult it is. Why? For many reasons, probably for this one most of all: we are being asked to challenge long-standing traditions, and often the leadership itself. What encourages me in my work as a facilitator in local churches is the attitude of parents when they realize that this is God's plan to *prepare* their children as part of the faith community for their mission in the world, even to the point that planting a new church may become part of that mission.

The Preparatory Approach to Youth Ministry
by Wesley Black

Responses
Nel: from an Inclusive Congregational perspective
Clark: from a Missional perspective
Senter: from a Strategic perspective

Rejoinder
Black

The Preparatory Approach to Youth Ministry
by Wesley Black

Scenario: The Great Commission is for youth groups, too

"Kevin, can you come up here and tell us what happened last weekend?"

At his youth minister's invitation from the platform during a Sunday morning service, Kevin rose from the pew and headed for the front of the church. The high school junior, who had been coming to the midweek youth group meeting, had become a Christian only recently.

Also invited up front was Charlie, Kevin's Sunday school teacher. The youth group had just returned from youth camp, and with Charlie's encouragement, Kevin had some exciting news to share with the whole church.

"After I came to faith," Kevin told the congregation, "I realized my dad wasn't a Christian. I asked the youth group to pray for him. It was really cool to hear them pray, but nothing much happened at first.

"Then my Sunday school teacher—Charlie, here—came over to our house and became friends with Mom and Dad. A few weeks later our youth pastor asked Dad if he'd help with nighttime security at youth camp, and he agreed."

Charlie picked up the story. "During the week several of the adult counselors befriended Kenneth—that's Kevin's dad—and I had a chance to share the gospel with him," he said. "On the last night of youth camp, Kenneth publicly professed his faith in Christ. The prayers of Kevin, his youth group friends, the sponsors on the trip, and others in the church family had been answered."

"So this morning," said the youth minister, "we celebrate the baptism of Kenneth Runge as a new member of God's family."

With the pastor, Kevin, and Charlie standing near the pulpit—and the youth group, packed into the front two pews, a significant player in this joyful event—the youth minister baptized Kevin's dad and welcomed him into the family of faith. Smiles rippled through the congregation, some "Amens!" could be heard from the older members, and outright applause exploded from the youth group.

Consider this a glimpse into a healthy, comprehensive church youth ministry. It is hardly a complete picture, but it at least introduces the concepts of a kind of youth ministry that expresses the overall mission of a church.

Definition of the Preparatory Approach

The Preparatory approach to youth ministry can be defined as *a specialized ministry to adolescents that prepares them to participate in the life of existing churches as leaders, disciples, or evangelists.* Students are viewed as disciples-in-training, with opportunities for service both in the present and the future. Developmental dynamics suggest that youth ministry be viewed as a laboratory in which disciples can grow in a culture guided by spiritual coaches.

Description of the Preparatory Approach

In the story at the beginning of this chapter, both Kevin and his father were brought into the kingdom of God through the youth ministry of a church. But who was responsible for evangelizing this student and his father? The youth minister? The youth leaders who befriended the father? The teenagers who prayed for Kevin and his dad? The church's pastor? The answer, of course, is yes to all of these—for everyone who had anything to do with this situation was responsible for the outcome.

Let's look at a snapshot of a typical youth group during a typical activity—say the first 10 minutes of the weekly youth meeting, while kids are up and socializing before the program gets down to business. Jason, the youth leader—the *only* youth leader in the room—notices that the group is having a great time. Then he spots Heather. At one time she was active in the group, but lately has dropped out.

"Hey, it's good to see you," Jason says. "We've missed you…you know, we really need to catch up with each other."

"Yeah," she replies, "I really do need to talk to someone."

Jason glances at his watch, looks around the room, can't help but notice that the seventh and eighth graders are on the verge of dismantling things, sees the older high schoolers drifting out the door to their own meeting.

"Tell you what, Heather," he says. "Right after this we're going to have a great discussion time. Stick around, okay?"

After the program, of course, Heather is nowhere to be found. Her only ride home was with a friend who had to leave early. Upshot? A prime time for ministry was missed in the press of a fun youth event.

Now let's look at another snapshot of the same social gathering, same teenagers. But this time most of the church's church adult youth leaders are there. Jason spots Heather, the same conversation takes place—except this time, when Heather says that, yes, she needs to talk to someone, Jason glances to the front of the room and notices that the volunteer Sunday school leader responsible for this meeting is starting the program. The high schoolers, instead of departing for their own meeting, are leading the games, music, fun, and devotional time. Adult youth workers and Sunday school leaders are there to guide the younger ones toward more creative, positive uses of their time, as well as to help integrate everyone into the group—even those who are paired off romantically or who stick to their own clique.

> He looks around the room and can't help but notice that the seventh and eighth graders are on the verge of dismantling things, while the older high schoolers drift out the door to their own meeting.

Meanwhile, Jason has begun a meaningful conversation with Heather. He gives a come-here-for-a-minute wave at Libby, who teaches the Sunday school class that Heather is in.

"Heather, this is Libby. She's been trying to contact you for a while now."

This is all the priming Heather needs to open up. She explains that she and her mother had to move to another part of town since her parents' divorce. She does not have a car, their phone number has changed, and she has to go to another school, so she lost contact with her church group. Libby offers to arrange transportation for Heather with a girl who doesn't live far from Heather's new neighborhood. The three of them keep talking, and ministry happens.

Activity-based or ministry-based?

There may be many models of youth ministry, but they mostly fall into two approaches: the activity-based approach and the ministry-based approach. They share many of the same techniques and principles, but there are important differences.

The *activity-based approach* is built upon a series of youth activities—a programming approach designed to appeal to youths by involving them in the youth group, building relationships with other youths and adult leaders, and keeping them too busy to sin. It is normally evaluated by the calendar and the calculator. The key questions are usually—

- *How many?*
- *How often?*
- *How big?*
- *How exciting?*

And if the answer to each is *More than last time*, success is thought to be assured.

The activity-based approach typically has little purpose and direction. It often has a theme or overarching slogan, yet the underlying goal is merely to attract more youths, do more things with more money, and have more fun than the last time.

A *ministry-based approach* is radically different in key areas. While on the surface it looks no different than an activity-based event, the ministry-based approach starts from a different stance and moves with different goals in mind. It grows out of the ministry of the church and is consequently related directly to the purposes of that church—out of which the youth ministries' activities, strategies, funding, and leadership grow.

While using many of the same activities, a ministry-based Preparatory approach has a clear purpose for every activity: *the development of mature Christians in the church, both now and for the future.* Activities, always carefully chosen, may be a starting place, but they are never the gauge by which the youth ministry is judged.

A ministry-based approach attempts to reach increasing numbers of youths and involve them in the youth ministry. Unfortunately, some youth ministries see only that aspect and believe they are ministry-based youth groups because their goal, too, is increasing the size of the youth group. In reality, however, they have settled for simply planning and conducting youth events while hoping the students will become involved in the church as a result.

If we are to touch the lives of youths in significant ways, we must also touch the lives of those who are in their world of influence. This includes parents, siblings, extended family, and peers.

Melinda had the good fortune to be in a youth group that was ministry-based. She grew up in the church and attended Sunday school and most youth activities. And youth choir—she loved to sing and had natural talents that led her to become a leader in her church's music ministry. She often led the music in youth group meetings. When she graduated from high school, Melinda moved into the college group and eventually into the adult music ministry of her church.

Now Melinda is a young adult, active in several spheres of church ministry. She sings in the adult choir and participates in many of the activities and ministries of the church. She has found ways to live out her faith and employ her spiritual gifts in the body of believers. Many of the adults she knew as a child and teenager welcomed her into the world of adulthood. They were pleased and affirmed her when she joined the adult choir and continued to serve God through her musical talents. Her transition from youth ministry into adult ministry was almost seamless , and the leadership talents that budded in adolescence now blossomed in young adulthood.

Key Distinctions of the Ministry-Based Approach

Youth ministry is the church's ministry to youth

Youth ministry belongs to the church. The church is the basic unit of ministry in the Great Commission, and youth ministry grows out of that scheme. Youth ministry is the expression of the Great Commission by a church toward teenagers and the adults who make up their world.

Youth ministry is not the property of parents, Sunday school teachers, or youth ministers, despite the commitment of all these people to providing a positive spiritual and moral influence upon their teenagers. Youth ministry is not merely a forum for issues facing young people (drug abuse, sexual activity, cultural questions, etc.). Youth ministry is more than Bible studies and fellowships, even more than pastoral ministry to adolescents. Youth ministry is everything a church does with, to, or for teenagers. In fact, under the banner of youth ministry is anything that a congregation does that touches the lives of teenagers in any way, formally or informally.

In a sentence, youth ministry is the *holistic Christian ministry of the local church under its leadership to young people and those who influence their spiritual growth.*

Even *this* is youth ministry: the church parking lot had become a favored hangout on Friday and Saturday nights—and not by the church's own teenagers, either. The kids turned up their car stereos, made out, and generally disturbed the neighbors. The first church members to take action, fortunately, were those who wanted to minister, not enforce private-property laws. These church members (who were not particularly young, either) took their plan to the elders, got the green light—and soon began spending their Friday and Saturday nights grilling hamburgers in the church parking lot. Needless to say, the free food opened a lot of conversations and friendship with the kids who parked there.

Youth ministry is not a separate program

Youth ministry is not a program to reach and involve teenagers while merely hoping they become involved in the church. Again, youth ministry is everything a church does with, to, and for teenagers that builds them into becoming the church. This may include such things as organized groups, elected leaders, planned programs, strategic experiences, and carefully designed curriculum materials. Or it may include such things as informal conversations at football games, intergenerational experiences with adults and children, worship times on Sunday mornings, and spontaneous happenings away from the church campus.

This is vastly different from what Mark DeVries calls "orphaning structures" found in many traditional youth ministries.

> **They carry students to the doorway of adulthood but often leave them there. For many young adults who have grown up with the youth group (or the Fellowship of Christian Athletes or Young Life or another such group) as their primary faith community, frequently their only hope is to try to recreate their youth group experience as an adult (by becoming a youth leader or**

finding a church that is as much like their youth group as possible). This is at least one cause of the amazing phenomenon of new, short-lived "hip" churches springing up across the country, where members over 40 are as rare as a snowstorm in the Sahara. These churches may simply be the perpetuation of a traditional youth ministry.[1]

Youth ministry is channeled through the ongoing programs of the church whenever possible. Sunday school is foundational to reaching and involving teenagers in all areas of the church's ministry. Discipleship, mission education and ministry, music, fellowship, recreation, and worship all serve to guide youths toward a lifetime of spiritual growth.

Youth ministry blends discipleship and evangelism

The Great Commission has at least two emphases—reach all you can and teach all you reach (Matthew 28:19-20). It is a human tendency to go overboard in one direction or the other. For example, we can spend a lot of energy reaching more and more teenagers, yet fail to disciple those we reach—despite the fact that we are called to make disciples, not just baby Christians.

On the other hand, others are inclined to go too far in stressing discipleship at the expense of reaching larger numbers of youths. Such youth workers major on going deeper in the Christian life, yet fail to reach out to those who are on the fringes or beyond. They tend to limit the number of youths who can take part in youth events, provide programs that appeal to only those youths judged to be "serious about the Lord," and neglect those who are not actively involved most of the time.

Youth ministry both separates and integrates

Theologically, there may be no division between youths and anyone else in the church. But developmentally, socially, and culturally there are major differences—differences that must be addressed if we are to be faithful to Christ's command to make disciples of all the world. Teenagers require focused attention to their needs in ministry, programming, and relationships.

Youth ministry has to be a two-headed creature in order to keep balance in this effort. There are times when the primary youth leader needs to remind the church that youths need different agendas, meeting times, and programming techniques. Effective youth ministry needs proper funding and provision that might not be cost-effective in a bottom-line mindset.

Likewise, the youths may need to be reminded that they are part of a larger enterprise. They are not building the world's largest banana split simply for fun: there is purpose and direction to what is happening, and it is tied to the overall purpose and direction of the church. It is good for youths to have a growing appreciation for the fact that, for example, someone's tithes and offerings help pay for the buildings in which they meet. The church cares enough for the future of their youths that they invest in many ways to nurture their lives toward Christ.

Youth ministry is shaped by families

Youths do not live in a vacuum. They originated in families and spend most of their childhood and teen years in the home. They are highly influenced by their parents—a point that some youth ministry approaches seem to ignore, and a point that Chap Clark makes when he writes that—

Church programs have evolved to the point that many now operate as parachurch programs within the context and under the umbrella of a local church. Perhaps this began with youth ministry, which a few decades ago modeled much of its programming after the successful pioneering work of Youth for Christ and Young Life in the 1950s and 1960s. Today nearly every ministry program in a local church operates as an independent entity. These programs vie for money, volunteers, and visibility as they attempt to carry out their ministries.[2]

In fact, Clark asserts, "such an individualistic approach eventually harms families in a local church." If we are to touch the lives of youths in significant ways, we must also touch the lives of those who are in their world of influence. This includes parents, siblings, extended family, and peers. It means that the church's youth ministry reaches out in significant ways to relate not only to the teenagers, but also to the adults who make up their world. A church that is serious about youth ministry will seek to relate to the parents of teenagers as energetically as it does to the teens themselves.

As Clark states,

> The church as Christ's body on earth must reverse this trend, remembering that we are all necessary to be a healthy community. Each program must see itself as a part of something bigger that God is doing. Every member of the body must be concerned about the other members. A unified vision for the local church is the first step in reshaping the church into God's family.[3]

I recently visited a church's youth leaders, a young couple looking for help for a high school girl—call her Ashley—who had begun dabbling with sex and drugs. She was even talking with her friends about suicide. The youth leaders had tried to talk to Ashley, but she was not interested in their help. I encouraged them to go to Ashley's parents and discuss the situation with them.

Ashley's mother was single, having just gone through an ugly divorce from a husband who had been neglectful and abusive. But now she was involved with another abusive man. It became clear how the influences were stacking up against Ashley, a girl who had once thrived in the youth group but was now headed down a destructive path. She was not going to pull out of this alone. She needed a more positive family environment to make some necessary changes. Both Ashley and her mom needed to respond to the life-changing power of Christ.

The Best Practices in Youth Ministry

An e-boutique, and the good-time girl

In an office just this side of luxurious, Nate has all the gimmicks, gadgets, and resources that youth ministers dream about. There's a video-editing suite in a side room, a fully loaded computer, enough books for a small college library, and a desk larger than many small apartments. He has a secretary, voice mail, e-mail, a Web site, and electronic organizers.

But Nate has a lousy youth ministry.

Yes, he has collected all the trappings of a current, high-tech, youth ministry. He has built an image but forgotten about the ministry in the process. He does not relate well to teenagers or leaders or parents. The rest of the staff is a bother to him. In fact, the very practice of ministry is his downfall, and he will probably crash and burn—at more than one church—unless he changes quickly.

Jean's office, on the other hand, could pass for a storage room—basketballs and in-line skates in the corner, lost-and-found blue jeans and sweatshirts from the last retreat under her desk, empty Coke cans under the beat-up couch. The phone cord is a knotted tangle, but ostensibly for a good reason: Jean is constantly in contact with all the kids.

But she has problems, too. Jean gets along well with a certain segment of the youths, while others go largely ignored. The jocks, cheerleaders, and popular kids all love to see Jean coming because she relates so well to them. But quieter, less popular kids do not get the same attention from her. Plus she has never been able to enlist adults to help her, because she is too busy building relationships with the teenagers. Parents smile and tolerate her because the kids seem to enjoy having her around. The truth is, Jean seems closer to an overgrown adolescent than a guide into adulthood.

Nate and Jean are common types of youth workers with common practices. Let's identify some of the better (if not the best) practices among youth ministers today, practices that pastors and church staff youth ministers have found to be most effective in youth ministry.

An educational base

Youth ministry calls for a multitude of ministry skills—worship leadership, pastoral ministry, counseling, family ministry, leader development, and teaching. Of these skills, it is common for youth workers to focus their efforts on the relational tasks—befriending teenagers, building trust. The social events, one-on-one encounters, informal gatherings, and trips that such

> The mention of recruiting volunteers usually starts a youth worker into a litany of excuses: people are busy and overextended...they have no time or energy for youth ministry...most have enough trouble dealing with their own issues, not to mention those of adolescents.

youth workers plan are aimed at building relationships and fellowship between the leaders and the youths, as well as among the youths themselves.

But there has to be more. Beyond the fellowship and trust building, there has to be teaching and proclamation of the message of Christ. Of all titles, Jesus was most often called *teacher* in the New Testament because of his approach to ministry: he taught. We would do well to follow his example.

Effective youth ministers must be competent teachers. They find themselves in teaching situations constantly—in small groups and large, one-to-one with youths, with parent groups and volunteer leader groups, speaking to the entire congregation, and standing before other youth ministers. The skills of effectively communicating to others, leading the learning process, and designing learning experiences are essentials in effective youth ministry.

Even the volunteer leaders should be able to teach. "The things you have heard me say in the presence of many witnesses," Paul instructed Timothy, "entrust to reliable men who will also be qualified to teach others" (2 Timothy 2:2). When youths meet in small groups with volunteer leaders, those leaders need teaching skills similar to those of the youth minister. If they can't teach, then it is the youth minister's responsibility to train the volunteers to be teachers (or provide training for them).

Finally, youth ministry needs to be built on an educational base—rather than, say, a relational base—because it is an integral part of one of the three basic church functions (ministry to believers—see page 55 for further discussion of church functions). Discipleship includes teaching youths and others to know and obey all that Christ commanded. Any youth ministry that ignores this vital function is lacking in a key area.

Weekday ministries

Like many youth ministry interns, Bryan visits the schools where most of the youths from his church attend. (In the process of visiting his young flock on their campuses, he has also developed a lifelong immunity to school cafeteria food.) Through contacts at the schools, he has opened up doors for relationship and ministry with unchurched kids who might never have met him in the hallways of church.

> Some youth ministers prefer that their students' parents would just deliver the teens to the youth room, then kindly step aside so the real professionals can do their magic.

And it is often those unchurched teenagers who see Bryan at Friday night football games, the district track meets, and the weekly home meetings. They might also see Bryan at the midweek youth meeting at the church—which is informal and attractive to a lot of unchurched teens, and where the music is played loud enough to irritate the adults.

Parachurch youth ministries developed these techniques through the years, yet church-based youth ministries adopted and honed them. Any youth worker knows that youth ministry cannot be confined to a church building or a Sunday meeting. It takes a 24/7/365 outlook to penetrate the adolescent world.

Which means that youth ministers and their volunteer leaders must find prime ministry moments between weekends. Students who see their Sunday school teachers at a concert or a recital or a game get the message that their teachers cares about them personally—that, to their teachers, the kids are more than just warm bodies filling chairs at church.

Many youth ministers today are building their weekday ministries into highly effective evangelistic tools. Midweek nights, for example, are terrific times for youths to gather at the church (or elsewhere) for worship, celebration, learning, fellowship, and discipleship. Larger churches often hold separate meetings for the younger and older youths. Youths themselves often serve as key leaders in music, worship, teaching, and leading games. The environment is one of joy, celebration, and youthfulness, such meetings can serve as an excellent entry point into the church for non-Christian youths.

Youth ministry council

In earlier days of youth ministry, churches attempted to reach and hold onto young people by throwing events *for* them—parties, banquets, picnics, trips. It wasn't long before youths wanted to have a part in planning and leading their own ministries.

So some churches began involving youths through a *youth council*, composed of students who would meet with a youth leader and plan some of their own activities—most of them social events. Often a youth council was overseen by an all-adult *youth committee*, which all too often believed their job was to keep the kids in line or to supervise the youth director. The adversarial relationship that developed was almost inevitable. The kids and the youth director would plan the fun stuff, and the youth committee would say that it cost too much.

Today a more effective practice has evolved that incorporates the best of each group. A *youth ministry council*—composed of teenagers, youth leaders, and parents—involves youths in planning and leading, while providing reasonable adult leadership. Teenagers typically comprise the majority of a youth ministry council, the point being to make it easier for them to speak up without being intimidated by adults on the council.

Youths are often selected to serve on the council by placing their names in the running for a position. They apply in writing, describe their school activities, their family situation, interests and skills, their spiritual life. The youth minister and a screening committee then draw from these applicants to be on the council. The adults that typically sit on the council are key youth leaders—leaders or teachers in Sunday school, discipleship groups, music ministries, mission and outreach, and the like. A few parents round out the council membership.

The usual purposes of a youth ministry council are to—

- Provide overall direction and coordination to the youth ministry.
- Give specific feedback to the youth minister about programs, activities, and strategies.
- Coordinate all items on the youth ministry calendar in view of the church calendar.
- Plan major youth events—camps, retreats, mission trips, and weekday ministries, etc.

Lead teams

Once a youth ministry council puts events on the calendar, the *lead teams* plan their details. Lead teams, involving a broader section of the entire church family than a youth ministry council does, consist of teenagers and adults who work together to plan and carry out one event or project: one lead team plans the winter retreat, another produces the youth group newsletter, etc. A lead team is typically composed of two to four youths, an adult youth worker, and two to three other interested adults (parents or otherwise). The size and makeup of these teams can vary according to the needs and size of the church.

All teams meet monthly, to work on their projects and give status reports. The youth minister moves from team to team, facilitating their work and helping as problems arise. But the key is for the teams to plan and conduct their projects themselves. They most often draw in other youths and adults to carry out the project, while the lead teams themselves serve as a steering committee. This is a beautiful picture of shared leadership among youths, youth leaders, other interested adults, and the youth minister.

Lead teams must be nurtured and developed by a youth minister with a vision for sharing the leadership across a broad spectrum. Churches who cherish the image of a youth director doing all the work with teenagers will have to come to terms with the concept of youth ministry throughout the church. The youth minister becomes the leader of the church's youth ministry, rather than the director of a series of activities and events called "youth ministry."

Enlistment, screening, and development of volunteers

The Lone Ranger had Tonto. But even a Tonto is in not enough for the multifaceted world of today's youth ministry. Effective comprehensive youth ministry demands a variety of people with all sorts of gifts and talents. Contemporary youth ministers must be willing and able to enlist and develop those persons into a cadre of leaders with a heart for God and for teenagers.

The mention of recruiting volunteers usually starts a youth worker into a litany of excuses: people are busy and overextended…they have no time, energy, or commitment to be involved in youth ministry…most candidates have enough trouble dealing with their own issues, not to mention those of adolescents.

Yet enlistment should be an ongoing lifestyle, not a seasonal campaign. Veteran youth ministers have learned to plant the seeds with potential leaders, nurture them in relationships, and pray for the time when they are ready to take a step into leadership.

The practice of screening prospective leaders has become a necessity. No longer is it acceptable to enlist someone who looks young, talks young, thinks young, or is simply willing to work with a church's teenagers. Too often churches or youth groups have suffered because of some inappropriate behavior of a youth leader who succumbed to temptation or sinful desires around youths. Given the world we live in today, and the need to protect the church against liability as well as the young against harm, steps must be taken to screen potential leaders—and especially those who will work with teenagers and children. Most churches now have procedures in place for background checks, references, and time limits before a person can begin serving in youth ministry in any capacity.

If youth ministry is to multiply and grow, leader development is essential. Volunteers need training and equipping in effective youth ministry knowledge and skills—which can be provided through local workshops, regional and national conferences, printed materials, and multimedia resources.

It is more and more common to see active youth ministers in their 50s and 60s. Youth ministry as a stepping stone into "grownup" ministry is losing steam. Youth ministry is now considered a valid, life-long vocation by growing numbers of churches.

Often prospective leaders learn on the job as they begin working with youths in informal ways and gradually assume more responsibility.

Churches with the best track records in this area provide some sort of potential leadership training experiences, which can resemble the following:

- Classes that take place over a series of weeks cover introductory material into the basics of leadership, biblical examples of leadership, help with leadership gifts, and suggestions for personal spiritual growth.
- A second training series is offered later, on the basics of youth leadership skills, under standing adolescents and their culture, and practical suggestions for teaching and learning with youths.
- Another series consists of an overview of the church's youth ministry and opportunties for service now and in the future.

Most youth workers learn that it is usually easier to enlist someone to take part in training for future service than to enlist someone for an immediate responsibility.

Parent enrichment

Youth ministry involves ministry to youths and their families. Parents are powerful influences—both good and bad—on teenagers. Adolescent psychologist Nancy Cobb says, "Despite the increasing importance of friends in adolescents' lives, parents continue to remain significant sources of strength and influence."[4]

Doug Fields echoes the need for attention toward parenting and the influence of parents on their teenagers.

> **Each student in our youth ministry is the product of a unique family system, a system responsible for forming beliefs, values, and actions. If we plan to effectively minister to students over the long haul, we must sincerely desire to minister to entire families, because a youth ministry that excludes parents is about as effective as a Band-Aid on a hemorrhage.[5]**

Still, youth ministers—particularly *young* youth ministers—tend to regard their students' parents as extra baggage. Some youth ministers would prefer that those middle-aged people would just deliver the teens to the youth room, then kindly step aside so the *real* professionals can do their magic. Other youth workers involve parents only by telling them the pertinent details about an event—just cost and schedule, usually.

These are serious shortcomings, both from biblical and ministry skills perspectives. A comprehensive youth ministry must relate to parents in more transparent and comprehensive ways, including—

- *Parent-teen experiences.* These are fellowships, retreats, discussions—whatever shared experiences can be created in order to foster family discussion of important issues, rather than just the rapid exchange of information (*Where are you going? Have you finished your homework? Who was that on the phone?*).
- *Parent discussion groups.* Parents provide feedback and input about youth ministry programming and strategies. On these occasions parents may provide information, express concerns, and offer suggestions to those who work most closely with their children.
- *Parent education and ministry.* This can occur in a variety of forms: classes for parents, special speakers to deal with parenting issues, parent support groups, parent discussion groups, and resources (books, DVDs, videos, audio tapes—to name just a few of the resources that the church can provide for Christian parents that are unavailable for meetings).
- *Parent information processes.* Newsletters, mailers, announcements during worship services and Bible studies, and informational meetings before major youth events—all these help families make informed decisions about the manner in which their young people will be involved in the discipleship ministries of the church.

> As long as volunteers are simply chaperons for group outings, they can hang around the outside of the group and be mere preventive influences. But if you want your adult staff to roll up their sleeves and do the work of the youth ministry, then they need training.

Campus ministry

Some of the most exciting and promising ministry among teenagers today is happening in the places where they spend a great deal of their waking hours. School clubs provide a way for teens to be ministers among their peers. Campus Bible clubs, Christian clubs, and the like provide a place for teens to meet with other Christian friends for support, prayer, encouragement, and outreach to their peers.

While students provide the leadership in many campus efforts, they still need the support and administrative expertise of adults. Take Scott and Chris, for example—seniors in our church youth group who wanted to start a community-wide meeting once a month for Christian youths, on a high school campus. Their first meeting was an overwhelming success: 400 teenagers came, representing several schools and a variety of Christian groups. The two boys soon saw they were in over their heads, at least logistically. So they called our youth minister for help. He responded with just the right amount of encouragement, affirmation, and adult guidance to avoid problems and make their new ministry run smoothly.

Schools are important places for church youth leaders to meet teenagers and build bridges. Yet this aspect of youth ministry must be handled with appropriate respect for the concerns many parents and school officials have for protecting teenagers against radical elements in society. Campus ministry, therefore, must have strong student leadership—which of course highlights the benefits of equipping youths to take the lead in reaching and discipling their peers.

It may be appropriate for an adult youth leader to visit with youths during their school lunch period, but it is another thing for that person to lead a Bible study or discussion group during school hours. Youths are looking for the challenge and opportunity to step into leadership, and church-based youth ministry provides the ideal training ground to prepare youths for the future and give them real experiences today.

The Role of the Youth Minister in the Church

Younger children are unrivaled at telling the ungilded truth. Our kindergarten son came home one afternoon with exciting news about school that day. The teacher had apparently asked the class what kind of work their mommies and daddies did. So what did he tell the teacher, I asked our son.

"I said my daddy plays with teenagers," the boy replied.

I could hardly wait to meet his teacher at open house.

Merely "playing with teenagers" is only one stereotype youth workers must live down. Of course, some stereotypes are more earned than others. When people ask what seminary subjects I teach, I sometimes answer, "Wildlife Management."

One stereotype at least is falling—the Hip Twenty-Something Youth Guy—as many churches discover the value of maturity in youth ministry leadership, and as a trend continues of longer tenure and longevity in youth ministry. It is becoming more and more common for me to know active youth ministers in their 50s and 60s; many I know are in their 40s. Youth ministry as a stepping stone into "grownup" ministry is losing steam. Youth ministry is now considered a valid, life-long calling and vocation by growing numbers of churches,[6] which is a welcome trend. Ministers who consider themselves "preachers in waiting" cheat youths out of valuable nurture and ministry that could and should be offered by those who are truly called to this area of service.

Of course, a minister is almost forced to look beyond youth ministry if it cannot provide realistic wages. Salary (including taxable and nontaxable monies) and protection benefits (insurance, medical coverage, retirement provisions) are appropriate budget items for church youth ministers. Recoverable expenses such as car allowance, books, and conference expenses are common budget provisions in churches today. As youth ministers grow older in ministry, they have additional expenses for their families—larger houses to accommodate a growing family, college expenses, and weddings, to name just the big ones.

Programming, too, requires funding. Bible study materials, curriculum materials for all educational groups, music, teaching supplies, and recreational materials are only a few of the expenses involved. Personnel expenses can include support staff, interns, and expenses for volunteer leaders. If a church intends to build a thriving youth ministry, then a budget needs to be provided through normal budgeting channels.

Youth leaders have many demands on their time and energy, and they shouldn't be saddled with raising funds for the basic costs of doing youth ministry. Certainly, some activities will call for special offerings or fundraising efforts—but the primary channel for undergirding the work of the church, including youth ministry, should be the tithes and offerings of the congregation.

Not too many years ago, budget items like these were an extravagant and impossible luxury to most congregations, because in many churches the youth leader was by no means perceived as a minister of the congregation, but only as a fun-loving adult who related well with teenagers. This perception has changed in many contemporary churches with full-time youth ministry staff. The youth minister is often seen as a full minister to the entire congregation. This is sometimes reflected in titles such as *associate pastor for youth ministry, minister to youth,* or *student pastor,* according to church polity.

The Value of Volunteer Leaders in Youth Ministry

Remember Kevin in this chapter's opening scenario, whose father became a Christian during a youth retreat? When Kevin first came to the church's midweek youth group program, "Backstage," he met many adults who love and care about teenagers—because the youth minister had encouraged all volunteer youth leaders, Sunday school teachers and otherwise, to come as often as possible. So during Kevin's first visit to Backstage, he was introduced to the man who'd be his Sunday school teacher, who in turned encouraged Kevin to get involved in Sunday school and other youth activities.

Furthermore, on the first overnighter Kevin attended with his youth group, he met some other volunteer youth leaders who worked in all kinds of educational and ministry programs at our church. They learned of Kevin's desire for his father to become a Christian and began praying for Kevin's dad. And eventually that prayer was answered—with the volunteer leaders on hand to rejoice with Kevin.

Youths need adult role models to see what a walking, talking, real adult Christian looks like. As one benefits from a guide in a foreign country—for help with language, customs, food, taboos, expectations—so youth leaders can be that same kind of guide for youths as they move into and through adolescence.

It is a sad youth who does not have wholesome, positive interactions with those outside his peer group. Intergenerational experiences provide the flavor and heritage that make life rich and full. Adults can help youths connect with the past as well as the future, while guiding them as they step into leadership roles of their own. Skillful youth leaders can provide positive images of adults, which youths need as they sort through the many identity decisions of adolescence.

I remember when the thought first hit me that I would never be able to reach and relate to some teenagers—that for whatever reasons, our personalities would not click, and consequently they would not join our church or youth group. But I eventually discovered that I

> Jesus did not say, "On this rock I will build my church and my youth groups," because the church is the primary unit of ministry. To be biblically and theologically valid, youth ministry must be related to the church.

could enlist and train *another* adult who *could* reach and relate to those students. And when that happened, the size of our group began to enlarge and our ministry was multiplied.

Though it didn't come easy. It took my deliberate efforts to recruit people who were different from me in order to reach the teenagers who needed those different personalities and role models. These volunteer leaders also brought with them life experiences that added depth and validity as they worked with the youth group. It was Ephesians 4:11-16 played out before my eyes: God calling different individuals in the church to do a variety of tasks according to their different abilities—all for the building up of the body of Christ.

These volunteers must themselves be prepared, too. They need to be equipped to relate to youths and to teach an assortment of biblical, ethical, and doctrinal subjects—and this calls for training in youth ministry skills and knowledge of content in their area of responsibility. As long as volunteers are simply chaperons for group outings, they can hang around the outside of the group and be mere preventive influences. But if you want your adult staff to roll up their sleeves and do the work of the youth ministry with you and alongside of you—as leaders of small groups, for instance, a model of youth meeting that is particularly needed for teenagers in this generation—then volunteer leaders must be enlisted, equipped, and supported in youth ministry.

Youth Ministry in the Church and Home

The ancient Hebrews recognized the home as the primary teaching institution.[7] They took seriously the commands that follow closely on the *Shema*:

> **Hear, O Israel: The Lord our God, the Lord is one. Love the Lord your God with all your heart and with all your soul and with all your strength. These commandments that I give you today are to be upon your hearts. Impress them on your children. Talk about them when you sit at home and when you walk along the road, when you lie down and when you get up.** (Deuteronomy 6:4-7)

The home was the context where children and parents encountered God—where teaching and learning occurred in natural, informal ways through example and loving words. Through an environment of warmth and acceptance, parents communicated the meaning of a personal relationship with God.

Youth ministers today yearn for homes such as that. Too often teenagers come to church alone or in spite of unbelieving parents. Church leaders are caught between being true to the biblical teaching of the role of homes in religious training and the reality of unbelieving parents who care little about the things of God.

So how do we sort through this? Some youth leaders try to make their youth ministry the one stop where teenagers can have all their spiritual needs met and ignore the parental dimension. Other youth workers just assume that parents intuitively know to have a family devotional life and can do it. A few confront the issue and do what is appropriate to help parents fulfill their biblical responsibilities.

Youth workers who do this best provide parents and guardians with the tools and encouragement to carry out the proper functions of home in the spiritual life of teenagers. They plan and conduct classes, workshops, and informal discussions designed to help parents address the needs of raising teenagers "in the training and instruction of the Lord" (Ephesians 6:4). They engage teens and adults in parent-youth dialogue sessions to build stronger bonds and improve communication. They make literature available to parents that strengthens the home in Christian education. They guard their programming schedules to allow for adequate time for families to be together. They offer suggestions for parents who don't know how to handle blocks of unplanned time with their own teenagers.

It is almost in the nature of a youth minister to assume a parental role, to be their students' mothers and fathers in absentia. Yet this is wrong, both biblically and socially. Youth leaders can provide needed adult role models and some measure of nurture, but they can never fulfill the role of parenting that is so often missing in today's families. They can, however, be a friend to families and offer help and encouragement to the parents of teens.

Justification for the Preparatory Approach

Youth ministry and the church

When one asserts that youth ministry resides in the very life and ongoing work of a church, it must be understood just what the word *church* means. In the New Testament the word *ekklesia*, translated *church* in most English-language Bibles, usually means a local body of believers gathered to worship, teach, fellowship, and spread the gospel of Jesus Christ. The word is never used to mean a building, and in most cases designates a local congregation of Christians.[8] Although we may speak of "the early church," or of all Christians collectively as "the Church," no New Testament writer used *ekklesia* in this way.[9]

The books of Acts, James, 3 John, Revelation, and the earlier letters of Paul always use *ekklesia*, or *church*, to mean a particular local congregation. While there is only one church in God's ultimate purpose, which includes all believers throughout all time, on earth its use is pluriform—that is, *ekklesia* is wherever two or three gather in God's name.

New Testament churches were gatherings of persons who professed faith in Jesus Christ, met together to worship him, and sought to enlist others to follow him in faith. Their practices included baptism in the name of Jesus, regular attendance at instruction, and regular fellowship that is described by Luke as the breaking of bread and prayer (Acts 2:41-46).

All this to say that, when we talk about the relationship between youth ministry and church, we mean a local congregation of believers. This does not rule out the larger context of working with other Christians in cooperative efforts. Groups of churches, parachurch groups, denominational and interdenominational groups, and even groups of individual Christians can work together in marvelous ways to advance the kingdom of God. But the approach to youth ministry described in this chapter is based on and resides in a local body of believers that we call "church."

A ministry base

To Peter's great confession of the Lordship of Christ (recorded in Matthew 16:16-19), Jesus responded with a pun, playing with the similarity between a pair of Greek words: *petros* (stone) and *petra* (large rock or bedrock). The upshot was this: Peter's confession was the bedrock statement of the church, in that it acknowledged the true identity of Christ, the Son of God.

"On this rock I will build my church," Jesus declared. Notice that Jesus did not say, "I will build my church and my youth groups," because the church is the primary unit of ministry. To be biblically and theologically valid, youth ministry must be related to the church.

Since the church is the home of youth ministry, then, it makes sense to look at how the church shapes the Preparatory approach for relating to teenagers—teaching them, guiding their activities, and helping them move into the world of adults. This biblical pattern provides the best framework for comprehensive, in-depth youth ministry with youths, their families, and the leaders who guide them toward spiritual maturity.

Youth ministry on purpose

The purposes of the church are the purposes of youth ministry. "Healthy youth ministries are built on these same eternal purposes," Doug Fields observes about the church-youth ministry relationship. "Fortunately, God has already given them to us in the Bible. It is our job to uncover them, communicate them, and put leadership behind them."[10]

Healthy youth ministry grows out of the three church functions, which are derived from two passages of Scripture:

> Jesus replied: " 'Love the Lord your God with all your heart and with all your soul and with all your mind.' This is the first and greatest commandment. And the second is like it: 'Love your neighbor as yourself.' (Matthew 22:37-39)

> Therefore go and make disciples of all nations, baptizing them in the name of the Father and of the Son and of the Holy Spirit, and teaching them to obey everything I have commanded you. And surely I am with you always, to the very end of the age." (Matthew 28:19-20)

From these passages we distill three functions of the church: *ministry to God* (worship), *ministry to believers* (nurture), and *ministry to the world* (evangelism). Note how the verses virtually outline the functions of the church—and of youth ministry:

- "Love the Lord your God with all your heart"—*worship*
- "Go therefore and make disciples"—*evangelism*
- "You shall love your neighbor as yourself"—*ministry*
- "Baptizing them"—*fellowship*
- "Teaching them to observe all that I commanded"—*discipleship*
- "Of all the nations"—*missions*

Youth ministry is anchored to the same intent that God has for the church. We may have a multitude of ways of fleshing it out and may use all kinds of gifts, talents, personality traits, and experiences; but we can agree that God has called us to walk alongside youths and involve them in fulfilling these purposes.

Changes Required in the Church

Youth ministry is alive and thriving in some churches, but in others teenagers endure boring traditional programs that lost their effectiveness long ago. Their pastors secretly wish the troublesome adolescents would just go away so they could settle in for comfortable mediocrity. Many youths and their parents have simply given up on the hope of any real change in churches.

In his research with innovative churches, Merton Strommen lists five reasons why stagnant churches resist change: tradition, personality, ideology, affiliation, and demonic power.[11] Yet these reasons need not deter pastors and youth leaders from moving ahead toward five changes that I believe today's churches must embrace if they want a vital ministry with youths.

Youth ministry must become a shared ministry

Youth ministry is a church-wide ministry that involves teenagers in all the functions of the church. These functions include worship, evangelism, fellowship, discipleship, ministry, and missions. Taken together, these provide a comprehensive picture of the Christian life.

As youths participate in church-wide events, they experience the purposes and functions on a larger scale. They see the scope of the Christian life through many ages. They build images and memories of role models for many aspects of life.

At other times, the youths spend time with the youth group, in smaller groups, and in one-to-one relationships with mentors and peers. They gain a variety of experiences that contribute to a more comprehensive picture of the Christian life.

Church leaders must view youth ministry in comprehensive terms. Youth discipleship is the responsibility of everyone. Young people are not a problem to be solved, but an opportunity for love to be expressed.

Youth ministry must become comprehensive

"We see high turnover in youth ministry because many youth workers try to do everything themselves," Doug Fields writes about the frustration that youth ministers often sense when they seek to enlist volunteer leaders. "Some youth workers tell me that they don't have enough time to find leaders; they don't have enough time because they are too busy doing everything themselves."[12]

The most effective youth ministers today seek to partner with parents and teachers in all ministries of the church to guide youths to know God and his love, to have a personal relationship with Christ through salvation, and to grow through a lifetime of discipleship.

Volunteer leaders in a church spend time with teenagers in and out of classes. They teach them the great truths of the Bible and model for them what adult Christians look and act like. They attend to their interests and guide them in positive ways toward Christ. A wise youth minister seeks to enlist and put into service leaders of all ages who can relate to teens in a variety of ways. A wise pastor evaluates the effectiveness of the youth minister on the basis of the manner in which she empowers the diverse gifts in the people of the church to mold the lives of young people.

> Churches must choose people who are capable of purposeful planning to minister to their youths. The selection of the youth minister must be taken with the same seriousness that goes into the process of selecting the preaching pastor.

Kenda Creasy Dean and Ron Foster relate the biblical account of Moses in Numbers 11.[13] The people have begun a giant, whining pity party that leads Moses to the point of exasperation when he cries out, "I cannot carry all these people by myself; the burden is too heavy for me. If this is how you are going to treat me, put me to death right now—if I have found favor in your eyes—and do not let me face my own ruin" (Numbers 11:14-15).

God told Moses to select elders from among the people to share the ministry with him. "What we overlook is the fact that God does not ask Moses to recruit volunteers for Moses' ministry," Dean and Foster write. "These volunteers share *God's* workload, not ours. 'Gather for *me* seventy of the elders of Israel,' God's instructs Moses, 'and they shall bear the burden of the people along with you so that you will not bear it all by yourself.'"[14] The secret to biblical youth ministry is to see it as God's ministry, not ours. Youth ministers must enlist volunteers for God's work, not their own programs or agendas.

Pastors must be willing to be the pastor of youths as well as of adults and children. They must also call forth the gifts of many persons to minister to youths in all aspects of their lives. There must be a sense of balance between pastors, church leaders, parents, and youth leaders as they seek to minister most fully to adolescents.

Youth ministry must become purposeful

Youth ministry often seems to be spontaneous and quickly changing. The postmodern world thrives on a fluid, ever-changing environment with little sense of permanence and direction. It's tempting to think of long-term planning as what they will do *tonight,* and give no thought beyond the immediate interests and needs.

Many other pastors and youth leaders have a better sense of purpose and direction for their ministry with students. Churches today often think in terms of a six-year span—the years between seventh and twelfth grades—in their ministry with youths. What would we like to see happen in the lives of teens before they graduate from high school? How can we best guide them through the teen years and into adulthood? What will we do each year to build on prior experiences, while always providing for those who just entered the youth division? How can we relate to youths at several levels of spiritual maturity through our programming and organization?

These are all questions that pastors, youth ministers, and churches must grapple with if they are to take seriously the biblical mandate of the Great Commission (Matthew 28:19-20) and the Great Commandment (Matthew 22:37-39). A six-year plan to deal with all areas of the Bible, all major biblical doctrines, mission lifestyle and strategies, and developmentally focused life issues will contribute significantly to a purposeful youth ministry.

Furthermore, the church must choose people who are capable of purposeful planning to minister to their youths. The selection of the youth minister must be taken with the same seriousness that goes into the process of selecting the preaching pastor.

Youth ministry must begin to bridge the gap between church and home

Youth ministry includes ministry to and with parents of teenagers. Teens grow up in homes, whether that home is positive or negative, traditional or progressive, intact or splintered, Christian or non-Christian. Youth ministry cannot ignore the influence and modeling that goes on in the home and church and the powerful effect it has on adolescents.

"Are we connecting our kids to nurturing relationships that will last them after they complete their teenager years," Mark DeVries asks, "or are we simply exploiting them as public relations tools to make our ministries appear successful?" He then makes the crucial point "that unless we are making intentional focused efforts at connecting kids with mature Christian adults in the church (not just their youth leaders), we are more like the vultures preying on kids at rock concerts and less like spiritual leaders praying that their children's lives would be founded upon eternal things."[15]

The point is that parenting teenagers is a tough job. It takes enormous energy and stamina. Today's families are stressed and worn from a world that is not often family friendly. Too often parents are eager to find relief by turning over their adolescents to others who seem hip and cool. They relish the thought of a night off from the duties of parenthood with teenagers who continually stretch their patience.

Parent support groups, discussion groups, parent-teen events and experiences, and other parent ministry efforts can play a key role in reaching and discipling families for Christ. And this in turn deepens the quality of ministry with youths in the church.

Youth ministry must begin including the pastor and church

The Preparatory approach to youth ministry has to have the support of the church, including the senior pastor. This support includes a priority in budget planning for youth ministry. The pastor is often a key in championing the efforts to support a thriving youth ministry.

While some churches want to have an effective youth ministry, they often settle for essentially sponsoring a youth ministry: that is, they provide budgeted funds, designate a meeting place, hire someone to do all the work, and wish them well. They just don't want to get their hands dirty with the grind of youth ministry.

This is not the biblical model or mandate, and youths can detect this attitude in a heartbeat. They sense when adults do not want them to be around. They know when the church is just going through the motions of youth ministry without the heart's desire to include youths in the life of the church. The pastor often sets the tone for all this.

Consistent support from the pulpit makes a world of difference. The pastor does not have to be at every youth event. He doesn't even have to keep up with the teenage slang du jour. A few appearances at youth fellowships, however, do not hurt the cause. A pastor who goes to youth camp and spends a week with the youths, building relationships and allowing the youths to know their pastor better, will reap the benefits for years to come.

Conclusion

Kevin and his father experienced the nurture and support of a body of Christian believers. The church—not merely the youth group—served as the context for youths to learn, grow, minister, and celebrate their faith.

In the past we looked upon young people as the "church of tomorrow." This was a sincere desire to help adolescents be prepared to someday step into leadership roles in their churches and the community. The mere desire to see this happen, however, is not enough. Adolescents are hungry for challenge and opportunities today. They are willing to pour enormous time and energy into service, meeting challenges all around them. Visit any athletic training field before or after school to see the kind of energy and enthusiasm that teens will put forth to make a winning effort. They will give themselves unselfishly to those causes they see as being worthy and wherever they feel needed and valued.

The best learning often comes on the job. Preparation for the future can best be learned through a combination of classroom experiences and hands-on learning. The church's youth ministry is an ideal setting for a learning laboratory for youths as they live today with eyes on tomorrow.

When Nathaniel recognized Jesus as God's Son (John 1:49), Jesus commended him—and went on to say, "You shall see greater things than these" (v. 50). When we see youths as active and involved in their churches, reaching out in ministry with their peers today, we can see that same promise fulfilled.

Notes

1. Mark DeVries, "What Is Youth Ministry's Relationship to the Family?", *Reaching a Generation for Christ* (Chicago: Moody Press, 1997), 485.

2. Chap Clark, *The Youth Worker's Handbook to Family Ministry* (Grand Rapids: Youth Specialties/Zondervan, 1997), 26.

3. Clark, 28.

4. Nancy J. Cobb, *Adolescence* (Mountain View, California: Mayfield Publishing Co., 1998), 280.

5. Doug Fields, *Purpose-Driven Youth Ministry* (Grand Rapids: Youth Specialties/Zondervan, 1998), 251.

6. This and other findings were mentioned at the Youth Ministry Educators Forum, October 30-November 1, 1999, in a research report by Dave Rahn and Karen Jones. The research was a national study done with ministers of youth, conducted by Link Institute for Faithful and Effective Youth Ministry, Huntington College.

7. Budd Smith, "The Family's Role in Teaching," *The Teaching Ministry of the Church* (Nashville: Broadman & Holman Publishers, 1995), 108.

8. *The New Bible Dictionary* (Wheaton: Tyndale House Publishers, 1962).

9. ———.

10. Fields, 45.

11. Merton P. Strommen, *The Innovative Church* (Minneapolis: Augsburg, 1997), 26.

12. Fields, 272.

13. Kenda Creasy Dean and Ron Foster, *The Godbearing Life: The Art of Soul Tending for Youth Ministry* (Nashville: Upper Room Books, 1998), 91.

14. ———.

15. DeVries, 485-488.

References

Benson, Warren S. and Mark H. Senter III. *The Complete Book of Youth Ministry*. Chicago: Moody Press, 1987.

Black, Wesley. *An Introduction to Youth Ministry*. Nashville: Broadman Press, 1991.

Clark, Chap. *The Youth Worker's Handbook to Family Ministry*. Grand Rapids: Youth Specialties/Zondervan, 1997.

Dean, Kenda Creasy and Ron Foster. *The Godbearing Life: The Art of Soul Tending for Youth Ministry*. Nashville: Upper Room Books, 1998.

Dettoni, John M. *Introduction to Youth Ministry*. Grand Rapids: Zondervan, 1993.

Dunn, Richard R. and Mark H. Senter III. *Reaching a Generation for Christ*. Chicago: Moody Press, 1997.

Eldridge, Daryl. *The Teaching Ministry of the Church*. Nashville: Broadman and Holman, 1995.

Fields, Doug. *Purpose-Driven Youth Ministry*. Grand Rapids: Youth Specialties/Zondervan, 1998.

Freudenburg, Ben and Rick Lawrence. *The Family Friendly Church*. Loveland, Colorado: Group Publishing, 1998.

Martinson, Roland. *Effective Youth Ministry: A Congregational Approach*. Minneapolis: Augsburg, 1988.

Robinson, Duffy. *Youth Ministry Nuts and Bolts*. Grand Rapids: Youth Specialties/Zondervan, 1990.

Ross, Richard. *The Work of the Minister of Youth, Revised*. Nashville: Convention Press, 1989.

Segler, Franklin M. Revised by Randall Bradley. *Christian Worship*. Second Edition. Nashville: Broadman and Holman, 1996.

Strommen, Merton P. *The Innovative Church*. Minneapolis: Augsburg, 1997.

Webber, Robert E. *Worship Old and New*. Revised Edition. Grand Rapids: Zondervan, 1994.

Response to the Preparatory Approach from an Inclusive Congregational Perspective
by Malan Nel

When I read your chapter, Wesley, I was once again excited about the possibilities of equipping God's people for ministry. Your chapter is very much in line with what was called catechism teaching during and after the Reformation. Being part of this tradition, I enjoyed your exploration of the approach. If I may quote one of your sentences around which I would like to build my discussion with you: "It was Ephesians 4:11-16 played out before my eyes."

Would you agree that a sad thing that happened was the development of a false dichotomy between equipping older people and Sunday school for children, on the one hand, *and* integrating youths into the full life and work of the total body of believers? In a way this led to a schism between being *prepared* for service, and *service itself*—and we have ended up with an adult membership who are involved in ministry in few ways. Isn't the intention in Ephesians 4 different? The total ministry is aimed at *katartizein* of the people of God "for works of service, so that the body of Christ may be built up" (Ephesians 4:12).

In your article you focus more on the discipleship metaphor, which of course explains the same truth. Whether we approach ministry from that angle or from the Pauline view-

> I am concerned that people might view the Preparatory approach as just another way of reaffirming an outmoded educational paradigm—especially if this approach is paired up with a theological departure point that is authoritarian and propositional in nature.

point, the fact is that we prepare people for ministry or for works of service. Why do you think we have created a gap between adults and children in this regard? Is it possible that we deem young believers unworthy of being equipped and only worthy of being kept busy?

What I point out here is not intended as a critique, but only to emphasize some points of yours that may enrich our attempt to get churches back into a comprehensive ministry of preparing children and adolescents for life and for ministry.

Old Testament moments

The background of the teaching ministry of the church lies in the Old Testament. The teaching concept involves three vital moments: initiation, guidance, and instruction in the way of wisdom.[1] In Jewish thought, life is seen as a way with a destination. Education is seen as the unfolding of life, giving it direction and meaning. In this context the *Torah* was not really viewed as the law of a far-away lawgiver, but as the ever-present voice of the God who cares and wants to give guidance in this unfolding of life. "It points out the way, offers guidance on the road," writes Firet. "It is the word of revelation in which God comes to a person."[2]

In order to sell this important and essential approach in youth ministry, should we not go a little deeper in the discovery of what preparation for life is? I am concerned that people might view the Preparatory approach as just another way of reaffirming an outmoded educational paradigm—especially if this approach is paired up with a theological departure point that is authoritarian and propositional in nature. I believe you would agree that what we want is to revitalize the ministry of *katartizein*, as explained to us in Ephesians 4 and through the metaphor of discipleship. In my own tradition, it is the older members that would identify with the Preparatory approach as you describe it, because they see it as getting back the old Sunday school they grew up with. This is probably not your intention. The norm is to prepare youths for life and ministry—to be contextually relevant.

Relational concerns

Secondly, there is the relational aspect of the preparational approach in youth ministry. I share your conviction that there has to be more than relationships. Like you said: "The social events, one-on-one encounters, informal gatherings, and trips that such youth workers plan are aimed at building relationships and fellowship between the leaders and the youths, as well as among the youths themselves. But there has to be more." Although I know you are not dismissing the importance of relationships, I want to ask you this: given the absolute necessity of pastoral relationships for teaching, should we not explore the relationship and *relational and preparational* aspects more in-depth?

Preparing youths for life and ministry implies change—and we know that people change only when they feel safe. Without a sense of safety, then, they will resist change—in particular, they will not see our preparational efforts as helpful. In *Dynamics in Pastoring*, Firet explores this issue in depth: after a psychological and educational exploration, his conclusion is that nurture focuses on the quintessence of being fully human. That is, when we want people to change into fully functioning human beings, they need to be nurtured. If we want to get adolescents involved in this process of becoming what they have been created to be, then a relationship aimed at change (what Firet calls an *agogic* relationship) is necessary.[3] This relationship is essentially a pastoral one and asks for a basic pastoral posture on the part of the nurturers.

My reason for bringing up this line of Firet's is to make a deduction concerning the approach in your chapter. I often ask myself how it came about that churches can do so much teaching with so little result. Observational research led me to the conclusion that because of the lack of a caring pastoral relationship, teaching has taken place without learning. In church, children and adolescents learn in direct relationship to the measure of care they experience.

How would you respond to this? You probably remember the findings and remarks of Larry Richards concerning advice-giving in youth ministry. "I've suggested that a ministry-facilitating relationship," I remember him writing, "is one in which the adult admits and expresses his equality with youth as persons by encouraging mutual self-revelation and in which youth and adult each learn to trust the other with his thoughts and feelings and experiences, knowing that he is valued and respected."[4]

> How can churches can do so much teaching with so little result? Because of the lack of a caring pastoral relationship, teaching has taken place without learning. In church adolescents learn in direct relationship to the measure of care they experience.

Ministry-based approach

My third observation has to do with the importance of what you call a ministry-based approach over an activity-based youth ministry. I think you are correct in this distinction. Even our activities should have ministry in focus.

Yet what about providing ministry opportunities that befit age-specific abilities and needs of children and adolescents? I would link this with your strong emphasis on family. Would it be fair to say that, in the long run, not many church youths will do what they have not seen their parents do as Christians? Some say that even up to 80 percent of all youths eventually take over the life and worldview of their parents. And we all know that "works of service" (Ephesians 4:12) is an attitudinal thing and needs to be modeled by significant adults.

Leadership development

Finally, I want to thank you for your words about the organization of leadership in the Preparational approach:

> **If youth ministry is to multiply and grow, leader development is essential. Volunteers need training and equipping in effective youth ministry knowledge and skills—which can be provided through local workshops, regional and national conferences, printed materials, and multimedia resources. Often prospective leaders learn on the job as they begin working with youths in informal ways and gradually assume more responsibility.**

Let me make two observations about this point. First, I assume that you work toward creating an atmosphere for this approach in which the leadership sees a local church as a training unit. If that is the case, I would be in full agreement. When we follow through on your discipleship emphasis, this is inescapable. The basic meaning of the discipleship concept (especially taking its Old Testament root seriously) is not so much *following* in the sense of imitating but *learning* (the Greek word *manthanein*). Being disciples of Christ indeed implies *learning*. The older but still relevant book of Wilson rightfully carries the title: *With Christ in the School of Disciple Building.*[5]

Second, I worry about how easy it is to turn a church into a school, which it is not. Would you agree that a safeguard against this temptation might be to develop the relationship training or service even stronger? This would help distinguish a church from a school—which, ironically, students tend to work to get out of, rather than embrace to become prepared for works of service.

Notes

1. J. Firet, *Dynamics in Pastoring* (Grand Rapids: Eerdmans, 1986), 53-58. (See his references to well-known Old Testament scholars.)

2. Firet, 55.

3. Firet, 179, 246. See also Duffy Robbins, *The Ministry of Nurture* (Grand Rapids: Youth Specialties/Zondervan, 1990).

4. L. O. Richards, *Youth Ministry*, 10th printing (Grand Rapids: Zondervan, 1978), 139-148.

5. C. Wilson, *With Christ in the School of Disciple Building* (Grand Rapids: Zondervan, 1979).

Response to the Preparatory Approach from a Missional Perspective
by Chap Clark

The article on the Preparatory approach to youth ministry was filled with assertions, practical suggestions, and philosophical assumptions that I found helpful and engaging. The many angles of youth ministry—what it is and what it needs to become—made it clear that there is much to be said for seeing youth ministry in a Preparatory way.

Too busy to sin

Your comparison between the activity-based and ministry-based youth ministry philosophies was an important reminder that so many youth ministry programs—maybe even most of them—operate in a knee-jerk, responsive entertainment mode of simply trying to keep the young people in the church. I believe that the article is absolutely correct in its stinging critique of an activity-based ministry that is created without purpose, vision, or strategic structure. Youth ministry *must* have a driving reason for being that goes beyond a baby-sitting mentality, beyond the need to keep students too busy to sin. Neither *raison d'être* will have any kind of significant or lasting impact. It is a stretch to even label this kind of thinking "youth ministry."

Laboratory

Another strength of your argument was your view that youth ministry is a laboratory where the adult leadership functions in the role of spiritual coaches. The Preparatory approach, more than the Inclusive Congregational and Strategic approaches, takes seriously the transitionary realities of adolescence.

When lifespan theorists recognized this eight- to fifteen-year process as a legitimate phase of human life, they acknowledged what people who work with youths had known and experienced for years—this is the only stage of life that is *transitionary* in essence. The entire phase is one massive transition, from being a relatively sheltered and safe child (ideally, hopefully, usually), whose life and being are defined within the external context of the family system, to living as an interdependent, relatively autonomous adult whose sense of self is determined and ordered from within. In between, the shift from being entirely reliant on outside influences for meaning, security, help, safety, satisfaction, and purpose to learning what it means to take personal responsibility for these things occurs while the teen learns how to function in a society where the "other" matters as well as the self. This shift comprises very difficult sociological and psychological processes. And as the culture fragments, deconstructs, and disavows any commitment to the rising generations' needs, the adolescent phase has become all the more difficult.

Youth ministry approaches and programs that do not take this complex, varied, and intrinsically dangerous process seriously, by providing an atmosphere of tender nurture, can do more harm to young people even than approaches that ignore them. The tenet that contemporary adolescents need adult coaches is the Preparatory approach's single most important contribution.

Belongs to the church

In addition, the assertion that "youth ministry belongs to the church" provides a theologically vital scaffolding to the youth ministry task in any church context. Youth ministry should not be delegated to the few, but rather embraced by the entire local expression of the body of Christ. Surely some people will serve as the direct, hands-on expressions of the church's ministry to the young. But those adults who are not directly involved must be just as committed, just as pro-kid, as any Sunday school teacher or youth worker volunteer, or even paid staff.

Ecclesiological status quo

Yet some of your assertions remained incomplete when compared to the missional mandate of the church as an organism. For example, the Preparatory approach seems to be a relatively traditional one (albeit the best of the traditional) to youth ministry. Programs primarily run by adults…student involvement in decision-making…a church that cares about ministry focused on adolescents—these all add up to what many churches are basically doing already. Some are doing a better job than others, of course, but in general this approach seems to support the ecclesiological status quo of youth ministry, at least from the 1970s onward.

> The tenet that contemporary adolescents need adult coaches is the Preparatory approach's single most important contribution.

My most serious criticism of what seems to me a traditional view of youth ministry, and thus of the Preparatory approach, is the lack of strategic focus on the missional mandate of the church. The goal of theologically appropriate youth ministry, like any ministry, if it is to fulfill the call of our Lord to be his witnesses (Acts 1), must be to "go into the world" (Matthew 28). Granted, the Preparatory approach *does* have a missional component, but it is far from strategic, is not an explicitly stated outcome of the entire ministry focus, and thus is relegated to the historical yet flawed strategic methodology of "kids bringing friends" to outreach events. The fact is, they usually do not bring friends; when they do, the friends they bring are almost always the kind of students already inclined to church involvement without the goad of evangelistic and strategic energy. The Preparatory approach edges closely to the reason why the church of the last 50 years has suffered: there is little strategic commitment to the "going" mandate of the gospel.

Take, for example, the adult church members who cooked the hamburgers for the students who were hanging out in the church parking lot. The effort was admirable, the reported initial results exciting, and as a result the church patted itself on the back for being concerned for the lost youths. But upon closer examination, this ministry arose and functioned more out of knee-jerk compassion than theologically reflective strategy for mission. You assert that "under the banner of youth ministry is anything that a congregation does that touches the lives of teenagers in any way, formally or informally." So this desire to cook some hamburgers implicitly falls "under the banner" of the youth ministry.

But this anecdote illustrates a tremendous flaw in traditional youth ministry. A real need of young people ignited a programmatic response out of a strategic context of the youth ministry program. So faced with this event, which on the surface has a missional component to it, I am full of questions: What happened to those kids? Who followed up with them? How were they assimilated into the youth ministry? Into the church? Your article states that this

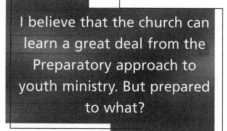

> I believe that the church can learn a great deal from the Preparatory approach to youth ministry. But prepared to what?

gesture "opened a lot of conversations and friendship with the kids who parked there," but did it *strategically* draw these adolescents into the family of faith? And, if so, *how?*

Prepared to what...?

I believe that the church can learn a great deal from the Preparatory approach to youth ministry. But prepared to *what?* The most significant preparation must prepare young people to become integral and committed believers. This implies, as presented by Jesus himself in John 15, a connection to the Vine and expressing that connection with a willingness to love the body. *Then* the church is ready and able to program and strategize what it means to be Christ's witnesses to the world (Acts 1). I fear that, as written, the Preparatory approach to youth ministry will do little to motivate an entire church to commit strategic resources toward reaching an entire generation that has yet to either hear or experience the power, love, and forgiveness of the gospel.

Response to the Preparatory Approach from a Strategic Perspective
by Mark H. Senter III

As I read through your chapter, Wes, I found a deep love and respect for the church. As you presented your Preparatory approach to youth ministry and the church, certain phrases jumped out at me, each suggesting how you envisioned youth ministry connecting to the local church:

- "A ministry-based Preparatory approach has a clear purpose for every activity: *the development of mature Christians in the church, both now and for the future.*"
- "Youth ministry belongs to the church."
- "Youth ministry is everything a church does with, to, and for teenagers."
- "Theologically, there may be no division between youths and anyone else in the church."
- "The church is the home of youth ministry."
- "The purposes of the church are the purposes of youth ministry."

Ownership

What seems so powerful to me about these statements is the idea of ownership. There is no *them* and *us*. It is all *we*. As you wrote, "There may be no division between youths and anyone else in the church." The church is the home not only of youth ministry, but also by implication of a wide cross-section of young people as they explore their ties to the family of God. At the same time, the church is home to people of all generations. For youth ministry to be effective, the church has to be vigorous. For such vigor to emerge and be sustained, everyone must have a sense of ownership of all aspects of the ministry.

Like you, Wes, I have concerns over churches where young people are viewed as problems to be solved. I wish there were more churches where older men (does that mean my age?) grill free hamburgers for unchurched teenagers who hang out in the church parking lot on Saturday nights. Unfortunately, I fear this is an exception rather than the norm.

Similarly, I worry about churches where young people have little commitment to the ministry as a whole. In these youth ministries, worship means "our" music and instruments. Witness lacks focus beyond "our" friends at school—not even including the families of "our" friends. Stewardship expects the money to support "our" own activities or mission trips. In these churches, adults are seen as obstacles to be avoided.

In both cases the church is impoverished.

Laboratory

Your idea that we view youth ministry as "a laboratory in which disciples can grow in a culture guided by spiritual coaches" is a helpful image. (Especially clever is the ambiguity of your use of *culture*. We could have some fun imagining a freshman in a petri dish.) One purpose of a laboratory is to allow learners to fail in a safe context and discover specific skills in the process. A lab is a hands-on place, where involvement is essential to learning.

Even apart from the petri-dish image, however, *culture* remains ambiguous. Are we talking about the youth culture or the church culture? Perhaps we should add one more: the heavenly or kingdom culture of God. Actually, a youth ministry is richest when young people learn to live in all three. If the *youth culture* is ignored, the youth ministry becomes inbred, and in time all its genetic flaws (so to speak) cause abnormalities to appear. If the *church culture* is ignored, especially in this postmodern age, young people lose an opportunity to learn the stories of godly people who have made possible the fellowship they are enjoying. If the *culture of God* is ignored, young people may assume that the flaws of the other two cultures are normal.

The image of the laboratory is not that of programs or discipleship. The idea that comes to my mind, Wes, is the idea of experimentation. I think this is what was happening as the disciples followed Jesus through the Galilean countryside. They were not squeezing themselves into an existing system of worshiping Jehovah—the Pharisees had all the formulas for that. Nor were they creating something entirely new—Christ constantly pointed out the continuity between the law and the prophets and his own teaching. What they *were* doing was trying out fresh ways of discovering and worshiping God. Our Lord called it "new wineskins."

Your Preparatory approach carried a new wineskin flavor. Unfortunately, too often the church prefers the old wineskins. I suppose that is why our Lord spent as much time outside the synagogues as in them. I suppose this is where camps, retreats, mission trips, and small groups on the high school campus fit in. They are all laboratories where young people test their Christianity.

Separate program

The major question I have, Wes, relates to how this laboratory called youth ministry brings about the growth and maturity you desire. The very nature of a laboratory is that it is a separate place. It is not the real world, but imitates the real world for the purpose of learning and understanding. While it is safe to say, "youth ministry is everything a church does with, to, and for teenagers that builds them into becoming the church," all you have described is culture (no petri-dish puns this time): the informal educational process through which the values and customs, language and symbols of a population of adults are passed to the next generation.

Before the Industrial Revolution and even today in small churches and congregations in preindustrial situations (Third World situations primarily), young people learn what it means to be a Christian by living among Christian people. There are no intentional Christian education programs. To rephrase the bumper sticker, learning happens. Culture is the most powerful teacher because the learners do not realize they are learning.

What I heard you saying, Wes, is that youth ministry *is* and *must be* a separate program, but never divorced from the larger church culture. In tribal cultures young boys and girls have

> About your idea of youth ministry as a lab: one purpose of a laboratory is to allow learners to fail in a safe context and discover specific skills in the process. A lab is a hands-on place, where involvement is essential to learning.

well-defined rites of passage as they move from childhood to adulthood—"separate programs," in essence, intended to initiate children into adulthood. They are within the culture but distinct from the rest of it. In fact, unless you are an adult male, you will never know what is involved in the initiation rite for young boys. The same is true for young women.

One aspect of the initiation rite is a naming process. With the tribal elder's approval, young boys in particular are given a name that describes or suggests how the boy sees himself. Perhaps that is what the Preparatory approach to youth ministry is all about. It is a naming process, preparing young adults for what they will be in the church. A name change in preparation for ministry is throughout Scripture: Jacob becomes Israel, Simon becomes Peter, Saul becomes Paul. While I do not see the naming process included in your description, I think we both can conceive of a number of places where it has happened informally and could happen formally with the blessing of the faith community.

But isn't confirmation, as practiced by many churches, such an initiation, such a naming process? I think not—unless confirmation is transformed into something very different than is usually practiced today. Today confirmation programs most commonly initiate young people *out* of the church, not into it. After the formal ceremony, young people tend to disappear from the church. I believe the problem is that the confirmation process is designed for just the head, not the whole person.

Now let me combine the laboratory idea with the initiation rite. If youth ministry is a laboratory that initiates young people into full participation in the faith community, then most of the structures you have described will play a role. As you say, the Preparatory approach will have "a clear purpose for every activity." Every activity will assist the young person to discover their "new name" and how they will serve the faith community.

One interesting side benefit of this idea is that it might defuse the arguments of a small but vocal group of former youth workers who claim that adolescence is not a biblical idea and therefore should not be used as a basis for ministering to people during their teenage years. Adolescence is a product of modern education, they claim, and was introduced by G. Stanley Hall in 1905 with the publication of his classic work, *Adolescence*. But even in the Bible there was a rite of passage from childhood to adult roles, illustrated (in part) by Jesus at age 12 going to the temple for the Feast "according to the custom" (Luke 2:42). If youth ministry is a contemporary expression of this rite of passage, it fits within even this more restrictive view of biblical ministry.

Changes in the church

If youth ministry is the church's primary means of preparing young people for full participation in the faith community, the most important question we can ask is this: *What are the values of the faith community?* All four authors of this book agree that the three essential functions of the church are ministry to God, ministry to believers, and ministry to the world. If the tribe/church places the highest value on these functions and demonstrates them in the life of the tribe/church, then initiated young people will quickly assume leadership in promoting the same values.

The five areas of resistance to change in the church, which you cited from Merton Strommen, must be tackled by the adults in the tribe/church before young people have a chance of becoming the church described in Scripture. If Strommen is right (and I fear he is), youth ministry as it is commonly practiced today is highly successful: for the young people who survive their contact with the church and are initiated into the tribe/church demonstrate the same disinclination to change that they learned from the adult community, and for the same reasons: tradition, personality, ideology, affiliation, and demonic power. Young people have very effectively absorbed these negative values and are perpetuating them into the next generation.

Unfortunately, this is not the kind of success we want. Yet it is not the fault of the youth minister or youth ministry. If we are not comfortable with the values of church youths, the place to look is at the adult members. Three questions about the adult congregation might help focus our understanding of the youth ministry:

- In what ways do the adults of the congregation minister to God?
- In what ways and with what frequency do the adults of the congregation minister to Christian people?
- In what ways and with what frequency do the adults of the congregation minister to people who have no relationship with Jesus Christ?

How can we expect younger members of the tribe/church to absorb Christian values that are not a part of the daily life of the church? Certainly, God has used young people to trigger renewal and missionary movements—but those examples are rare and serve as stinging rebukes to the carnality of adult believers.

While your suggested changes for the church might be small steps in a healthy direction, Wes, I think much more is needed if our young people are to be prepared for a biblical model of what the church is all about. Anything we wish for among our young people must first be true among our adults.

Conclusion

I may owe you an apology, Wes, for taking your chapter and building on your definition while ignoring much of your descriptive material. It is my conviction, however, that the Preparatory approach has in its heart a biblical image based in the church that we must explore.

I must confess, however, I am not optimistic about the willingness of the church to change. Was it Thomas Jefferson who said, "What a democracy needs is a revolution every 20 years"? I would say the same thing about the church—which is why I proposed the Strategic approach to youth ministry. Youth ministries need to become the breeding grounds for baby churches at least once each decade. It is my firm conviction that as churches birth new churches, both become healthier—and the new-generation church quickly takes on a vitality that the parent church could not recapture or perhaps never had.

Rejoinder from the Preparatory Approach
by Wesley Black

Notwithstanding your reasoned, informed, and often intriguing observations, I still believe the Preparatory approach is the best stance for effective Christian youth ministry. Perhaps a little more discussion in three areas will clarify my position.

Preparation is more than a one-way street

The very title of this approach indicates its biblical source. Ephesians 4:12-13 says that we are "to prepare God's people for works of service, so that the body of Christ may be built up until we all reach unity in the faith and in the knowledge of the Son of God and become mature, attaining to the whole measure of the fullness of Christ." The Preparatory approach is part of the overall mission of a church, which is to prepare (equip or perfect, as used in some translations) God's people (including God's younger people) to do his will in the world.

Malan, you expressed concern about the nature of preparation in two enlightening ways. You wrote that you are "concerned that people might view the Preparatory approach as just another way of reaffirming an outmoded educational paradigm." I agree wholeheartedly. Preparation might easily be seen as simply a process whereby adults pour knowledge into passive receivers (youths) who have nothing better to do than absorb the traditions from the past. It reminds me of the old cliche in which the teacher instructs the students to "sit still while I instill." I think we can agree that this is neither good educational practice nor good discipleship.

> Adults do their best teaching when they walk alongside youths, providing a loving, nurturing environment in which youths see the model of adult Christians learning and growing along with them. Teaching and discipleship are more than just telling and advice-giving.

Mark, you also pointed to this with your comments about confirmation programs that "initiate young people *out* of the church." This is a problem that many mainline denominations face regularly. You summarized it well: "The problem, in my opinion, is that the confirmation process is not designed for the whole person—just the head." The result, as you noted, is rejection by young people of the whole process. They sense they are considered unimportant and have nothing to contribute. Therefore, they leave as quickly as possible in search of something that involves and challenges their youthful energies and commitments.

Perhaps in these churches the young people really are "viewed as problems to be solved" and the best way is to see preparation as a one-way street. After all, if the older generation has all the wisdom, insights, experience, and knowledge why, should youths be involved in the teaching or learning process other than as passive receivers? Malan, you captured this idea when you said that in your own tradition "it is the older members that would identify with the Preparatory approach...because they see it as getting back the old Sunday school they grew up with. This is probably not your intention."

Relationships with youth

Part of the solution to this dilemma, I believe, lies in the idea of relationships with youths, as Larry Richards pointed out in Malan's chapter on the Inclusive Congregational approach: "A ministry-facilitating relationship is one in which the adult admits and expresses his equality with youths as persons by encouraging mutual self-revelation and in which youths and adult each learn to trust the other with thoughts, feelings, and experiences, knowing that both are valued and respected."

Discipleship is a lifelong process, not just a short body of knowledge dealing with select-ed topics and skills. We are all on the road of discipleship leading to "perfection", and adults do their best when they walk alongside youths in the discipling process. This provides a loving, nurturing environment in which youths see the model of adult Christians learning and grow-ing along with them. It makes discipleship a lifelong journey, not just something to endure as a child or youth. Teaching and discipleship are more than just telling and advice-giving.

I did emphasize that youth ministry has to be more than building relationships with youths. Perhaps I should have illustrated this more in the sense of those who see relationships as simply entertaining youths and hoping they will somehow grow closer to God in the process. This is an inadequate view of youth ministry that neither builds Christian fellowship nor discipleship. As you said, Chap, "It is even a far stretch to label this kind of thinking 'youth ministry'."

On the other hand, we make a mistake when we rule out the social elements of adoles-cence. Malan, you expressed your concern "that it is so easy to turn a church into a school, which it is not." This would be going to the opposite extreme. I fear there are some youth min-isters and pastors who sincerely want to avoid the "silly fun and games" and go to the extreme of "serious Bible study" without considering the need for balance in adolescent social needs. You stated this well in the formula, "The norm is to prepare youths for life and ministry. The form is to be contextually relevant."

Mark, I liked your discussion about laboratories. You added to our understanding when you said, "Laboratories are designed to allow the learner to fail in a safe context and discover specific skills in the process. It is a hands-on place. Involvement is essential to learning." Involvement in this case means we must be sensitive to adolescent levels of learning and needs, and approach them in relevant, meaningful ways.

Separating and integrating

Second, I want to reemphasize the concept of separation and integration, which I believe is a key distinction between the Inclusive Congregational and Preparatory approaches. The Preparatory approach takes seriously the need to deal with youths as adolescents. As Chap said, this approach "takes seriously the transitionary realities of the adolescent phase of the life span." Yes, youths need to be involved in the life of the local body of Christ, but they also need focused ministry that is generationally specific. It is a balancing act between separating and integrating.

> The Preparatory approach does a better job of balancing evangelism and discipleship. Any shortfall of evangelism and mission in the Preparatory approach is due to inadequate leadership, not the approach itself. The Preparatory approach calls for an equal effort in both directions.

Chap, you described adolescents well when you reminded us that they are learning how to "shift from being entirely reliant on outside forces and influences for meaning, security, help, safety, satisfaction, and purpose, to learning what it means to take personal responsibility for these things."

Mark, you also hit on one of my current concerns, dealing with the "small group of former youth workers who now claim adolescence is not a biblical idea and therefore should not be used as a basis for ministering to people in their teenage years." I liked your ideas of the rite of passage as seen in the life of Jesus (Luke 2:42-51) and as practiced by both ancient and modern Jews. It is both biblically and developmentally correct to deal with adolescents in a focused way.

Further, Mark, I agree with your assessment that, "youth ministry *is* and *must be* a separate program, but never divorced from the larger church culture." Again, there must be a balance between separation and integration.

Malan, you reiterated this when you said, "Why in the world do you think we have created a gap between adults and children in this regard? Is it possible that we deem young believers unworthy of being equipped and only worthy of being kept busy?" Perhaps it is far too easy to put forth the efforts to disciple teenagers on an age-appropriate level, so we simply fall back to entertaining them separately from others and hope they will behave until they reach a magical age when they can contribute something to the kingdom of God.

Relationship between families and the church

In this separation-integration context, Malan, you brought up the issue of the relationship between families and the church. I agree that many youths (perhaps even the 80 percent you mentioned) will tend to become more like their parents as they mature. They tend to take on the life and worldview of their parents, and I think this fact alone calls for intentional efforts by pastors, youth leaders, and churches, to equip parents for their proper role as spiritual coaches for youths. This, of course, is the biblical pattern (Deuteronomy 6:4-7; Proverbs 22:6; Ephesians 6:1-4). Churches that view youth ministry as only focused on adolescents, apart from their family context, are missing an important element. Youth ministry must face the challenge of discipling both teenagers and their families if they hope to make significant life changes. This is a whole-church effort, not just something that can be done by a few youth workers.

Mark, you raised an interesting dilemma in the separation versus integration arena. You mentioned that youth leaders and young people "have little commitment to the ministry as a whole." When we try to be generationally relevant, we sometimes mistake ministry, worship, evangelism, and stewardship to be only age-specific activities, and ignore the larger church family. Teens do need intergenerational experiences to broaden their life and worldview. This can only be accomplished with a proper balance between separation and integration.

You mentioned your concern with the three cultures: youth culture, church culture, and kingdom culture. You voiced my desire when you wrote that "actually, the youth ministry is richest when young people learn to live in all three." I think we make a mistake, however, when we think that discipleship in the Preparatory approach is simply teaching youths how to be good *church members.* This falls into the trap that some confirmation and even some Sunday school approaches enter. In these contexts (the weaker ones) the task is assumed to be simply passing along the traditions of the past generation and ignoring the culture of the youths and the larger kingdom of God.

The answer has to be a youth ministry that grows out of the purposes of God for the church and his kingdom. Youth ministry that is a knee-jerk response to planning entertainment for youths, teaching outdated traditions, and keeping youths under control ignores the possibilities of developing young disciples in intentional, purposeful ways.

Initiation rites

One additional comment along these lines, Mark, has to do with your idea of the initiation rites. I like this possibility. For years I have bemoaned the fact that in contemporary life we have very few markers and initiation rites for adolescents. As David Elkind said in the title of his book, we have a generation that is all grown up and no place to go. Youth ministers, pastors, parents, and churches should develop some markers along the way to guide young people in their journey toward adulthood. This would help develop their identity and their place in the kingdom of God. You said it well: "Every activity will assist the young person to discover their 'new name' and how they will serve the faith community."

Finally, this process can only be accomplished when the church sees its larger responsibility in youth ministry. Chap, you nailed this when you wrote that "youth ministry should not be delegated to the few, but rather embraced by the entire local expression of the body of Christ." The entire congregation has to accept the marriage of youth ministry with the total mission of the church.

Balancing reaching and teaching

Finally, there is the issue of the balancing act between reaching and teaching—evangelism and discipleship. This grows out of the dual facets of the Great Commission (Matthew 28:18-20). Jesus commanded us to make disciples (reaching out) and teach them to observe all that he had commanded (teaching).

Chap, the Missional approach obviously majors on the evangelism facet. We both agree that "youth ministry *must* have a driving reason for being that goes beyond a baby-sitting mentality, beyond the need to keep students too busy to sin." However, we disagree that the Preparatory approach "seems to support the ecclesiological status quo of youth ministry from the 1970s onward."

Perhaps the answer lies in the mistaken view that the Preparatory approach equals the outdated mode of youth work with its "lack of strategic focus on the missional mandate of the church." I would assert that the Preparatory approach does a better job of balancing both elements of the Great Commission. If there is a lack of emphasis on evangelism and mission in the Preparatory approach, then it is because of inadequate leadership, not the basic approach. The Preparatory approach calls for an equal effort in both directions.

"Kids bringing kids" approach to evangelism

Chap, you really made me rethink the "kids bringing kids" approach to evangelism. Your comment is insightful: "They usually do not bring friends; when they do, the friends they bring are almost always the kind of students already inclined to church involvement without the goad of evangelistic and strategic energy." According to your assessment, this is the reason for stagnation in evangelism and church growth.

However, I'm not ready to give up on this strategy. It's still an effective way to reach out to peers who may be friends in a school or community context but not a part of the Christian family. Sensitive, generationally aware adults can aid in the process by strategizing to reach out to the fringe youths, to those outside the church family, and to secular neo-pagan teenagers. It will take honest, intentional efforts for this to happen, but it can and is happening in churches that take seriously the mandate of the Great Commission.

This will take more than status quo youth ministry. It will take conscious, intentional efforts to plan youth ministry with the evangelism purpose in mind. In the best sense this involves youths as vital parts of the equation, with adult coaches who have a heart for reaching the whole world for Christ.

But then, Mark, you pointed out that many adults do not have this heart for evangelism. Resistance to change "must be tackled by the adults in the tribe/church before young people have a chance of becoming the church described in Scripture." The reason for much of the stagnation lies in the fact that, as you put it, "Young people have very effectively absorbed these negative values and are perpetuating them into the next generation."

I tend to agree with much of what you said. "Anything we wish for among our young people must first be true among our adults"—I still believe this is possible within the context of the Preparatory approach. God can and does bring renewal and revival among his people. We have seen this in many of the great youth movements of history. But it most often happens with the support and encouragement that adults provide to youths.

The best contemporary expressions of evangelism and spiritual renewal—True Love Waits, See You at the Pole, and the growth of campus Christian clubs—are all youth initiated and youth led. But they could not become reality without a base of adult support and encouragement. To separate youths into a baby church, even with adult oversight, tends to separate them from the ongoing coaching and support that adolescents need. I believe the Preparatory approach provides for this adult spiritual nurture in the best way.

Revival and renewal to the entire congregation

The beauty of this can also be seen in the way young people can bring revival and renewal to the entire congregation. Youthful idealism and exuberance, in the midst of a loving and nurturing congregation, can inspire adults to renew their faithfulness and commitment to the Lord's work. In this way, God can use youths to prepare his people, "with everything good for doing his will, and may he work in us what is pleasing to him, through Jesus Christ, to whom be glory for ever and ever. Amen" (Hebrews 13:21).

The Missional Approach to Youth Ministry

by Chap Clark

Responses

Nel: from an Inclusive Congregational perspective
Black: from a Preparation perspective
Senter: from a Strategic perspective

Rejoinder

Clark

The Missional Approach to Youth Ministry
by Chap Clark

Scenario: stranger in a strange land

Tony is a high school sophomore. Typical of everyone he knows, he has never been to church and doesn't plan to go. God is a power he respects. Religion, however, just gets in the way of life.

But Tony has a friend who has been badgering him about going to church with her. "Not really *church*," she says, "more like a youth group." *Whatever* that *is,* Tony thinks. So just to get her off his back, Tony says he'll go—but just once.

When the sophomore arrives at youth group, he finds a cluster of people in one corner playing guitars and others standing around talking in small groups. After some very long moments, Tony finally spots his friend.

They sit together on the thin carpet and talk for a few minutes before a 30-year-old guy wearing an earring plugs his guitar into an amp and, with a kind of garage-band style, plays and sings a few songs; some students sing along, others don't. Tony has never heard any of the songs before.

Two students from Tony's school do a dialogue kind of skit about lying to parents. Then a guy jokes about being homeschooled (which Tony *has* heard of, but never met anybody who actually was) and gives some announcements. Another student, one of the guitar players whom Tony recognizes from school, asks everyone to form groups of five to share (*share?*) and pray. Tony sits quietly, declining to speak (even when asked), watching for his chance to break for the door.

After the prayer time ends, the earring guy tells a story about a student who was caught lying…then says something about God and Jesus…and finally reads from a book Tony assumes is the Bible (though, having never *seen* a Bible before, he can't be sure). The speaker talks about how "non-Christians" think and why "they do what they do." Gradually it dawns on him that that this guy is talking about *him*. Anger boils inside Tony, but he manages to keep a lid on his feelings.

The speaker then makes a joke about how boring the minister is and suggests that the students hold a tic-tac-toe contest during next week's sermon—for prizes. (Tony thinks it's curious that one church leader would talk this way about another.) He then finishes his talk by pointing out that there are "student leaders" who "are always there for you, if you want help with lying." He mentions a guy Tony knows from cross-country, the same one he saw trip another runner during a meet last fall but later denied it happened. *Sure,* Tony thinks, *that's the first person I'd go to for advice about lying.*

When the speaker finishes, Tony bolts for the door, but his friend is right on his heels.

"I've gotta go," Tony explains.

"Thanks for coming" is her only response. No questions about what he thought or how he felt. If she had asked, Tony might have said something like, "They sang songs I didn't recognize—or even like—made me *pray* with strangers, used words I didn't understand, and insulted me and my friends. I *knew* church was going to be like this." But she never asks, and so the visitor leaves quietly, never to come back.

On his way home, it occurs to Tony that if this is what religion is all about—some private club where he obviously isn't a member—then who needs it? Then he mellows for a moment. *Maybe I should try the church service someday.* Then he remembers what the earring guy said about the pastor's sermons. *Why bother? That guy's boring, too!*

Heart of the problem

For those raised in the church, a youth group may not *feel* like a private club with its own culture, rules, and norms, but to many of those on the outside that's how it has felt for decades. As the secular culture becomes increasingly post-Christian, the gap widens between those who feel qualified for membership and those who don't. The gulf between the church youth culture and the secular youth culture increases, but the official-yet-unwritten mandate of contemporary youth ministry has stayed the same for years:

- Keep the church youths (and their friends) happy, interested, and safe.
- Teach them the basics of the Christian worldview and appropriate political ideology.
- Place them in virtual charge of the program and mission of the ministry, whether or not they are sociologically or developmentally ready for that level of relational responsibility.
- Make sure they are not contaminated by the world.
- Keep them interested in coming to church.

But there has been a subversive movement in youth ministry that has gained momentum over the last several years. For many in youth ministry, even among the leaders of the movement, the church—that umbrella organization that sponsors youth ministry—is considered a necessary nuisance. The prevailing view? Churches do not really care about the needs of kids.

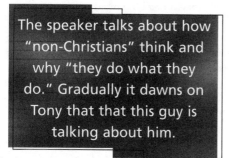

The speaker talks about how "non-Christians" think and why "they do what they do." Gradually it dawns on Tony that that this guy is talking about him.

The church staff, especially senior staff, do not understand kids. Parents and lay leaders are usually the greatest threat to effective youth ministry. Among some youth workers, pastors are the brunt of jokes, worship services are ridiculed, music ministers are written off, and parents are contradicted.

Is this what youth ministry is supposed to be about? Programs that highlight those mid-adolescents who are lifted up as exemplars and leaders, who somehow have more than usual influence over their peers? A separate, exclusive discipleship program that uses the resources of a church while it bites the hand that feeds it? Can youth ministry be simply described and explained by listing the meetings, events, and programs that sociologically define who is "in" (that is, those who know and appreciate or resonate with the songs, the language, and the expectations of the youth ministry) and who is "out"?

As outlandish as these dubious goals of ministry sound, the fact is that for large numbers of adolescents (probably the majority), youth ministries in churches (and even in parachurch organizations; *parachurch* roughly meaning *alongside the church*) represent a world that is foreign, irrelevant, and even occasionally offensive. Despite all the focus, energy, history, and money that has gone into youth ministry over the last several decades, secularized and disenfranchised adolescents are not any closer to viewing the local church as a viable sanctuary for relational stability, peace, and hope. It's not even an option for them. "The curtain must be pulled back," Mark Yaconelli writes. "If we are to keep young people involved in the church and if we are to renew our congregations, we first must acknowledge that many of our current forms of youth ministry are destructive."[1]

A Definition of the Missional Approach

"The gospel is always conveyed through the medium of culture,"[2] declares D. L. Guder. The Missional approach to youth ministry recognizes that there are cultural barriers that separate adolescents from adults. This is not only true of the *secular* adolescent world, but also the world of churched young people. Therefore, youth ministry as *mission* is defined as the community of faith corporately committed to caring for and reaching out into the adolescent world (of both churched and unchurched young people) in order to meaningfully assimilate them into their fellowship. "Even when I am old and gray, do not forsake me, O God, till I declare your power to the next generation, your might to all who are to come" (Psalm 71:18).

Description of the Missional Approach to Youth Ministry

Since its inception, youth ministry has evolved out of a *mission* conviction. Generationally focused ministry programming has emerged from a concern that the church was losing its ability to impact an increasingly distant and discontented segment of the population. Thus youth ministry pioneers and entrepreneurs took the foundational mandates of the church—worship, Christian nurture and training, and social commitment and evangelism—and contextualized it for this evolving subculture. Ultimately, regardless of denomination and tradition, mission is often cited as the basic reason for youth ministry. In light of increasing cultural fragmentation, this commitment and focus have never been more necessary.

Adolescents now represent both a definable culture *as well as* a legitimate phase of the life span. The church really has no choice, then, but to *reach out* to this group of people, to bring the gospel to the world of the adolescent, with the ultimate goal of assimilating each child into the greater body of Christ as expressed in the local church. As F. F. Bruce states: "No member (of the body) is less a part of the body than any other member: all are necessary. Variety of organs, limbs and functions is of the essence of bodily life. No one organ could establish a monopoly in the body by taking over the functions of the others. A body consisting of a single organ would be a monstrosity."[3]

The Missional approach views Christian adults as missionaries and adolescents as a people to be reached with the gospel of Jesus Christ. Principles that guide cross-cultural ministries around the world apply to youth ministry. Lingenfelter and Mayers suggest six orientations in ministering cross-culturally: time versus event, task versus person, dichotomistic versus holistic thinking, status versus achievement, crisis versus noncrisis, and concealment versus vulnerability orientations.[4] Missional youth ministry accepts the fact that each of these orientations will shape the manner in which young people will be reached, evangelized, and made part of the body of Christ. Consequently the church that ministers to youths must embrace the culture in which adolescents live, just as Christian churches in India or Brazil or Nigeria have contextualized in order to become the kingdom of God in their various cultures.

Justification for the Missional Approach

Theologically, few would argue with the idea that youth ministry is an important mandate of the church, regardless of how it is defined. Ecclesiologically, however, youth ministry has become in many cases a praxeological nightmare, for in a wildly changing culture the church is hard-pressed to address such a dynamic force as youth culture. The vast majority of churches want a vibrant youth ministry; but the bulk of them want to create and sustain a healthy youth ministry out of pragmatic need, rather than theological and ecclesiological conviction. This is the paradoxical quandary of contemporary youth ministry: churches are screaming for youth ministry (an "excellent one," at that—high-powered, entertaining, and theologically and sociologically safe), but there are few pastors, parents, and even boards who are *convinced* that God has called them *as a church* to mobilize their resources in order to penetrate a distant and disruptive generation.

But the church is clearly *called* to influence and care for the secular culture and, more specifically, the youth subculture. The church is *missional* in that its mandate is clearly focused on God *sending* his people into the world as light and salt—"You will be my witnesses in Jerusalem, and in all Judea and Samaria, and to the ends of the earth" (Acts 1:8). "We have come to see that mission is not merely an activity of the church," writes Darrell Guder. "Rather, mission is the result of God's initiative, rooted in God's purpose to restore and heal creation. 'Mission' means 'sending,' and it is the central biblical theme describing the purpose of God's action in human history." The missional church then becomes "the instrument of God's mission."[5]

In terms of youth ministry, then, the church is called less to take care of its own by creating an isolated private community, and more to be a dynamic force of intentional penetration into the adolescent world. A missional youth ministry will contain *elements* of community, but never for the community's sake (in other words, to acculturate churched young people, or to "keep our kids safe and healthy"). The goal is *not* to simply focus on those who already are involved in a given church's youth ministry program. The theologically driven missional mandate of youth ministry is to bring the gospel and the kingdom to every adolescent. The church must step up and allow this theological axiom to shape and alter ecclesiological traditions and norms.

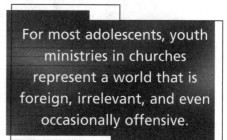

For most adolescents, youth ministries in churches represent a world that is foreign, irrelevant, and even occasionally offensive.

As the church attempts to realize its biblical mandate of missional youth ministry, the issue is to rediscover its historical and fundamental missional commitment and focus and proceed accordingly. In the world of contemporary youth ministry methodology, models are everything. From the frenzied merchandising of youth ministry products to the hype of the newest program, event, or philosophy, the North American youth ministry movement seems to be increasingly susceptible to fame, marketing, and spin. Most professional youth workers who are struggling with uninterested and disengaged students, complaining parents, uncommitted leadership, and unsupportive senior level staff and laity will too often jump at anything and everything that may help to jump-start the ministry. This eventually translates into a youth ministry methodology that ultimately measures success by the interest and enthusiasm of students (and their parents), the pat on the back from the leadership of the church, and the perceived relative stability of the program. Then when the current model, plan, or program fades or students lose interest, the youth worker frantically searches for the next hot thing to get the machine up and running one more time.

Segmented generations

But if youth ministry is faithful to its missional commitment, to assimilating students into the life and faith of the local church, then none of these indicators—student or parental response, pleased leadership, or programmatic stability—are suitable for measuring success. While each of these are potent and legitimate markers in understanding how people *feel* about youth ministry in a given church environment, none of them use the end goal of youth ministry as the significant or even a single criterion for measuring ministry success. As a mission, a church must keep before itself the primary reason for having a youth ministry program: The world has segmented the generations. God has called his people to be a family, and so the church must create a bridge of love, trust, and support to encourage the disenfranchised adolescent to be welcomed as a member of the family of God. The apostle Paul puts it this way: "Therefore, as we have opportunity, let us do good to all people, especially to those who belong to the family of believers" (Galatians 6:10).

This means that the only true measure of success in a youth ministry program is the ability and willingness of a church to fully assimilate growing adolescents into the adult fellowship. This does *not* necessarily mean letting them come to church with earrings or even expecting them to attend services. A church committed to adolescents will create a worship environment and church community where the generational differences, tastes, and life situations and experiences are equally appreciated *and* equally valued with any other segment of the church community. This inclusiveness has not been the hallmark of the contemporary church community for several decades. But, as theologian/psychologist Dennis Guernsey put it, the church that resists stylistic, material, and substantive change in order to avoid embracing and assimilating new kinds of people into it's fellowship is making a grave mistake. "If we preach a gospel that neglects the welfare of the whole in exchange for the happiness of the individual, then the Church as a living, pulsing body is weakened, as is the welfare of the family. We must recover the priority of interrelationships."[6]

> Most churches want to create and sustain a healthy youth ministry out of pragmatic need, rather than theological and ecclesiological conviction.

Then and Now—A Brief History of Modern Parish Youth Ministry

The scenario described at the beginning of this chapter, while grossly reductionistic and exaggerated, depicts an often stale and culturally ignorant state of parish (or local church-based) youth ministry. The youth ministry forms of the past 30 or more years have changed very little, for the identical program described in the opening scenario could have taken place in 1972—in fact it did! Yet in most settings a *commitment* to the programmatic structures and forms seems to be etched in stone.

Although the roots of the ministry movement targeting the adolescent population have been active for several decades, what is now called *youth ministry* is really not that old. The youth ministry we see today, now a worldwide movement, recognizably began to emerge as an ecclesiological force in the mid- to late-1930s, around the time of mandatory high school.[7] The teenager subculture was taking on a power and identity all its own, and (not surprisingly) the churches were left behind in these sweeping cultural changes. The church was seen by many to be inherently irrelevant, boring, and out of touch with the modern and youthful world of adolescents.

Beginning with youth ministry pioneers like Jim Rayburn (Young Life), whom Dean Borgman calls "the founder of modern youth ministry,"[8] and Jack Hamilton (Youth for

Christ), so-called parachurch youth ministry movements emerged, as people committed to church-based ministry sought to address this generational disloyalty and discontent. Mark Senter describes this movement:

> Jim Rayburn forged the high school club methodology which would be perfected in the Young Life movement in the 1940s and 1950s. A nearly identical strategy was adopted by the Youth for Christ International club division in the 1960s and then found its way into church youth groups during the decade of the 1970s. Rayburn's contribution was at the heart of the parachurch contribution to church youth ministry.[9]

Prior to 1970, parish youth ministry relied primarily on volunteers and occasional interns.[10] The parachurch movements, driven by a commitment to professional trained staff, were building tremendous momentum and influence. The church had a choice—stand back and disparage these ministries for stealing kids from the parish's programs or learn from them and bring the parachurch program into the parish. Increasingly, most church programs (that could afford it) chose the latter tack and essentially created what Stuart Bond referred to in 1989 as a "one-eared Mickey Mouse": a parachurch program under the structural umbrella of the local parish.[11] To many this was the final step in the evolution of youth ministry. The church had the best of both worlds—an attractive, relationally sensitive, culturally relevant program for their own students; and a mechanism to keep them involved in their church. Now there would be no need for church kids to leave ecclesiological home and get involved with Young Life or Youth for Christ. In this scenario, the church could provide the program they wanted—and their kids would never want to leave the church.

The Great Divide

But, as history has proven, this proved to be a debilitating flaw in church youth ministry. As Senter notes,

> Once again the church copied the technology of parachurch agencies, this time Young Life and Campus Life, and employed their methods to maintain youth groups of Christian adolescents in church settings while practically ignoring the vast majority of young people who had not made a commitment to the Christian faith.[12]

Thus the great divide between the church and the secular adolescent world began to take shape, all in the name of youth ministry. Church youth groups, designed to ensure adolescent congregant loyalty to the church, by default built systems, norms, and attitudes that implicitly (and sometimes explicitly) excluded secular students. In an increasingly secularized society, the gulf widened to the point where today the majority of kids would not even consider attending a church or religious event or program.[13] In 1986, Jim Burns claimed that "programs attract kids; relationships keep them."[14] That may have been true in the early years of modern parish youth ministry, but not today. For the vast majority of church-based adolescents, programs are seen to be irrelevant at best and aggressively oppressive at worst.

The problem historically was not what the church programs copied from the parachurch, but rather what they did not copy. What was modeled was not the essence of the parachurch youth ministries (especially Young Life and Campus Life) but the form of the program. Jim Burns, in a 1997 *Christianity Today* interview, stated, "We who did youth ministry took the Youth for Christ and Young Life models—they were the best models—and brought them into the church."[15] The methodological models practiced by Young Life (and later by Campus Life), and the domestic evangelistic club-based program of Youth for Christ were created as tools to achieve one purpose—to reach out to young people where they lived in order to bring the gospel to this disenfranchised culture.[16] The vision behind these and other organizations was a missional commitment of the church toward the lost, in this case adolescents. The model itself, and especially the specifics of the program, was not the commitment. The vision and mission is what mattered. Historically the youth parachurch movements were far more concerned with the core of their mission than the delivery system or programmatic methodology. For example, for years Young Life shunned the club as the key to Young Life ministry, for the organization's theology held fast to the idea of "adults reaching kids for Christ" as the core value, whether or not a club, camp, or small group was ever methodologically involved. This focused commitment is perhaps the single key factor to the historic success of these ministries over the years.[17]

But when church youth ministry began to move toward modeling itself after the success of the parachurch methods, by concentrating on highly produced youth groups, flashy programs, and relevant talks targeting the least-common-denominator student, it unknowingly abandoned one of the local church youth ministry's primary missions—to create an environment where churched adolescents are communally nurtured in their walk with Christ in order to ultimately assimilate them into the larger body of the local church. The church is to be the place where care, training, teaching, discipling, and spiritual formation can flourish *with a missional end goal*—"Go and make disciples of all nations" (Matthew 28:19). Now secular young people discount the church as a viable influence, and for so many anything that sounds religious is instantly and forthrightly rejected. What went wrong?

When churches and denominations chose to focus parish youth ministry on the prominent youth minister and a series of programs, they failed to recognize that, up until the 1970s anyway, at the core youth ministry had been more concerned with mission and less with program. The power and impact of a missional youth ministry approach was due to its focus—to contextually care for and thus reach the student who did not want to be reached and to share the love of Jesus Christ with the student who did not know that Christians cared. A student touched by this missional emphasis would naturally be prone to experience the church as a caring community who accepted her as she was. But the local church allowed itself to define youth ministry as one *program* of the church, instead of a basic theologically driven *mission* of the church. Thus the last 20 to 30 years have seen youth ministry move from a mission-driven, outreach-oriented, culturally sensitive expression of God's incarnational care for all people to an entertainment-based series of events, programs, options, and classes.

Saddleback and Willow Creek

Two particularly influential programs have sought to change from a program-driven to "purpose-driven" focus—Saddleback Community Church's Purpose-Driven Youth Ministry and Willow Creek Community Church's Student Impact. Each organization (and resultant resources) seeks to bring a missional focus to the church's ministry to adolescents. Both of these programs are highly missional—but define mission differently. According to Bo Boshers, Willow Creek targets "three groups of people: seekers, believers, and leaders."[18] In this philosophical schema, the seeker is defined as "someone who is interested in spiritual things and is investigating the claims of Christianity."[19] By this definition the missional commitment of this program excludes

> The only true measure of success in a youth ministry program is the ability and willingness of a church to fully assimilate growing adolescents into the adult fellowship.

those who are not actively seeking. Saddleback's philosophy, on the other hand, does not define its ministry focus to only those who are interested, but also targets "community students," defined as "teenagers living within a realistic drive of our church."[20] The programmatic philosophy behind the first of Saddleback's "five purposes of the church" is "Mission: We communicate God's Word through evangelism."[21]

So although both programs, key leaders, and resources are held up as cutting edge youth ministry programs, in print at least, Saddleback's purpose-driven philosophy is more in line with historic parachurch focus on the mission of the church than is Willow Creek's. In defense of Willow Creek's philosophical position on reaching out to uninterested adolescents, the argument has been made that their position considers all uninterested nonbelievers as at some level, and therefore is targeting the same types of students that Saddleback tries to reach. This apologetic, however, rings hollow given a careful reading of Student Impact materials. With all of the emphasis given to philosophical focus and vision drivenness, Willow Creek's basic philosophy remains that of the contemporary church youth ministry: students must first *come* in order to be drawn into the ministry (italics in the following are mine).

> **At Student Impact, we want every student *who walks through the door* to feel accepted. Some who *come* have mohawks and tattoos, while others look as if they just shopped at the Gap. No matter what these students look like, each is accepted into a team with other students from his or her high school. New students are introduced to other team members and get an overview of the night. It's like a party just for them.[22]**

This is absolutely appropriate for a seeker because a seeker will not mind coming to something he or she finds interesting in the quest for information and truth. But this philosophical focus, while important and significant, is still not entirely missional in that a nonseeker will likely show her lack of interest by *not* showing up.

Saddleback, on the other hand, seeks to take the uninterested student more seriously by including him in the community. These students are therefore specifically targeted and sought out. Like historical youth ministry philosophy, programs for these students are usually logistically connected to the church facility, but this is not always the case. Home-based Bible studies and discussion groups are designed to address and alleviate the uninterested student's innate fears. Even this commitment, however, can be overshadowed by an emphasis on a "come to us" programmatic mentality and methodology.

> Church youth groups, designed to ensure the loyalty of its adolescent congregants, by default built systems, norms, and attitudes that implicitly (and sometimes explicitly) excluded secular students.

These two programs—Willow Creek and Saddleback—are unquestionably the most significant forces in church-based youth ministry philosophies to date. Even with the popularity and unquestioned success at several levels, however, these and other church-based youth ministry programs must continue to evaluate their missional programmatic commitments and strategies. Every youth ministry must constantly ask itself *Who are our targets? How do we best reach out to them? Where do we want these students to end up when they leave our program?* This is especially true in a youth ministry climate that has relegated youth evangelism to early and middle adolescents by committing to a philosophy that leaves evangelism entirely up to the students. For when the essence of a program's evangelism is simply encouraging students to bring their friends to a church-based program, this immediately sets out of reach that vast number of young people who have no Christian friends to bring them.

Willow Creek clearly holds to this strategy when Bo Boshers states, "There can be no outreach without Christian students who care for their non-Christian friends."[23] Saddleback's *Purpose-Driven Youth Ministry* nuances this view in acknowledging that even the most devoted young disciple needs adults to partner with the core students: "Youth ministries that successfully reach unchurched students are almost always led by a leader with a burden for the lost."[24] But even Saddleback's primary method for reaching out is to encourage the core students to bring students to *their programs*, which they refer to as the "friendship evangelism challenge."

Peer to peer

The movement to peer evangelism as the main thrust of a youth ministry's missional focus is an inadequate strategy for at least three reasons. First, the latest research on peer relationships makes clear that adolescents choose friends who are most like themselves. Somewhere in the

> Thus the last 20 to 30 years have seen youth ministry move from a mission driven, outreach-oriented, culturally sensitive expression of God's incarnational care for all people to an entertainment-based series of events, programs, options, and classes.

early onset of mid-adolescence (13 to 14 years of age), peers become more important in the lives of young people. The current form of grouping has become known as *clustering*, where mid-adolescents choose three to eight students to bond with based on their self-concept during this roughly five-year period. These clusters then choose other clusters with whom to align, again based on similar self-concept, identity, and ego strength. The interesting thing about the clustering phenomenon is that these groupings of clusters, or "cousin clusters," consistently struggle against social participation with other cousin clusters for fear of being either tainted (if they perceive the other group is less socially competent) or rejected (if they perceive themselves to be less socially competent). The upshot of this newly emerging, adolescent social structure is that when someone is encouraged to bring their friends to a church-sponsored event, few outreach students actually attend because the potential target group—their friends—comprises a relatively small group of students. By default, then, those programs that rely on student-to-student come-to-our-church evangelism attract only those students who are similar to the church's young people![25]

The second way that peer evangelism is lacking as the sole methodology for a missional commitment to youth ministry is that adults are asking students to do what they themselves are deathly afraid of and do quite poorly at best. Adults rarely bring a friend to church-sponsored events, unless they are absolutely convinced that this friend will positively respond to both the invitation *and* the experience. There seems to be a worldview in youth ministry, however, that believes that students are more socially secure than adults and can therefore risk alienation and stereotyping as they are challenged to "do" evangelism. The research on mid-adolescence and peer relationships shows exactly the opposite. Mid-adolescents, by definition, are far *less* socially secure than adults are. Identity has yet to be formed, the peer group is taking on enormous power and influence, and the rules and norms of the adolescent experience are in constant flux. Youth workers who push students in this area risk limiting students' growth in Christ in several ways:

- Forcing students to limit their circle of friends to only those who are willing to attend a church program,
- Teaching young people how to justify their way out of an expected norm of the faith (at least as communicated by the leadership), and
- Creating an understanding of evangelism that communicates that the only people God is calling us to are those just like us—people we consider to be our friends.

Lastly, limiting a missional commitment in youth ministry to peer or friendship evangelism creates a mission mind set that is *program centered*. When we ask students to bring their friends, our responsibility as adults is reduced to providing a program that is designed to draw those friends into our ministry. Our goal, then, becomes active participation in *our* ministry. We are thereby forced to continue a cycle of attractive and relevant programs so that our students' friends will continue to be enticed to come. In a program the staff is responsible to make certain that the machine continues to run. The program becomes the product, and the congregation (in this case the students) becomes the consumer. This cycle continues where expectations of programmatic excellence become the bottom line for ministerial evaluation and effectiveness, with the goal being students who like the program.

While it has its place within the broader context of a youth ministry philosophy and methodology, peer-to-peer ministry is inadequate as the *primary* missional thrust because it only draws kids who are like the students already participating in a given program. We ask of adolescents what we hardly ask of mature Christian adults, and it can create a program-centered ministry. These three issues, however, are exponentially magnified when youth ministry is defined as a *mission* of the church with an end goal of full assimilation into the locally expressed body of Christ.

As stated, youth ministry *is not* simply about attracting and keeping students involved in one of the generationally focused programs of a large, disconnected body. It *is* about bringing young people into full participation in the local church family. Missional youth ministry takes adolescents and their culture seriously enough to provide them a sociological and theological bridge from the secularized world of the young into a broad, rich community of faith, hope, and love.

For a church to be truly *missional*, the goal is clearer and more central. The staff, lay adult leadership, and even the entire congregation are missionaries to a specific population—whether they are involved or not, willing to come or uninterested, seeker or lost wanderer. A missional commitment to youth ministry means that a congregation sees adolescents—regardless of their current involvement—as deserving love, focus, and care. Programs shift and change, methodology is fluid, and young people are encouraged to pursue Christ in the context of an accepting community of adults who care.

A widening gulf: today's adolescent world

As mentioned above, the target or goal of youth ministry must clearly be established. If the goal of a parish-based youth ministry is to provide an environment where the congregation's young people can be nurtured, cared for, and disicpled, then in some ways what is happening in the secular community may not matter. However, if youth ministry is more broadly defined within the context of the church universal's missional mandate, where every young person is our mission field, then it is essential to understand what is happening in the world of secular adolescents.

The distinction between secular and sacred in the adolescent context is far too narrow, for two reasons. First, a kind of cultural spillage will have some effect on even the most spiritually cloistered of young people. It is important to recognize that even an appropriately acclimated Christian student will carry at least some of the marks of the dominant generation. Nearly all churched students carry the baggage of the culture in their psyches.

But second, and even more theologically and ecclesiologically important, is that churched adults and leadership must not be allowed to deny that the church *must* be a place of refuge and welcome for the most desperate of the lost. If the church has created a sociological climate that makes assimilation or even casual interest difficult (if not impossible, at least in some cases), then the church has ceased to be the church and has become a members-only club.

People, even young people, have not changed all that much over the years; but the world has changed dramatically since the beginning of the modern youth ministry movement. In the last 30 years we have experienced great change in technology, geopolitical structures, cultural rules, norms and values, and even what many believe to be the most profound shift in thinking in several hundred years (the move from a modern to a postmodern worldview). This rapid change has caused church leadership to become reactors rather than responders. Most have made attempts to keep up with the many changes occurring in the culture around us, but there is always something else to worry about, something new to understand, and someone else to listen to. Amidst all of this turmoil, adolescents have been on their own to make sense out of life.

> When the essence of a program's evangelism is simply encouraging students to bring their friends to a church-based program, this immediately disqualifies that vast number of young people who have no Christian friends.

The cluster phenomenon mentioned earlier is but one of the significant societal changes that has had a deep effect on modern adolescents. In the mid-1980s, Canadian youth minister Donald Posterski noted that the adolescent social scene was changing and Canadian students were gathering in smaller groups than in the previous decades.[26] Although his data were helpful in pointing to a sociological shift in the high school world, there was not enough clear information available to fully develop the implications. The survey Posterski and his team used uncovered an emerging trend, especially in the United States, and many believed that he had discovered something very important to the future of youth ministry.

Jim Burns and Duffy Robbins both note Posterski's research, but neither provides any other collaborative data for the shift or detail methodological changes that will need to be made to recognize something is going on in the world of young people.[27] The idea was too new. In 1992 Mark Senter rightly noted this as a future "megatrend of the coming revolution" when he stated that, based on his research, "Posterski proposed the best way to minister to young people was through their cluster of friends."[28] Senter went on to give an example of an East Los Angeles pastor who had used this concept to "evangelize (adolescents) in group Bible study settings."[29]

If the church is not going to strategically and proactively address the sweeping cultural shifts of the past 30 years, the vast majority of young people—who will soon be our mainstream adults—will enter adulthood believing that the church is basically irrelevant and cares about them only when they show up at church. The target of every form of ministry in the church must have, at least as an end goal, a missional mindset in order to fulfill its call in Christ. Every student must be sought out and relationally and incarnationally enveloped with the aroma of Christ.[30] As Dean Borgman insists, "More than ever, today's youth ministers must function first as missionaries, then as social workers, and finally as pastors. Furthermore, these professionals are effective only if youth ministers have proved themselves as real friends of particular individuals *and* groups. Communities and churches need to see youth leaders as critical bridges to youth culture."[31]

The missiological mandate of the gospel (Go!)

To many, youth ministry is healthy, effective, and has come of age as a movement.[32] To others, however, parish or local church-based youth ministry is in need of a major overhaul. As in the church, our historic assumption has been that all we need to do to minister to the uninterested and disenfranchised is to open the doors of the church, offer a program, and get our constituency to bring their friends. We actually believe that the church is a safe, attractive place for those who have been culturally and relationally removed. But as New Testament scholar Darrell Guder claims, "Neither the structures nor the theology of our established Western churches is missional. They are shaped by the legacy of Christendom. That is, they have been formed by centuries in which Western civilization considered itself formally and officially Christian."[33]

The same can be said of modern youth ministry. We have become convinced that our programs, music, and ethos of youth ministry are enough to reach the lost, uninterested, and disenfranchised. Even if we have made some programmatic and philosophical changes in how we "do" youth ministry in the attempt to win the seeker, any programmatic, "come to us" methodology for evangelism, Christian witness, and mission in the world will, by its very assumptions, exclude the masses. When we fail to acknowledge how far away from us the culture has moved, we also fail in our ability to impact this broken generation. This is especially true in the vast majority of adult worship services. Even when a youth ministry program is able to reach a secularized adolescent, any attempt to assimilate that student into the life of the larger church is often doomed from the start. Very few churches see youth ministry as *their* missional mandate. That's why they hired a youth minister, after all. Yet this attitude and spirit destroys any hope of fulfilling the ultimate goal of youth ministry.

Missional youth ministry is a youth ministry that is driven by an entire congregation's commitment to reach the adolescent population, both those who show up and those who do not. In a missional youth ministry, youth ministers and pastors are equippers of the laity who do the face-to-face, incarnational, hands-on ministry to those who will come to us *and* those who will not. But they are *not* called to be program directors or, as one elder put it, party planners. Youth ministry paid staff and volunteers make up the hands, arms, and feet of the body of Christ to the young of a congregation and community.

The church, however, has become a place where we do not *want* others around who force us to talk openly about what we believe and why, who cause us to constantly rediscover who we are in Christ, and who push us to tell others our unique stories. The church seems to want to program the relational intimacy and interconnectedness of our lives right out of the equation. But the very presence of the young and vibrant threatens the security of our stained-glass system. Yet openness to that kind of pressure is exactly what it takes to have a missional commitment to the adolescent world—that pressure is exactly what it means "to go." The church is not the church without this kind of relational struggle and give-and-take. "Life is not to be lived through autonomous selfhood but through relational connection," writes Steven J. Sandage. "Our individual stories are shaped and constrained by the stories of others."[34]

In a missional youth ministry, there is a commitment on the part of the staff to "go" into the cultural settings and world where modern secularized adolescents live. Outreach to the "community," to use Fields' term, is seen to be a three-way partnership between the church at large, the youth ministry adult staff, and the "core" students (defined as those who experience the church environment as *their* spiritual community). Evangelism is thus the cumulative conviction of the entire local family of God to reach out to students on their turf (to borrow a historic parachurch term). Relational, no-strings-attached contacts are made with students in settings—both relational and physical—where the target student feels safe to encounter another person, regardless of their age, who genuinely cares.

Changes That Must Be Made

For a church to recapture the Missional approach to youth ministry, the following people or groups must commit to substantive changes regarding the youth ministry task: the youth ministry leadership team, the youth minister or youth pastor, the senior pastor (and other church staff), and the lay leadership of the church.

Youth ministry leadership team

This group must refocus on the heart of the youth ministry task in every aspect of the program and ministry. There must be a willingness to receive students who walk through the door and to become a ministry that has a go-to-them mentality of adolescent ministry. The leadership, lay and paid, must see themselves as representatives of the entire congregation, being ambassadors and representatives of the church at large. Here are some specific changes that can be made. The youth ministry leadership team will:

- Respect, honor, and seek to understand the culture where secularized adolescents live;
- Seek, along with committed students, to be relationally connected with students in the context of their clusters on their own turf;
- View programs as incidental tools that facilitate relational trust and confidence, as opposed to being the end goal of the ministry; and
- Make certain that every program, every event, and every methodology employed is centered on the end goal of full assimilation into the larger body of the church upon graduation from the youth ministry program.

Youth minister/youth pastor

The staff leader of the youth ministry must see herself as both a point person for a specific ministry, as well as a member of the leadership of the whole. Youth ministers must constantly resist the temptation to fight for their own programs or exclusively focus on the rights and needs of adolescents or strategically seek to move the youth ministry agenda ahead of other needs and concerns of the church. As with all associate level staff positions in a church, it is vital that the youth minister remember that Christian leaders must model Scriptural body life: "Do nothing out of selfish ambition or vain conceit, but in humility consider others better than yourselves. Each of you should look not only to your own interests, but also to the interests of others" (Philippians 2:3, 4). Here are some specific changes that can be made.

Youth ministers will be wise to—

- Resist typical youth ministry mentalities that divide a church staff, such as being a Lone Ranger or having a "We're the only ones doing it right" attitude.
- Submit personally and in ministry to being primarily a member of the overall church's leadership team.
- Seek to connect students with other people and programs in the church.
- Partner with parents and other adults in the church in ministry to students.
- Strategically commit to and plan for the goal of full assimilation into the life of the church for each student.

Senior pastor and other church staff

In the life of any church, the single most influential person is the senior pastor. Over the last several years, many senior pastors have sought to stay out of the day-to-day running of their church, hiring competent staff to run their ministry so they don't have to think about it. But inherent in the role of senior pastor is the responsibility to oversee the theologically appropriateness of each program and to ensure that each program moves the congregation into com-

> Missional youth ministry takes adolescents and their culture seriously enough to provide them a sociological and theological bridge from the secularized world of the young into a broad, rich community of faith, hope, and love.

munal conformity into the image of Christ. We are the body and Christ is the Head. Every program must be held accountable for its commitment to the whole.

In addition, the senior pastor has to lead the way to receive the young of the congregation *and* the community. A senior pastor has tremendous influence over a community's willingness and ability to create an environment that is warm, relationally and sociologically safe, and an inviting place of refuge for the young or any other member of the congregation. Here are some specific changes that can be made. Senior pastors should—

- Create a systemic structure and relational community where *all* people are welcomed and cared for, especially in the worship services.
- Preach to the needs, environment, and situations of the *entire* congregation.
- Build meaningful relationships with adolescents and youth ministry staff.
- Take decisive leadership with those who, by their actions, deny adolescents' access to experiencing community in the larger church body.
- Invite the youth staff into the inner circle of leadership in the church.

The lay leadership of the church

Theologically, the laity are the mainstay of any church body and the staff are employees. Thus, the real influence of any church, should they choose to express it, is in the lay leadership. Therefore, for any tangible change to take place in how a church body will receive and envelop adolescents, lay leadership is most in need of a strategic commitment to a Missional approach to youth ministry. Even a few strong lay people who are convinced that it is the spiritual responsibility of a local church to reach out to *all* young people and make a place for them in their community can effect great change. Here are some specific changes that can be made. Lay leadership should:

- Ensure that all programs and staff are committed to a holistic body view of the church;
- Create and hold others accountable in maintaining a corporate ethos where adolescents *know* they are both accepted and taken seriously in their gifts and ministry;
- Allow no one—lay or staff—to view young people as merely "the youth pastor's job."

Conclusion

Missional youth ministry is an extension of the local body of Christ, where every person who desires to belong to the community is welcomed. Programs, then, are useful tools to attract and win those who are ultimately willing to come to a church, but they are never the end goal or focus of evaluation. In a missional youth ministry, each program is specifically and strategically analyzed to ensure that the focus is an intentional reaching out to those who may feel unconnected, with the goal of seeing that they are ultimately connected to the church at large. When students do feel relationally safe enough to attend a program, even then the program is not the end-all. Instead, a new student who attends a missional youth ministry event is embraced by the core students and adult leadership in such a way that there can be no doubt that their personal value to both the person *and* the church body has nothing to do with any level of programmatic participation. As Rollie Martinson, youth ministry expert for the Lutheran (ELCA) church, states, "Youth ministry belongs to God through the ministry of God's whole church."[35]

This type of approach does not presuppose that student leaders will not be able to use their gifts with their friends. Rather, they will be allowed to be adolescents themselves, on the journey that requires, by definition, the freedom to walk tall and occasionally fall down. The youth group is a community of broken people who are committed to loving one another, but it is not the *only* community of the church. The other programs and members of the church family are always respected and valued, parents are friends and partners of the leadership, and the worship service and other church events are cherished opportunities to celebrate the life of Christ as a body. Missional youth ministry seeks to present the community of the church as the end, not simply another (and often less desirable) community.

> If the church will not address the cultural shifts of the past 30 years, then most young people will enter adulthood believing that the church is basically irrelevant and cares about them only when they show up at church.

God's call is for the *entire church community* to create a relational environment where people, young and old alike, can experience a deep, rich, family-like environment where discipleship, equipping, nurture, training in spiritual disciplines, and mentoring all occur. This is what all people, and especially young people, need from the church.

In the evolution of church youth ministry, the focus has been on two things: the students that attend the church, as the target of the ministry; and outreach, defined as "bringing your friends to youth group." While these two programmatic and philosophic focuses have served the church, with varied results, for the last several decades, a gap has widened between the people who have grown up in the church, own the church, and love the church, versus those who live outside of the sociological and spiritual boundaries of the local parish. This has created a family crisis. The church, especially as expressed in and through youth ministry, must recapture its historical theological roots and redefine its mission. Youth ministry *and* the local church are called to be a mission community with a missional commitment to rich Christian community that spills over into the secularized adolescent world. As Darrell Guder reminds us, "A missional ecclesiology must clearly identify and resist all attempts to equip the church merely for its maintenance and security."[36]

Notes

1. Mark Yaconelli, "Youth Ministry: A Contemplative Approach," *The Christian Century*, 28 April 1999, 2.

2. Darrell L. Guder, "Missional Context: Understanding North American Culture," *Missional Church: A Vision for the Sending of the Church in North America* (Grand Rapids: Eerdmans, 1998), 18-45.

3. F. F. Bruce, *1 and 2 Corinthians* (Greenwood, South Carolina: Attic Press, 1971), 121.

4. Sherwood G. Lingenfelter and Marvin K. Mayers, *Ministering Cross-Culturally* (Grand Rapids: Baker, 1986), 27-26.

5. Darrell L. Guder, "Missional Church: From Sending to Being Sent," *A Vision for the Sending of the Church in North America* (Grand Rapids: Eerdmans, 1998), 4-5.

6. Dennis Guernsey, *A New Design for Family Ministry* (Elgin, Illinois: David C. Cook, 1982), 99.

7. Dean Borgman, "A History of American Youth Ministry," in *The Complete Book of Youth Ministry* (Chicago: Moody Press, 1987), 67-74.

8. ———. 69.

9. Mark Senter, *The Coming Revolution in Youth Ministry* (Wheaton: Victor, 1992), 125.

10. This overview and timeline is to be viewed as a macro-historical analysis. The actual dates and programmatic/philosophical influences vary greatly. Every church, locale, and denomination can trace its youth ministry roots in different ways and at different times.

11. Stuart Bond, "The One-Eared Mickey Mouse," *Youthworker* (Fall 1989). Presbyterian youth pastor Stuart Bond addressed the issue of fragmentation in the church by describing the relationship between the youth ministry program as a "one-eared Mickey Mouse" with the church at large as Mickey's head. In his description of church youth ministry, the point was made that youth ministry had become more and more separate as congregants. To take this illustration further, youth ministry has become, in essence, a semi-parachurch community loosely connected to the local congregation.

12. Senter, 142.

13. Although there are some who claim that there are more church-going young people than not (George Barna among them), there is no reliable empirical research even close to supporting this assertion. In nearly every community in North America, the number of adolescents that willingly attend a church, even on an infrequent basis, is vastly outnumbered by those that do not. This is an unchurched and religiously disinterested generation.

14. This comment was made by Jim Burns, President of the National Institute of Youth Ministry, during a seminar at the Youth Specialties 1986 National Youth Workers Convention.

15. Jim Burns, quoted by Wendy Murray Zoba in, "The Class of '00," *Christianity Today*, 3 February 1997, 21.

16. *Subculture* may bit a bit more accurate categorization of the adolescent community, but the differences between the Christian cultural world and the secular adolescent world are great enough that fully demarcating the difference with the term *culture* seems appropriate.

17. Perhaps this acclaim is not quite justified today, for there are those who critique many of these organizations for being as committed to their methods as are parish youth ministries. If so, then the concept of "missional" youth ministry is even more necessary to lift high, for if the parachurch organizations have capitulated to elevating form and method over vision and end goal, then the parish must take action in not neglecting this lost generation.

18. Bo Boshers, *Student Ministry for the 21ˢᵗ Century* (Grand Rapids: Zondervan, 1998), 95.

19. ———.

20. Doug Fields, *Purpose-Driven Youth Ministry* (Grand Rapids: Youth Specialties/Zondervan, 1998), 88; Fields, 51.

21. ———.

22. Boshers, 99.

23. ———. 224.

24. Fields, 105.

25. For further adolescent clustering research, see—

• Curran, P. J., E. Stice, and L. Chassin. "The Relation between Adolescent Alcohol Use and Peer Alcohol Use: A Longitudinal Random Coefficient Model." *Journal of Consulting and Clinical Psychology*, 65 (1997):130-140.

• Oetting, E. R. and F. Beauvais. "Peer Cluster Theory, Socialization Characteristics and Adolescent Drug Use: A Path Analysis." *Journal of Counseling Psychology*, 34 (1987):205-213.

• Posterski, Donald. *Friendship: A Window on Ministry to Youth*. Scarborough, Ontario: Project Teen Canada, 1985.

• Urberg, K. A., S. M. Degirmencioglu, and C. Pilgrim. "Close Friend and Group Influence on Adolescent Cigarette Smoking and Alcohol Use." *Developmental Psychology*, 33 (1997):834-842.

• Dekovic, M., and W. Meeus. "Peer Relations in Adolescence: Effects of Parenting and Adolescents' Self-Concept." *Journal of Adolescence*, 20 (1997):163-176.

• Giordano, P. C., S. A. Cernkovich, H. T. Groat, M. D. Pugh, and S. P. Swinford. "The Quality of Adolescent Friendships: Long Term Effects?" *Journal of Health and Social Behavior*, 39 (1998): 55-71.

26. Donald Posterski, *Friendship: A Window on Ministering to Youth* (Scarborough, Ontario: Project Teen Canada, 1985).

27. Jim Burns, *The Youth Builder* (Eugene, Oregon: Harvest House, 1988); and Duffy Robbins, *The Ministry of Nurture* (Grand Rapids: Youth Specialties/Zondervan, 1990).

28. Senter, 177.

29. ———.

30. Phillip Yancey, lecture to a course on spiritual formation at Denver Theological Seminary, Winter 1996.

31. Dean Borgman, *When Kumbaya Is Not Enough: A Practical Theology for Youth Ministry* (Peabody, Massachusetts: Hendrickson, 1997), 6.

32. Although this point is too broad for this discussion, many, if not most, youth ministry professionals and leaders believe that the observable success of Doug Fields's *Purpose-Driven Youth Ministry*, the Student Impact movement of Willow Creek, and Youth Specialties is proof that youth ministry is healthy and on solid ground. For reasons I have stated throughout this chapter and several others, I am not so convinced.

33. Guder, "Missional Church: From Sending to Being Sent," 5-6.

34. Steven J. Sandage, "Power, Knowledge, and the Hermeneutics of Selfhood," *Mars Hill Review*, No. 12 (Fall 1998): 65-73, 72.

35. Roland D. Martinson, *Effective Youth Ministry: A Congregational Approach* (Minneapolis: Augsburg, 1988), 12.

36. Guder, "Missional Connectedness: The Community of Communities in Mission," *Missional Church: A Vision for the Sending of the Church in North America* (Grand Rapids: Eerdmans, 1998), 268.

References

Clapp, Rodney. *Families at the Crossroads: Beyond Traditional and Modern Options*. Downers Grove, Illinois: InterVarsity Press, 1994.

Clark, Chap. *The Youth Worker's Handbook to Family Ministry*. Grand Rapids: Youth Specialties/Zondervan, 1997.

Elkind, David. *Ties That Stress: The New Family Imbalance*. Cambridge: Harvard University Press, 1994.

Garland, Diana and Diane Pancoast (eds). *The Church's Ministry with Families*. Waco: Word, 1990.

Justice, Mike. *It Takes a Family to Raise a Youth Ministry*. Kansas City: Beacon Hill Press, 1999.

Guder, Darrell L., ed. *Missional Church: A Vision for the Sending of the Church in North America*. Grand Rapids: Eerdmans, 1998.

Mueller, Walter. *Understanding Today's Youth Culture*. 2d ed. Wheaton: Tyndale, 1999.

Stringer, Doug. *The Fatherless Generation: Hope for a Generation in Search of Identity*. Shippensburg, Pennsylvania: Destiny, 1995.

Weissbourd, Richard. *The Vulnerable Child*. Reading, Massachusetts: Addison-Wesley, 1996.

Response to the Missional Approach
from an Inclusive Congregational Perspective
by Malan Nel

The understanding of the church as being missional in identity, Chap, is basic to my own theology, and I am excited about this emphasis in your chapter. In my main field of interest—namely, helping local churches understand and find their identity (what in German and in Afrikaans we call *Gemeindeaufbau*)—it is crucial to develop an ecclesiology that is missiological in nature. It is this golden thread that runs through your whole chapter, and of the utmost importance in any approach to youth ministry. In my comments here, I am in truth in full agreement with you. I just want to explore some of the basic issues you raise, and I'm interested in your response to the statements made below.

Your discussion of the church and the role it plays (or does not play) ties in with my basic belief that our problem is not so much youths and youth ministry, but the adult *gestalt* of the local church. We have allowed what you call the "club mentality." And a club is not typically missionary in nature. This ingrown nature of churches is a major obstacle for the mission approach.

Along these lines, I've listed some observations that you may want to respond to:

- The church's lack of a missional understanding of youth ministry has to do with a misunderstanding of what it means to be a Christian. The practice of theology in local churches over many years is mainly responsible for this. Being a Christian does not mean (at least not in the first place) going to heaven. It is about being recreated back to our original purpose to serve this world. It has everything to do with the restoration of life and everything which is true of life and life eternal.

- The "come" mentality of churches in their mission is a historical result of an informational and propositional theology of evangelism: we know the Answer, and the lost world does not. If they come, we will tell them what they do not know. If they do not come, then we claim for ourselves the sinful luxury of remaining the way we are—and then blaming the world for not coming. Who would dare come then? This approach may have worked during the so-called Christian eras, but it will not be enough in years to come.

- I don't know of any reference in the Bible for lost sinners to come, but the Bible is full of references to the church going or being sent. As you pointed out, "The church is *missional* in that its mandate is clearly focused on God *sending* his people into the world as light and salt." The reference in Matthew 11:28 for people to come to Christ was not made to the world but to religious people who were so tired of their religion that they seriously needed the rest from religion and moralism, rest that Christ offers.

- Developing a missional character as a local church includes a real conversion to what is commonly called the servanthood of the church. This dimension may need further exploration in your chapter. It seems to me that this understanding of the church in mission changes the way we do mission. The emphasis on our followership of Christ focuses on the needs of persons (youths, in our case) far more than on conversions. Serving people takes on a new meaning.

- To be in service of the gospel is to be in service of the gospel *of the kingdom* (cf. Luke 8:1). To use your own words: "The theologically driven missional mandate of youth ministry is to bring the gospel and the kingdom to every adolescent. The church must step up and allow this theological axiom to shape and alter ecclesiological traditions and norms." My fear, however, is that this may still communicate that we just bring the gospel—and when people get saved, the kingdom has come.

I know this is probably not your intention. My history in evangelism makes me sensitive to this possibility. The coming of the kingdom that is served by the communication of the good news is so much more. Or to state it differently, salvation is so much more. In my country salvation so often means having only one meal, having shelter for one more night, or getting a job. I remember a Sunday morning in my quiet time when I read through Isaiah 58. I was stunned once again by the concrete nature of the kingdom.

> The propositional theology of evangelism: we know the Answer, and the lost world does not. If they come, we will tell them what they do not know. If they do not come, then we can remain the way we are—and then blame the world for not coming.

- Would you agree that it is partly because of the heavenly-mindedness of churches that youths often have no interest in the church? They just don't expect anything real and concrete from the church. The world they live in cries out loud for concrete help, yet they see more real help coming from big businesses, government, and other institutions than from God's agent for real kingdom help. Why then consider church (and by implication God and the gospel) as an option for life? The Germans have a saying that ministry is *lebenshilfe* (counseling). When youths find no help to live by, they quit seeking it from that institution.

- This brings me to a rather subtle distinction that I would like to test out on you. You explained in a wonderful way the necessity for what is generally called "friendship evangelism." This is a great way of doing youth evangelism. In *Service Evangelism*, R. S. Armstrong distinguishes between two styles of evangelism.[1] May I state it this way: there are many similarities between the two styles. There is a lot of friendship in service evangelism and vice versa. But there is one obvious difference: friendship evangelism, as it is normally practiced, is not need-oriented, but conversion-oriented: You befriend in order to convert. In service evangelism, as it is normally practiced, you serve irrespective of conversion. It is an honest attempt to take after our Father: Accept, love, and care irrespective of whether or not they respond positively to that care and love. Does this makes conversion irrelevant? Not at all. It is almost modeling the love of God to whom we want people to give their lives—allowing and trusting God to draw people to himself.

- This builds upon a very important theological issue. If we believe that faith in Christ as *the Christ* is ultimately a gift of God, it frees us from arguing anyone into faith. We serve in the spirit of Christ; do faith sharing, as we win the right to be heard; and when we have won that right, we leave the gift to God. He is the ultimate converter of hearts. I think Christian youths need this freedom from what is often an authoritarian go-tell approach.

May I underline a very important statement you made: "…churched adults and leadership must not be allowed to deny that the church *must* be a place of refuge and welcome for the most desperate of the lost." I believe it was Hebbard, in his book on family ministry, that made the same point: Nowhere should broken and hurting people (including youths) feel and be more at home and accepted than in the local body of believers.

Do you think it is possible that we are too middle-class in our churches? We seem to present a picture that the church is the place for those who have made it in life—successful people. Then how terribly difficult is it to help them change into helpless people who realize how broken they are, and to understand that we are but a fellowship of broken healers and healed broken ones? Kromminga referred in this regard to the local church as receiving fellowship.[2]

Finally (I am not criticizing here, and I can understand the absence of the argument in your chapter) let me ask you this: should a missional approach in youth ministry take family (or what is left thereof) seriously?

Let me explain my question by referring to a story Peters told concerning his plea for what he called "household evangelism." A missionary in Japan led a young man to Christ one night after a rally. Knowing how difficult it would be for this young man to go through with his decision to follow Christ, given Japan's emphasis on family, he asked the young man to wait for him. He went home with the man and met his parents, whom he told about the crucial decision their son had made. He also promised them that the church would in no way interfere with the family structure and would respect them as parents. He also invited them to come and

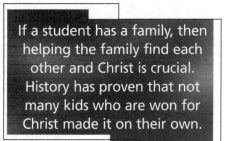

If a student has a family, then helping the family find each other and Christ is crucial. History has proven that not many kids who are won for Christ made it on their own.

see for themselves what new religion their son had accepted. It so happened that they did visit in a few weeks' time and eventually came to Christ themselves.[3]

My contention is that, irrespective of the age and state of family in a given case, the focus in mission is the family. If there is a family, then helping them find each other and Christ is crucial. History has proven that not many kids who are won for Christ made it on their own. The natural family (if in place) is a wonderful habitat in which to grow. But even where no family is in place, the future family of the young new believer should be our focus. Do you think this dimension can be part of the Missional approach—or even should be?

Notes

1. R. S. Armstrong, *Service Evangelism* (Philadelphia: Westminster, 1979).

2. C. G. Kromminga, *Bringing God's News to Neighbors* (Grand Rapids: Baker, 1976).

3. G. W. Peters, *Saturation Evangelism*, 6th printing (Grand Rapids: Zondervan, 1977).

Response to the Missional Approach from a Preparatory Perspective
by Wesley Black

Church as private club

I have to say first that I appreciate your insights into the critique of the church and its lack of emphasis on mission. We have too quickly relied on programs rather than an urgency in mission. As you say in the definition of the Mission approach, we need to reach out to "both churched and non-churched young people." And again, "The theologically driven missional mandate of youth ministry is to bring the gospel and the kingdom to every adolescent." It is far too easy to settle for the kids who come to our programs and forget about the ones outside the doors of the church.

One of the penetrating statements you made really hit home: "For those raised in the church, a youth group may not *feel* like a private club with its own culture, rules, and norms, but to many of those on the outside that's how it has felt for decades." We may mistake a warm, inviting fellowship for a closed club.

I also agree that one of the stress points for modern youth ministers is how to do the job in such as way as to be true to the calling and satisfy the gatekeepers, those who pay the salary and provide the resources for ministry. I felt like standing and cheering when you wrote that "this is the paradoxical quandary of contemporary youth ministry: churches are screaming for youth ministry (an 'excellent' one, at that—high-powered, entertaining, and theologically and sociologically safe), but there are few pastors, parents, and even boards who are *convinced* that God has called them *as a church* to mobilize their resources in order to penetrate a distant and disruptive generation."

This was spelled out in stark clarity with the list of expectations for youth ministers: keep the youths happy, teach the Christian worldview and political ideology, thrust them into leadership too quickly, and keep them interested and involved. This list would almost be humorous if it weren't so true.

Part of the problem, I think, grows out of the commonly held sense that church involvement leads to spirituality. As Darrel Guder first reminds us, "They have been formed by centuries in which Western civilization considered itself formally and officially Christian.... A missional ecclesiology must clearly identify and resist all attempts to equip the church merely for its maintenance and security." The people of God must keep their eyes focused on the world that needs a message of hope from God.

I liked how you reminded us that "youth ministry programs must continue to evaluate their missional programmatic commitments and strategies" by asking "Who are our targets? How do we best reach out to them? Where do we want these students to end up when they leave our program?" This is difficult to accomplish because, as you well stated, "Very few churches see youth ministry as *their* missional mandate. That's why they hired a youth minister, after all." But exactly how is that done? How do we reach out to youths, especially following your criticism that "any programmatic, come-to-us methodology for evangelism, Christian witness, and mission in the world will, by its very assumptions, exclude the masses"?

A gift of an earring

One discussion of yours particularly got my attention: "A missional commitment to youth ministry," you wrote, "means that a congregation sees adolescents—regardless of their current involvement—as deserving love, focus, and care.... This means that the only true measure of success in a youth ministry program is the ability and willingness of a church to fully assimilate growing adolescents into the adult fellowship."

This reminded me of a conference I led a few years ago for volunteer youth workers. As my luck would have it, one of the small groups included an 80-year-old lady and a 19-year-old male youth leader (with an earring, of course). I was curious about how they would get along during the week. The last day the small-group members brought small gifts of remembrance for each other. The octogenarian had bought a small earring set in the gift shop, just so she could give one of them to the 19-year-old she had befriended during the week. It was a reminder of how God's love can help us bridge the gaps between generations.

I also agree with your insight about sociological groupings and the problems with relying on peer ministry. When I read the statement, "The movement to 'peer evangelism' as the main thrust of a youth ministry's missional focus is an inadequate strategy," I was a little surprised but still intrigued. Peer evangelism is exactly what we've been stressing for years. *Get the kids involved and you will reach more kids* has been a prime organizing principle for most outreach strategies. But you added a new twist.

Your point is well made that "peer-to-peer ministry is inadequate as the *primary* missional thrust" because it only draws kids who, like the students, are already participating in a given program. We ask of adolescents what we hardly ask of mature Christian adults, and it

> I appreciated your list of expectations for youth ministers: keep the youths happy, teach the Christian worldview and appropriate political ideology, thrust them into leadership too quickly, and keep them involved. This list would almost be humorous if it weren't so true.

can create a program-centered ministry. I will take some issue with this later, but especially with your phrase "primary missional thrust," you give us reason to reevaluate our strategies for evangelism.

It reminds me of those who sterotypically speak of adolescents as "the typical teenager" or "the typical high school campus." The world of teenagers is complex and multifaceted. Anyone who misses that point will have a hard time understanding the world of adolescents. So when we urge our youths to evangelize their friends at school, we often picture everyone at school as being similar to the youths in our groups at church. It just may be our blind spot.

Unnecessarily harsh on the church

I feel, however, that you have been unnecessarily harsh in your criticism of the church, although I also see in modern North American churches many of the shortcomings that you pointed out. Furthermore, I don't see a lot of answers to the question of *how* to bring non-Christians into the family of God and eventually into the church. (Of course you would naturally expect me to respond to the criticism of the church, since it squarely hits the Preparatory approach.)

One statement of yours especially got my attention: "For many in youth ministry, even among the leaders of the movement, the church—that umbrella organization that sponsors youth ministry—is considered a necessary nuisance." That's a pretty strong statement. It almost appears cynical, as if you have written off the church as having no redeeming value.

"The fact is," you write elsewhere, "that for large numbers of adolescents (probably the majority), youth ministries in churches (and even in parachurch organizations...) represent a world that is foreign, irrelevant, and even occasionally offensive." Reading this is like getting a root canal—you know there's something good for you in it, but it still hurts.

By the way, I wonder about the accuracy of this statement. Do you have any research to indicate the numbers when you say "large numbers" and "probably the majority" of adolescents? A little later you write that "in an increasingly secularized society, the gulf widened to the point where today the majority of kids would not even consider attending a church or even religious event or program." Are these your perceptions or actual segments of the adolescent population?

I would like to raise the issue about *how* to move non-Christian adolescents from a secular world to the church. "As the church attempts to realize its biblical mandate of missional youth ministry," you wrote, "the issue is to rediscover its historical and fundamental missional commitment and focus and proceed accordingly." But I did not see a clearly stated process for proceeding to reach this goal. You mentioned some excellent ways that the church must change, mostly in attitude and acceptance; but what kind of strategies, programs, methodologies, organizations, or training should take place to reach the goals you mentioned?

Again, I appreciate your emphasis on *going* instead of simply making the invitation to *come* to programs at a church building. But this leads me to another point concerning the Missional approach. Among the needed changes you mentioned was a willingness on the part of the youth ministry leadership team to "make certain that every program, every event, and every methodology employed is centered on the end goal of full assimilation into the larger body of the church upon graduation from the youth ministry program." And you wrote that the youth minister or youth pastor should "seek to connect students with other people and programs in the church" and "strategically commit to and plan for the goal of full assimilation into the life of the church for each student." I am with you here completely—but how do we do that without falling into the trap of a *come-to-us* methodology? Sooner or later, they will *have* to come to us if they are to be fully assimilated into the larger body of the church.

> I feel that you put excessive emphasis on reaching, and neglect teaching. Yes, the church probably reaches more than it teaches—but it takes both to be faithful to Christ's Great Commission to us.

The Great Commission has at least two prongs—*reaching* all we can and *teaching* all we reach. I feel that you put excessive emphasis on the former and neglect the latter. Yes, the church probably reaches more than it teaches—but it takes both to be faithful to Christ's Great Commission. In fact, churches often fall into the entertainment trap, as you said: "Thus the last 20 to 30 years have seen youth ministry move from a mission driven, outreach-oriented, culturally sensitive expression of God's incarnational care for all people to an entertainment-based series of events, programs, options, and classes"—a potent indictment of the church. But could this also be said of many parachurch youth ministries? Both kinds of ministries stand in need of your reminders to be on mission with God.

Professionals or laypersons?

Your section about generational youth ministry approaches and parent-teen issues contains some confusing ideas.

You point out that "generationally focused ministry programming has emerged" in recent years. This is commonly accepted as a necessary process to be relevant to today's youths. But I believe we can twist that view until it presents a false picture of the world of adolescents. You cite Dean Borgman's statement that "communities and churches need to see youth leaders as critical bridges to youth culture"—meaning, he writes, that we function as missionaries, social workers, and finally as pastors. Yet I disagree with Borgman's implication that the youthful generation cannot be reached by untrained laypersons, but only by professionals with advanced degrees and unique skills that enable them to relate to a culturally distant generation.

The research simply does not bear this out. The work of Search Institute and many developmental psychologists consistently show that teenagers desire to have better relationships and to communicate with other generations, including their parents. Certainly, we must be generationally and culturally relevant to those we are targeting—but does this mean that pastors should turn over all youth ministry tasks to professionals and experts? That's the very point you were arguing against.

Finally, I was a little surprised that you did not include more about the families of adolescents. It almost sounded like this approach ignored the tremendous influence of parents on their teens. It is a common misperception that adolescents live in a world dominated by peers and isolated from adult influence, especially the influence of their parents. We all have to admit, in the end, that teens are strongly influenced by their parents and tend to be very much like them (more so than teens would ever desire to admit). If we are serious about reaching out to adolescents, we have to include strategies for reaching their families. We cannot evangelize teenagers and ignore the rest of the family.

Youth ministry must be more than simply going onto the turf of adolescents. We must also look for ways to bring them into relationship with other generations of the family of God, the body of Christ that we call church.

Response to the Missional Approach from a Strategic Perspective
by Mark H. Senter III

I commend you, Chap, for the manner in which you avoided the land mines laid by both sides in the church-versus-parachurch discussion. By now most thoughtful students of youth ministry recognize that the vast majority of resources (people, materials, facilities, and money) invested in youth ministry have been concentrated on less than 25 percent of the adolescent population—the bulk of whom are church kids.

Simultaneously, those same observers look at young people who come to faith through the efforts of missional activities and bemoan the fact that so few of them are assimilated into Christian churches, especially upon graduation from high school. Instead of becoming bogged down in that discussion, you framed the dialogue from the perspective of what *should* happen. You have leveled the playing field. A real discussion can now begin.

True measure of success

I loved your statement that "the only true measure of success in a youth ministry program is the ability and willingness of a church to fully assimilate growing adolescents into the adult fellowship." The context of your statement is the observation that "the primary reason for having a youth ministry...[is to] create a bridge of love, trust, and support to encourage the disenfranchised adolescent to be welcomed as a member of the family of God." The burden of this statement cannot be on the disenfranchised kid but on the church. That young person, with at least as many insecurities as experienced by the average church kid, should never be expected to worm his way into the family of God. As in the story of the prodigal son, the father should be the one who runs to the alienated son.

If anything, Chap, you could have been tougher on the church. Your comments about the role of the senior pastor to create a "systemic structure and relational community where *all* people are welcomed and cared for, especially in the worship services" is an excellent start. Your observation that lay leadership must maintain a "corporate ethos where adolescents *know* they are both accepted and taken seriously in their gifts and ministry" spreads the responsibility from the pulpit throughout all the pews. The greatest obstacle to the Missional approach is not the pagan youth of an MTV culture, or even the self-serving Christians in the youth group. The greatest obstacle is the failure of adults to build relationships and begin to love newcomers, especially young people.

Peer-to-peer youth ministry

Another point I find refreshing, Chap, is your critique of "peer-to-peer youth ministry." The idea of clustering into social units at the early onset of mid-adolescence has a rather profound impact upon the possibility of young people successfully evangelizing their peers beyond a very limited circle of friends or their cousin clusters. What I hear you saying is that even if young people in the church successfully evangelized all of the people in their cluster and cousin clusters, none of the disenfranchised adolescents, whom you say we should be reaching, would have a possibility of being included. They are all in their own clusters.

In addition, your comment about adults doing evangelism among their peers was quite telling. It does seem counterproductive if adults are asking young people to do peer evangelism when few of them are modeling what they expect from the kids. Perhaps the same cluster factor is at work in their worlds. They may not know people outside their circle of friends, most of whom are active in the church. Young people are no dummies. They know what people do is far more important than what they tell others to do. They can tell where the values of church leadership rest.

I am not as concerned about the program-centered aspects of peer-to-peer youth ministry as you are, Chap, because every missional effort I know of has a program component. To call something "program-centered" is more a matter of perspective than a factor that hinders peer evangelism. However, your other two factors do raise major questions about the potential effectiveness of this approach to mission. The alternative that adults are the missionaries, capable of reaching across cultural lines into the world of young people, is an idea that deserves further elaboration.

Children of the church

Now before I throw my arm out of joint slapping you on the back, I must hasten to mention two issues that left me a bit puzzled. First, what happens to the church kids? Our friends with a reformed theology perspective would refer to them as "children of the covenant." Do they become second-class citizens of the kingdom by virtue of being born into a Christian family? It would seem that we have the distinct possibility of a spiritual form of reverse discrimination here.

I recognize that young people born into Christian families have many advantages over the disenfranchised adolescent you are so rightfully concerned about, Chap. It reminds me of the apostle Paul's question, "What advantage, then, is there in being a Jew, or what value is there in circumcision?" (Romans 3:1). I would ask the same thing about being born "Christian." What advantage is there to being a part of a Christian family if the church is not encouraged to "take care of our own" young people?

There was a time when the family had lots of help passing the values of the Christian faith from generation to generation. The school system actively taught the importance of Christian virtues. Neighbors modeled a Christian lifestyle. Even the popular culture (primarily books and even early programming on radio and television) assisted the Christian family to raise their children in conformity with biblical standards. The church was just one of many voices assisting the Christian family to raise their children in the nurture and admonition of the Lord.

Today the only support left for the Christian family is the church. While I agree that the church should not create a Christian ghetto where Christian kids are "isolated [in a] private community," I am not sure these are the only alternatives to your Missional approach to youth ministry. We must not get caught in an either/or mentality. Perhaps we should look at some both/and options wherein we do a better job of living a missional lifestyle and teaching Christian youths to honor what you have called the "official-yet-unwritten mandate of contemporary youth ministry"?

After all, Chap, the world of the adolescent is a very unsafe place. People like you and Dean Borgman have been very effective in reminding us of this fact. So what is wrong with keeping church youths happy, interested, and safe if this does not mean deemphasizing the missional mandate of

> The world of the adolescent is, after all, a very unsafe place. So what is wrong with keeping church youths happy, interested, and safe? In fact, this safety in a loving community may become one of the most attractive features of Christian youth ministry in a postmodern world.

the church as it relates to youth? In fact, the safety factor in a loving community may become one of the most attractive features of Christian youth ministry in a postmodern world.

Don't misunderstand me. I am not saying that youth ministry has achieved this balance between being a safe place and doing the required missional work. Your emphasis on evangelism is sorely needed. Your focus on the relational aspects of being Christians in a non-Christian world is prophetic and I applaud you. What I do *not* see in your chapter is how we should function with youths in the faith community.

In my chapter on the Strategic approach, I have tried to build on the Missional approach, but also to give youths an intentional community in which to be safe and outreach-focused. The church-planting concept will be a miserable failure if church growth is based on people transferring from churches with less appealing worship styles or more obnoxious people. The Strategic approach is an inside-out approach to youth ministry. It is both/and.

When disenfranchised become enfranchised

The second concern I have with your chapter relates to what happens after mission. How are the disenfranchised adolescents who have been evangelized transformed into Christian worshipers? While worship may be done privately, the concept of the church requires an assembling of Christians and some corporate expressions of love for God.

You touched on the assimilation issue, and that is a very important starting place. Young people (church bred or disenfranchised) must feel the church is a safe place, a welcoming place, a relational place. But assimilation alone does not produce worshipers, it merely tears down the most obvious barrier to worship. To assume that worship will happen naturally, once a young person is enfolded by an intergenerational group of Christian believers, is to suggest theology is equivalent to sociology.

Let me frame it another way. Once the disenfranchised adolescents have become enfranchised participants in a local church, how does the church take care of them? The Missional approach, as you presented it, leaves the question wide open. Obviously, the missioner will retain some form of relationship with the new believer, but what should that be? Does the

> But assimilation into a church does not in itself produce worshipers—it merely tears down some barriers to worship. To assume that worship will happen naturally, once a young person is enfolded by an intergenerational group of Christian believers, is to equate theology with sociology.

missioner become a guide to help the youthful pilgrim pick her way through the maze of church life into the presence of God? Or perhaps a mentor with whom the mentoree consults as he discovers the alternating currents of richness and barrenness of corporate worship? Or does the missioner continue as the primary shepherd of a special flock of newly enfranchised Christians and gradually move her focus of ministry from mission to pastoral care?

I would assume all of these relationships would be options for the Missional approach, but what I hear you saying is that the responsibility for transforming the newly enfranchised into informed worshipers lies not with the missioner but with the church in the power of the Spirit of God. I do think the responsibility for training the church to disciple their youths, of necessity, must lie with the youth ministry specialist (in other words the missioner). This person not only understands the youth culture where the kids are coming from, but also the church culture where they now find themselves and the heavenly culture to which they aspire.

As you know, Chap, the history of enfolding new converts who are reached through missional approaches, such as you describe, is extremely weak. I recently contacted Young Life, Youth for Christ, and Fellowship of Christian Athletes and asked people in their national offices how successful their organizations have been in discipling young people into the church. Although all three claim this as part of their mission, none has ever tracked the question. They simply have no idea where most of their converts are five years after graduation. In defense of our parachurch friends, the information would be exceedingly hard to track because these organizations are not communities like churches and schools.

One would think that Willow Creek and Saddleback would have stronger records of "turning irreligious high school students into fully devoted followers of Christ." I assume that these church-based "fully devoted followers of Christ" would remain active worshipers in the years following high school. Yet even in these church-based missional efforts, the results appear to be far less than desirable.

I would love to see advocates of the Missional approach develop stronger intentional strategies for assisting the church to become the community of faith for newly enfranchised adolescents. Yet I wonder if it can be done, except on an intermittent basis. The church has a wonderful capacity to absorb occasional refugees from foreign cultures but little success in synthesizing diverse culture into new forms of worship. When communities undergo ethnic transitions, Protestant churches have a dismal record of reinventing themselves with a blended form of discipleship and worship. Is the expectation of such a blend theologically necessary? If so, the church, not just youth ministry, has a very long way to go. I would suggest that racial reconciliation should have priority over generational reconciliation, though a healthy approach to the latter may make a major contribution to the former.

My reading of the Scripture suggests that the expectation of cultural blending is at the heart of the gospel. It is a corrective to becoming conformed to the world (spirit of the age). If the Missional approach to youth ministry could view as its other "mission" the blending of cultures within the body of Christ, the impact would be profound. As you know, Chap, this is the problem of neither church leaders ("them") or missioners ("us")—it is the problem of the entire body of Christ. As such we must aggressively address the problem. Our credibility as the faith community before a watching postmodern world is at stake, as is the credibility of our Lord and Savior Jesus Christ.

Conclusion

To move the discussion of youth ministry and the church to the next level, Chap, I would encourage you to become even more specific in identifying how the church must change to make her missional friendly, especially as it relates to youth ministry. I think we agree that the greatest obstacle to missional youth ministry is the church—not as it should be, but as it is. Like Martin Luther, perhaps you should tack your theses to a Wittenberg door, but this time you should put them somewhere on the Internet and allow a free flow of discussion on how the church should behave in the 21st century. All of us are smarter than any one of us. Together the body of Christ should be able to resolve the problems created by the cultural blinders we bring into our attempts to worship.

Rejoinder from the Missional Approach
by Chap Clark

Let me speak frankly: no approach but the Missional seems to take seriously the mandate to disciple all of the youth culture. Unless I missed something, the vast majority of the energy you suggest we put into youth ministry begins and ends with church people. With that off my chest, let me respond to your critiques of the Missional approach.

Malan, your insights into the distinction between bringing the gospel as verbalized explanation of the gospel and the call of the church to bring the *whole* gospel (Luke 8:1) was helpful. I intended to include *both* emphases, for I try not to delineate between the two aspects of the gospel mandate. To love and to witness to Love is part and parcel of the same communicative event. But the reminder that not everyone initially recognizes this was great.

You asked me if "this is a reason why youths reject the church?" I tend to think that the general impression of the church being filled with hypocrites is the closest I would come to saying this. I rather doubt that most postmodern adolescents reject the church based on such reflective insights as this, but rather I have sensed a systemic abandonment from Christians in general and therefore do not trust those who wear that label like a badge. I believe kids respond to an authentic, loving, passionate, compassionate follower of Jesus Christ. It is this caricatured idea of what a Christian is that is shunned.

Incarnational witness

Also, Malan, in your discussion of the distinction between friendship evangelism and service evangelism, I see the incarnational witness as being the overarching theological premise guiding both. These two concepts you mention may and often do overlap, but the men and women who represent Christ and the church are called to go—to intentionally *incarnate* themselves into a *different* world. This reflects itself in friendships and service, and therefore both are subsets under the broader umbrella of incarnational witness.

I greatly appreciate and fully endorse your insights on family and relational sensitivity when the church does somehow connect with a lost adolescent. My own mother still carries an emotional scar from how I, as a new convert, denied the seeds of faith she (and my father, and my extended family) had given me. The missionary you mention is very wise indeed, and my approach is strengthened by this reminder. Thanks.

Cautions and adjustments

Yes, Wes, much of the thrust of my focus *does* question and challenge many if not most of the assumptions underlying the Preparatory approach. But, as you allude, my emphasis was *not* to replace or throw out the Preparatory approach, but only to offer theologically and sociologically driven *cautions* and adjustments to the way we think about youth ministry. I honestly believe there is much to the Preparatory approach that is right and good.

My commitment to the Missional approach means that I seek to influence the "bookends" of youth ministry—how do we care for and relate to those who do not feel safe or interested in coming to us? How do we send our adults *and* students into the world as representatives of Jesus, offering both the verbal gospel and the hope of the kingdom?

I understand how you were a bit put off by my critique of the church (although, as you can see, Mark felt I was too kind—oh, well, you can't please everyone!). Yes, I did report a cynical view of the church, but from the generalized perspective of youth ministry practitioners. There are many youth ministry folks who honestly feel this way about the church. I agree that this attitude is wrong, and sad, and must be addressed by leaders in the movement, but I also know that many hold this view.

Ten percent of potential students attend a Christian youth program

Regarding specific studies or research supporting my contention that most young people see the church as "foreign, irrelevant, and even occasionally offensive," it is true that there is not much solid research out there. But as a secularly trained social scientist who has spent my entire career studying the world of unchurched adolescents, I am convinced that it is even worse than I presented it.

An easy study would be to compare the number of students in junior and senior high in a given community with the number of students who attend a church or youth ministry program even, say, once a month. For accuracy's sake, factor in those who go to multiple meetings (in other words Young Life and a church youth group), then add those who are home-schooled. In the informal settings where I have encouraged this type of study, students have reported back to me that not even 10 percent of potential students attend a Christian youth program on a monthly basis! This may vary greatly across regions, but I have little doubt that even the most religiously welcoming community will not be able to consistently reach even half of a town's students with Christian programs. I contend that this is a major problem in a post-Christian society.[1]

> Yes, I did report a cynical view of the church. But Idid so from the generalized perspective of youth ministry practitioners, many of whom honestly feel this way about the church, however sad and wrong this perception is.

Called to connect people to people

As I read on I got the impression that you may be ready to concede that many if not most unchurched students have turned their collective backs on the church. The next question you raise, then is "How do we, then, do what you are saying?" My impression is you indict the Missional approach because it lacks the programmatic specifics for making transition and assimilation happen (in some ways Mark does the same thing). But that is exactly the point (although I have made it better in different articles with far more clarity): The church *is not* primarily called to programs and events in order to build a vital community of believers. It is, rather, called to *connect* people to people. I disagree that "teaching all we reach" is the goal, for example, unless you mean holistic teaching that Jesus himself implores in Matthew 28 (where the emphasis is on "obey" rather than the educational, cognitive component of historical youth ministry).

The "how" is not nearly so important as the "who" in creating a welcoming place for the person who seeks to know Christ and commit to the church. I am convinced that kids are not so much concerned about the kind of programs we offer as they are concerned that they fit, that they matter, and that they are important players in the grand scheme of life. Any number of models and programs with a missional commitment can accomplish this, and every model I know can fail miserably, too.

Your final comments were great—for, as with Malan's and Mark's comments, they helped me to see the holes I had left scattered about in my approach. I did not intend to communicate that we need anything other than "frail mortals" to do missional youth ministry. In fact, I teach exactly what you argue for—the best kind of youth leaders are those who are "culturally goofy" enough not to be a threat to fragile adolescent egos. When I use the notion of a "critical bridge" I mean that the one going must become a *relational* expression of the local church. This only means that they love God and love kids, period. You are right, Wes, and I fully agree—kids need people who love and care for them *as they are.*

In the context of the family system

Regarding the family, see what I wrote to Malan above. I am a published advocate for a family-based youth ministry approach (which is possibly why you expressed a sense of surprise at my article). But, Wes, I do not believe that the Missional approach negates his theological strategy. I see the church caring for all adolescents in the context of the family system. This may look differently in different programs and with different pragmatic strategies, but it is the *mindset* of those in youth ministry that makes or breaks this commitment. It is true that I have studied the impact of families on teenagers as much as anyone, and I know that real change generally occurs within the framework of familial systemic change.

But the flip side of this is that many unchurched adolescents break from spiritually antagonistic family systems when they respond to a Missional approach. If we wait for families to come around *prior* to reaching out to unchurched disinterested adolescents, we will lose far too many kids in the process. When it comes to the families of students we serve, we need to be aware, and sensitive, and smart. But we must not allow this commitment to keep us from strategically targeting the world of lost kids.

Thank you, Mark, for your perspectives on the issues raised by the Missional approach. As with Malan and Wes, in many ways we are obviously in the same chapter if not on the same page. Since you address many of the issues already covered in the above responses, I will note just a few.

A place that is safe

I must admit, your first critique struck a nerve in me (in a good way). As a result, I am going to have to take some time reflecting on the implications of the Missional approach on Christian families and churched young people. It is interesting to note that this is precisely what I struggled with in the Strategic approach! What about those dear kids who love God, want to grow, and need a place that is safe *for them?* You state that your approach attempts to do just this, but I found it could create just the opposite situation. Let me try and state my position on this *now*, with the promise that I will continue this personal reflection in the future.

I believe that most Christian kids, especially those who have grown up in the church, have been acculturated to view the church as a sort of private, "we own this" club. Although a church does not intend for this to happen, the ownership of a given sociological grouping is defined by those who have helped create and define it. The way we have learned how to "do" church—fragmentation of age groups, specializations of leadership, "church" on Sunday or Wednesday night (instead of being part of a worshiping community at *all* times and gathering on special days)—has caused the systems and structures which order the way we "do" church to become institutionalized. This in turn locks out others who are not acculturated. When cer-

> I am convinced that kids are not as concerned about the kind of programs we offer as they are concerned that they fit, that they matter, that they are important players in the grand scheme of life. Any number of programs with a missional commitment can accomplish this.

tain students are in a school classroom, for example, it is far easier to accept and embrace one new student than five who come in with expectations for inclusion and ownership. In other words, the nature of the contemporary beast creates an instant conflict—either the church kids will lose what they thought they owned, or the converts will dominate. I have seen this happen repeatedly.

But the church does not have to be this way. Youth ministry can be a place that creates community *with a purpose*. The Mormons have used this strategy with great effectiveness, even while propagating a theology of works, which is not supposed to fly in a postmodern culture! I believe your concern is valid but should be addressed and dealt with head-on, without sacrificing the Missional mandate of youth ministry. For years I have seen churches criticize Youth for Christ and Young Life for failing to get kids into church, only to find these same churches unwilling to embrace these new converts. This cycle must be strategically addressed, but not at the expense of the lost.

Not a prophet

And yet, Mark, that is exactly your challenge to me. Where does the solution lie? How do we get along in the church, even *before* we bring in alternative subcultures who do not feel moved by a well-played organ? You invite me to "be more specific in how the church must change to make her Missional friendly." I am a youth worker, a theologian, and a communication scholar. However, I am not a prophet, a magician, or a miracle worker. My voice is neither loud enough nor credible enough to cause sweeping change in how churches view themselves in relation to those outside. But as we all talk, teach, lead, and model what we know to be true, perhaps the Holy Spirit will wake scores of us up and cause the church to have the courage to be the church! My hope lies not in nailing my theses to the church doors so much as it does in all of us doing our part to call the church to account.

By the way, did any of you notice that we *all* agreed the church *must* change, but we all felt very little power to make it happen. That God would cause the church to have the heart of Jesus for those that he came to seek and save!

Notes

1. The exception to this is in communities where the Catholic church has a virtual cultural monopoly on the world of adolescents. I would say, however, that even where this is clearly the case—such as the Hispanic community in Los Angeles county—the vast majority of young people *may report* church commitment and may even attend, but they are not as personally active as their physical presence may imply.

The Strategic Approach
to Youth Ministry
by Mark H. Senter III

Responses
Nel: from an Inclusive Congregational perspective
Black: from a Preparatory perspective
Clark: from a Missional perspective

Rejoinder
Senter

The Strategic Approach to Youth Ministry
by Mark H. Senter III

Scenario: Foster kids

No one in the reunion committee of the Launchers Adult Fellowship foresaw how disappointing the turnout would be for their 10-year youth group reunion. After all, 40 or 50 high schoolers had typically attended the weeknight youth meetings, and twice that number came on Sundays. At least that is how Sheila Wolfe remembered it, and nobody wanted to argue with her because she had been the social glue that held the youth group together.

Yet only 19 people showed up for the reunion—and that included four spouses. No one expected their old youth pastor Geoff to be there, since he was now serving a church in another state. But at least he e-mailed a greeting. Hardly anyone else bothered to do even that.

"What happened to all of that unity we experienced in Bible studies, on mission trips, at camp?" asked Sheila. "It feels like some sort of dream that never really happened."

"Maybe it was a dream," said Roger. Every youth group has its skeptic. Roger, who performed that function in the youth ministry, was one of the remnant who showed up for the reunion. "Not a dream like it never happened, but an illusion as to what was really happening while we were absorbed in all of our good times."

"And what is that suppose to mean, Mr. Skeptic?" replied the ever-protective Sheila.

"Foster kids don't go to family reunions. The youth ministry wasn't really part of the church family. We were foster children. It was like the church fathers wanted to keep us from getting into too much trouble so they hired Pastor Geoff to create this virtual reality. He did a great job, too. For a lot of us it became a powerful spiritual experience, but the church never expected us to become a vital part until we got married, had children, and became just like them."

"So what did you expect the church to do, make *you* the pastor?" Since high school days Sheila had bristled when critical comments were made about her parents and their friends who had done so much to build the ministries of their church.

"Now that's an interesting idea…"

"You've got to be kidding! You haven't even been to seminary."

By now Roger's mind was working at warp speed. No, he did not want to be the pastor of *their* church because they had so many traditions, musical styles, and bothersome customs that made their church seem like—well, a foster church. But to be a leader (or even a pastor) in a church that actively sought the contributions of youths…now *that* was intriguing.

"I was kidding," confessed Roger, "but now that I'm thinking about the idea, it may not be as hare-brained as you seem to think. For example, if I were pastor, I could just about guarantee that more people would be here for the reunion. Not because of me, but because they would have a greater ownership in what the church is and what it does."

A realistic appraisal of youth groups a decade after graduation suggests a disappointingly small number of alumni remain in either their home church or other churches. The absence of alumni from Fellowship of Christian Athletes huddle groups, Young Life, and Youth for Christ is more startling. Unless the youth leader maintains a meaningful contact with graduates and encourages them to attend church together, very few establish a lasting relationship with a local church.

Heart of the problem

At the core of the reunion problem faced by Launchers Adult Fellowship were two obstacles: marginalization of youths and discontinuity in spiritual nurture. While the church wanted young people to mature in their Christian faith, maturity was defined in terms that the older generation understood and to which the younger crowd was expected to conform. Outside of the sheltered enclave of the youth ministry, Sheila and Roger were mere spectators in a middle age church. Young people lived on the margins of the church.

Hymnology, while punctuated with occasional praise choruses, found much of its style and substance in a world far removed from urban or suburban America. Evangelization rarely influenced decisions about how money was spent. Expectations of lifestyle found its motivation more through fear than Christian love. Prayer was an activity rather than a relationship. Public communication appealed more to the mind than to the total person. In general, young people were not valued for what they brought to the church family as much as for what they would someday become.

> Outside of the sheltered enclave of the youth ministry, Sheila and Roger were mere spectators in a middle-aged church. Young people lived on the margins of the church.

While Sheila and Roger were apparently content to be spectators until such a time as when they could begin shaping the vision and priorities of the church (the leadership of most churches begin listening to "the young people" when they reach their mid-30s), most of their peers were not that patient. Most dropped out of church. Some would return in a few years with children in tow, determined to force-feed their children the same Christian faith they had been force-fed.

The slate of church leaders to whom Sheila, Roger, and their friends looked for spiritual leadership changed every one to four years as they grew up in the church. The youth ministry was built upon a flawed discipleship model that was firmly rooted in modernity: based on the twin assumptions of specialization and discontinuity, the youth ministry resembled a factory model of nonformal education, which came to dominate formal education in the latter part of the 19TH century.

Factories, schools—and churches

Factories utilize an assembly line to create a product. As an automobile moves along the assembly line, workers contribute toward the finished product by inserting a part, tightening bolts, or welding a joint in place. At the end, a car rolls off of the conveyor belt ready to be sold to the public. No one person builds a car. Even a limited production car such as a Lamborghini is a product of many hands all contributing in specialized ways.

Schools follow the same model. The initial specialization is determined by the age of the child. A person may spend a lifetime teaching first graders and promoting them to the second grade specialist. Early in the process additional specialists enter the picture. The music teacher, gym coach, and art teacher bring their specializations to the education of children. As children approach adolescence, the various educational disciplines are isolated into specialty areas. Math, sciences, language skills, and history join the list of subjects being taught in different rooms by certified specialists. Discontinuity of relationships and specialization of content become the normal way of doing education.

Churches like Sheila and Roger's adopted a schooling model of discipleship. Sunday school divided youths from adults. Age-graded classes further sorted students into chronological ghettoes. Discontinuity and specialization expanded with the introduction of the youth group and eventually the youth minister. Even church architecture reflected the changes. Educational wings followed the model of public schools. Eventually gymnasiums became a normal part of church building programs. Discontinuity and specialization were set in stone. Any change in approach to discipleship through the church became extremely difficult. The church became a factory.

Specialization in the discipleship ministries of the church initiated a holistic ministry to youths. Very quickly, however, it was discovered that one rather large component of discipleship ministry was absent from youth ministry in the church: the evangelization of youths was less and less a normal part of church youth ministry. To put it bluntly, it simply was not happening.

Once again specialization and discontinuity entered the picture. As has happened throughout the history of the church, special orders formed outside the church by spiritually minded Christian people. Their purpose was to fill a gap created by the church's inattention to a value found in Scripture. Thus the concern for the evangelization of youths brought into being a series of parachurch youth ministries. They saw themselves as being alongside the church, as being the evangelistic arm extending from the church out into the youth culture.

Specialists gifted in youth evangelization championed the Young Life, Youth for Christ, and Fellowship of Christian Athletes movements. Hosts of similar youth evangelization agencies followed, including some associated with denominations. Their profound desire was to disciple youths into local churches. Yet discontinuity and specialization produced such a gap that few adolescent converts found their way into fellowship with believers in local churches.

British youth ministry specialist Pete Ward finds a similar concern in his country, where church attendance now tallies less than ten percent of the population. He comments, "This trend is extremely alarming. In the past parachurch ministries could assume that young people would somehow connect up with a suitable church. This is less likely to be the case, however, because of the decline in church-going among the youth's parents and immediate family. Wider changes in contemporary culture also make long term allegiances to institutions much less acceptable."[1]

In time, local churches like Willow Creek Community Church brought the parachurch strategy into the church. That church, for example, used team competition much like campus clubs to feed students into Student Impact, their weeknight "supplemental witness"—which was followed by the Student Insight meetings for worship on Sunday nights. Willow Creek brought Youth for Christ's club-rally small group strategy under the roof of the church. Yet even with church buildings housing specialized youth ministries, young converts rarely assimilated into the larger church family.[2]

> Churches that have grown out of parachurch agencies often begin as discipleship efforts before becoming worship services and then local churches. Other churches result from youth pastors who use the leadership developed in their youth ministries to start new churches.

Definition of Strategic Approach

How then should youth ministry relate to the local church so that young people both shape and are shaped by the faith community throughout their lives? The church must view youth ministry not so much as a means of turning out models of Christian living in order to perpetuate existing church ministries, but as the best opportunity to launch a vital Christian witness to shape the faith community for the next generation. We call it the Strategic approach to youth ministry.

The Strategic approach creates a community of leaders and youthful Christians that enables a parachurch or church-based youth ministry to establish a new church to maintain a theological continuity while expressing faith in a community relevant to both Christ and culture. Why do we call this the Strategic approach to youth ministry? Primarily because it calls upon the youth ministry to be and become a holistic intergenerational church that is relevant to the world in which it lives.

Description of the Strategic Approach to Youth Ministry

Strategic approaches might be a better way to describe the way in which churches grow out of youth ministries. Some ethnic groups—especially Chinese and Korean congregations—use an English-speaking youth service as a means of creating an American-style service within the same church. Some Gen-X worship services follow the same model. Churches that have grown out of parachurch agencies frequently begin as discipleship efforts before becoming worship services and then local churches. Other churches result from youth pastors who use the leadership developed in their youth ministries to start new churches.

Yet the basic approach remains constant:

1. *Solid youth ministry*
The ministry includes a blend of evangelism, discipleship, and worship that attracts both students and adult leaders. Through the ministry a faith community is built that delights in serving God. Instead of forcing people to leave the community as they graduate from high school, ways are sought to maintain continuity in discipleship relationships.

2. *Vision for continuity*
With the blessing of church leaders, the youth minister begins painting a vision of a new church that would allow the fruit of the youth ministry to be extended over a number of years, as adult and student leaders buy into the vision and begin shaping a strategy.

3. *Leadership team*
The team the youth minister has assembled to reach and disciple youths needs to commit themselves to the strategic vision. While some will choose to remain with the youth ministry in the mother church, a significantly large group of gifted youths and adults will need to leave their comfort zone to begin a multigenerational church.

4. *A critical mass*
In most of the youth ministry genesis churches that have formed in recent days, there has been an initial group of people committed to the idea that number close to 200 people or more. These are people who have been touched by the youth ministry and believe in the faith community that is being created.

5. *Relevant ministry style*

A ministry style grounded in scripture and appropriate to the rising generation of Christians begins in the youth ministry and then develops into an intergenerational ministry where worship, nurture, and ministries of evangelism and mercy build up the body of Christ and glorify God. Worship (*leitourgia*) is shaped in a holy tension between biblical concepts of preaching (*kerugma*) and holistic forms of communication and reflection. Nurture shepherds the flock with a balanced blend of fellowship (*koinonia*) and teaching (*didache*), while ministries of evangelism and mercy facilitate relevant witness (*marturia*) and pastoral care (*paraklesis*).

6. *Time and support*

Even in the best of circumstances, church planting takes time. During that time the youth ministry continues in the home church or parachurch club while the new ministry is taking shape. This means the mother church or parachurch agency may have double expenses as a new youth minister is groomed and the new ministry with all its expenditures begins. The start-up period may be as short as a year but may extend over three to five years.

7. *Location*

Some youth ministry genesis churches meet initially in the building of the mother church, others choose to gather in school buildings, theaters or shopping malls. In the initial stages this proves satisfactory, but eventually most new church choose to purchase property and create a place of worship appropriate to their vision. If the support base is not adequate to secure a permanent location, the new church may languish or fail. The mother churches may have to remain supportive through this stage of the ministry.

Justification for the Strategic Approach

Complexity and the youth culture

While some would call for a return to the simplicity of the old days, this option simply is not available to youth ministry in the 21st century. It would be much like returning to the one-room schoolhouse in public education. While a much more solid community might be built through returning to a 19th-century intergenerational approach to learning, the explosion and breadth of knowledge necessary to prepare young people for the challenge of sharing the planet with six billion people makes the possibility impractical.[3]

The complexity of the world is complicated by a distinct youth culture that gnaws on the fiber of all value systems, including the Christian worldview. The 1955 movie *Rebel Without a Cause* was a watershed for adolescence in America and proved to be the birth announcement of a youth culture. Rock and roll, movies targeted at the baby boomers, the anti-Vietnam war movement and accompanying experimentation with drugs, MTV, and the Internet have brought about such complexity in the world of young people that parents find their culture difficult to comprehend and more challenging to respond to.

A youth culture appears to be spreading across the developed world. While underlying cultural values separate youth cultures in Seoul or Beijing from those in Los Angeles or London, the need for generational differentiation fed by a popular culture depicted in the mass media make traditional ideas of community virtually impossible to obtain.

The influence of the youth culture's aggressive presence on radio, television, CDs, magazines, novels, and the Internet leave a return to simplicity in youth ministry a practical impossibility. Though some families provide safe places through homeschooling and some churches build loving networks of adult mentors in hopes of building a distinctly Christian counterculture, the task is overwhelming. Apart from a spiritual revival on the order of the Great Awakenings, a position of Christ against culture appears hopeless as the central thrust of youth ministry.

Confused by the cultural complexity faced by Christian young people and the desire of Christian adults to be a redemptive force in the lives of the rising generation, youth ministers stepped in to fill the gap. Before James Dean's *Rebel Without a Cause* there were fewer than 500 professional youth ministers (church and parachurch) in the United States and Canada.[4] By the end of the 20th century, the National Network of Youth Ministries in the United States alone had a membership of over 3,000 professional youth ministers. In 1998, Young Life reported 994 full-time field ministry staff.[5] For the same year, Fellowship of Christian Athletes reported 422 field staff, while Youth for Christ identified over 800 full-time employees, the vast majority of whom are field staff. Sonlife Ministries recounts training 49,420 youth leaders (lay and professional) in their Strategy Seminars since 1980.[6,7,8] In addition, youth ministry boasts thousands of local church and parachurch professionals not associated with these more visible groups.

The church as a community

In the rush to fill the spiritual vacuum that was created as the youth culture exploded, two essential questions hardly attracted any attention: "What is the church (faith community) and what should the church do to shape the values and spiritual journey of young people?"

Youth workers' glib but seldom spoken answer to the first question was, "We are." After all, most youth ministers (church and parachurch) attended church with some degree of regularity and thus assumed that since they were part of the invisible church (true believers), their ministry was synonymous with that of the church. Little thought was given to questions of spiritual development before or after youth ministry.

The second question received similarly slick but seldom stated responses ranging from, "Trust me. I will figure something out," to "I'll do my best to show them the attractiveness of Jesus, and after that let's hope they will want to return to the rather boring things Christian adults do." So the function of the church in the lives of adolescents had been reduced to individualism in the person of the youth minister. For the most part youth pastors are relational and purposeful, most are biblical and accountable to spiritual leaders. But youth ministry based on individualism, no matter how qualified the individual, is individualism just the same. Any person, no matter how relationally skilled, can maintain a spiritually sensitive contact with only a limited number of young people, either right now or over a period of years.

> The influence of the youth culture's aggressive presence on radio, television, CDs, magazines, novels, and the Internet leave a return to simplicity in youth ministry a practical impossibility.

Satisfaction with these responses ranges widely. Parents of adolescents, as well as senior pastors and church leaders, agreed that they needed help if the church was to be a redemptive force in the lives of youths. But how?

The spiritual formation of youths has always found its primary influence in the nurturing relationships of the family and community of faithful believers. Kings, priests, prophets, and pastor-teachers each played a role in passing the faith from generation to generation, but the primary responsibility for nurturing youths remained with the family. The family, in turn, drew from the larger faith community a shared understanding of what it meant to be the kingdom of God. A continuity of relationships with parents and godly people from another generation appears to be the dominant means of spiritual formation in scripture. Lawrence O. Richards comments, "When we look at the ideal community sketched in Exodus, Leviticus and Deuteronomy, we find little explicit instruction on child rearing. But we do find a clear expression of the social context that God designed for the nurture of faith. That context can be simply defined. Children are intended to be brought up as participants in a loving, holy community."[9]

What does it mean for young people in the 21st century to be participants in a loving, holy community? Jimmy Long, writing 15 years after Richards, asserts, "[C]ommunity, not self (in other words individualism), is the basic relational foundation...for creating small group communities, which in most situations need to be the basic framework for ministry with Xers in a postmodern environment."[10]

The church as continuity

Scripture is filled with metaphors for the church. Perhaps the biblical writers found it easier to describe what the faith community was like than to provide a precise definition. Major analogies for the church share one characteristic—continuity. All require a continued relationship over an extended period of time. Family images (Matthew 12:49; 2 Corinthians 6:18; 1 Timothy 5:1-2; 1 John 3:14-15), farming images (Matthew 13:1-30; John 4:34-38; 15:5; Romans 11:17-24; 1 Corinthians 3:6-9), the body of Christ analogy (1 Corinthians 12:12-14; Ephesians 1:22-23; 4:15-16; Colossians 2:19) and even the "living stones" metaphor (1 Peter 2:5) convey the idea of life and growth in a healthy organism over time.

Families grow and develop over the lifetimes of the family members. Crops spend at least a season maturing before harvest starts the process all over again. Vines and trees grow for many years and are made more productive through a pruning process. The organs and limbs of a body are organically connected for the cycle of life. While scriptural analogies are not intended to be detailed prescriptions for doctrinal matters, the persistence of the continuity image in the metaphors for the church does not appear to be random.

Perhaps the most vulnerable point in youth ministry is continuity in discipleship relationships. Three years in junior high school with some changes in personnel each year, give way to four years in high school with more turnover among youth leaders. College or a ministry to young adults follows with even greater changes in spiritually mentoring relationships. This disruption of continuity in relationships is exaggerated even more by the mobility of families and the likelihood that the family will move beyond the sphere of influence of the church family.

Maturity in Christian growth provides another glimpse of what should be happening in the church. While the maturing process is the responsibility of each individual believer and is often associated with personal

> The spiritual formation of youths has always been found primarily in the nurturing relationships of the family—which in turn drew from the larger faith community a shared understanding of what it meant to be the kingdom of God.

difficulties (James 1:2-8), maturity is seldom achieved in isolation. Perhaps the clearest picture of the relationship between the faith community and the spiritual maturity of each believer is found in Ephesians 4:7-13, where the apostle Paul links the gifts given to the church with all believers becoming "mature, attaining to the whole measure of the fullness of Christ."

One of the strong features of youth ministry in the last decade of the 20th century has been the determination of Christian youth leaders to identify the outcomes they feel God desires from ministry to high school students. Drawing a profile for a discipled student has helped focus many high school ministries. Gone are many of the activities designed merely to entertain youths. In their place are purpose driven activities. Discipleship is a professed value of most serious youth ministry.

Yet spiritual maturity is not something that takes place in a four-year span, especially during the high school years. The process began in childhood, even before the child learned to speak. The nurture of mother and father (or lack thereof), social exchanges with siblings (positive and negative), informal and formal communication of biblical content, and models of spirituality in the faith community (good and bad), all play a role in the spiritual maturation process both before and after youth ministry.

Even Jesus' own disciples, after three years of following our Lord, showed very few of the characteristics that should distinguish fully devoted followers of our Lord. Only after the trauma of the crucifixion, the euphoria of the resurrection, and the ecstasy of the Spirit's filling did the disciples suddenly show signs of maturity. Immediate persecution from their fellow Jews brought about a new continuity among the apostles (Acts 8:1-2), while other believers were scattered first throughout Judea and Samaria, and then—through the vision of the church at Antioch—throughout the Roman world (Acts 17:6).

The greatest passage on continuity in discipling relationships, however, is found following the second reading of the Law. Preparing the Israelites to enter the land they had been promised, Moses tells parents that the way to ensure that their children would remain true to Jehovah would be to talk about what Jehovah did for the Israelites throughout the normal flow of family life (Deuteronomy 6:4-9). A look at the context suggests this was to be a long-term strategy reinforced by a cycle of festivals celebrated by the nation of Israel.

While Scripture places responsibility on the individual to respond to God's call and to the Holy Spirit's work of sanctification, the whole purpose of Scripture is to provide instruction whereby the faith community nurtures and supports people in that process. As the African proverb declares, "It takes a village to raise a child."

The discontinuity fallacy

At the heart of the problem faced by a youth ministry that is shaped by modernity is the fallacy of *discontinuity*. Adults earn the right to nurture young people and then, somewhat artificially, attempt to hand their young friends to another discipler three or four years later. The dominant philosophy of church and parachurch alike has been that the mission of student movements has been to establish or retain the Christian faith and lifestyle of a particular age group—primarily high school and college-aged people, but recently middle school students have been included in the mix as well.

Even where the primary focus of a ministry has been evangelism and discipleship (especially effective in parachurch ministries), there has been a structural restriction on continuity of relationships. Meaningful contact beyond high school was a rare exception. The span of a ministry limited the discipleship process to four years or less. Converts in campus-based ministries were expected to leave the persons most influential in their initial spiritual growth to be nurtured through existing churches.

Training union concepts of traditional youth societies were age-group specific. The approach of African-American churches has been healthier, yet limiting, in that they seek to prepare a new generation to take on leadership roles in the parent church when the young people come of age. Even the current innovative generation of youth ministry specialists find themselves restricted by the expectation that the term of their ministry will normally be four years before they hand off their students to another pastor, or cut them loose to find niches in a church that had its primary growth spurt during another generation. Organizational expectations lock them out of continuity in discipling relationships.

The net result is that the church has created an entire profession that has no choice but to ghettoize both youths and youth ministers. Expectations are more akin to baby-sitting than missiology. Youth ministers are frustrated by constant resistance to theological reflection and strategic thinking about students' roles in the local church at the very time in life when adolescents should be adopting kingdom priorities.

Church leadership has treated youth ministers as novice adults rather than permanent parts of the church's strategy of discipleship and world evangelization. It's as if the church of middle-class America has been willing to pay "big kids" to play with its children. Consequently the expectation has developed that these big kids will grow up and move away, leaving behind another class of graduates who have weathered adolescence, grown in their faith, and brought a few people into the kingdom. Continuity in the nurturing process is a foreign concept.

Youth ministry as church-birthing

Perhaps the answer to the problems created by discontinuities in discipling relationships lies in a new vision of youth ministries: Youth pastors should become spiritual midwives and assist in birthing new churches. They would begin as age group specialists (they would still need some of these skills throughout their ministries) but would be chosen to work with a group of students from the time the young people entered high school until they reached their mid-20s. The primary objective would be to develop a team of spiritually mature young adults and start a new church.

Every activity of the youth group would be evaluated by its short-term impact upon students and its long-term effectiveness in preparing the volunteer staff, students, and their families to become a new church. Evangelism would be their responsibility or the infant church would not be born. Disciplines of discipleship, stewardship, eldership, prayer, social concern, and worship would rest on the shoulders of the youth pastor and emerging church leaders.

At the appropriate time the mother church would make a decision: The new church could become either a church within the mother church or a freestanding church apart from it. If the new church remains within the existing church, the youth pastor would turn over the youth ministry to another person and assume pastoral responsibility for the adult flock he has been shepherding. The test of the former youth pastor's ministry will be in the effectiveness with which the values that were emphasized during the high school ministry years are sustained and enhanced in the church-within-the-church setting.

If the mother church elects to establish a freestanding church, then it will fund the project as a mission endeavor; and a new church would be strategically hived off. While the new church may begin by meeting in the mother church (for example on Saturday night or Sunday afternoon), within a relatively short time the new congregation would commence worship services in rented facilities in a target location. Initially the mother church would have to share the expense of the rented facility and pastor's salary, but the church plant should rapidly move to an autonomous status. The long-term success of the venture may be tied to the securing of real estate in the new community. In most cases the mother church will have to make this commitment early in the process.

In both cases youth staff and students evangelized and discipled through the youth ministry would become the nucleus of the new church. The families of the students and former students under the youth minister's care would be encouraged to participate with their children in the project. Though the idea has some inherent weaknesses, most of them could be minimized by careful selection of the youth minister, along with a mentoring relationship with the senior pastor. The concept would require a paradigm shift both on the part of church and within the youth ministry fraternity.

Parachurch high school and college ministries are in unique positions to become birthing midwives. The whole argument about parachurch (literally, *alongside the church*) versus church ministries could easily be laid to rest if the parachurch ministries targeted their efforts toward the unchurched, pioneering strategies for turning these collections of believers into socially relevant and biblically based churches. Parachurch staff members would gradually leave the campus and begin ministering to a body of believers, including a core of mature believers who served as volunteer leaders, high school converts who left for college or the workplace, and parents of those converted or discipled through the ministry.

Post-high-school fragmentation

Post-high-school fragmentation of the youth ministry will be a fatal flaw to the church-birthing process if not addressed from the very beginning. Early ownership of the project by the young people and volunteer staff will determine the long-term success. A nucleus of parents and other adults need to be early adopters of the idea. Students could be encouraged to select their college or employment based on their involvement in this ministry. For those who attend school out of the area but wish to maintain committed to the church-birthing process, the youth minister or pastor will sustain a mentoring or shepherding relationship. Some will not return; but the choice will be made consciously, not by default based exclusively on career considerations.

While it can be shown that college ministries have been relatively successful in channeling their new believers into existing churches, many times the kingdom momentum that is established during the college years dissipates as eager young believers have to accommodate themselves to the social systems and political realities of established churches. Staffers from high school ministries, by contrast, have lamented for years that students who establish a vital relationship with Jesus Christ through their ministries frequently are lost in either a local church or campus-based college ministry. When the spiritual bond between the initial discipler and the adolescent severs because the parachurch person must concentrate on a new batch of freshmen, an ecclesiological vacuum is created and spiritual accountability frequently is lost.

Many youth ministers are prepared to accept the challenge. It is time for many youth specialists to stop thinking of youth ministry as a lifetime commitment and begin viewing their youth ministry as giving birth to a biblically and culturally relevant church that will, in time, give birth to additional churches in response to the needs of future generations. Viewing

Even the today's innovative generation of youth ministry specialists find themselves restricted by the expectation that the term of their ministry will normally be four years before they hand off their students to another pastor, or cut them loose to find niches in a church that had its primary growth spurt during another generation.

themselves as strategically placed ministers of the gospel of Jesus Christ, they must re-examine the presuppositions of their callings.

Youth groups into churches: it's been done

Though it sounds idealistic, the idea of youth groups becoming full-fledged churches has worked with startling success all over the world. From Marseille, France, to Mt. Prospect, Illinois, the strategy has established churches in postmodern cultures. In the Hindu kingdom of Nepal, a similar concept is associated with the explosive church growth that has more than tripled the size of the Nepali Christian church during the last decade of the 20th century.

Situations in Chicago, Ontario, and Brazil deserve special attention. A look at these settings might give a clue to the possible success of such strategic thinking. (It is worth pointing out, however, that only one of these youth-group-derived churches was initiated by a mother church, and none of them selected the minister of youth with this strategy in mind.)

- **Willow Creek Community Church (South Barrington, Illinois)**. More than two decades ago, South Park Church in Park Ridge, Illinois, hired David Hulmbo and Bill Hybels as youth pastors, who built the youth ministry to over 1,000 high schoolers. Willow Creek Community Church was launched from this youth group—perhaps the most emulated church in America during the 1990s.

  After 25 years of dynamic growth, the church is now attended by over 15,000 people on a weekly basis. Over 300 ministry staff members provide leadership for a bewildering array of ministries. The Willow Creek Association, a spinoff ministry of the church, now services 2,000 churches that share a passion for seeker-driven ministries.

- **Lawndale Community Church (Chicago)**. The Lawndale neighborhood on Chicago's West Side was ravaged by rioting following the assassination of Martin Luther King Jr., and with the riots began two decades of poverty and crime. Wayne Gordon, by merely providing a weight machine for the football players at Farragut High School, gained a foothold for his ministry through Fellowship of christian Athletes. Using his contact with high school leaders, he began a Bible study that eventually became Lawndale Community Church—assisted, sadly, by the reputation of Lawndale churches, which were considered irrelevant by the community's young people.

  Today Lawndale Community Church is a model of a holistic urban ministry. Worship services and youth ministries are complemented by a medical and dental clinic, counseling services, food and clothing resale shops, housing rehabilitation, and job referral ministries. Students from nearby Christian colleges still work with children in the community, but the church has grown far beyond its youth ministry roots.

- **Ginger Creek Community Church (Glen Ellyn, Illinois)**. When his Campus Life club strategy began to falter in the mid-1980s, John Henderson began Son City (now known as Student Impact), an evangelistic program modeled after the Willow Creek high school ministry. They replaced clubs with teams, led by student leaders from the area high schools. The ministry soon attracted hundreds of students.

  But the first wave of graduating seniors left a vacuum in the ministry. After failing to convince Campus Life's leadership to drop its long-standing prohibition of CL staffers starting churches (even though at this time the president of the national organization was a preaching pastor for a church only a few miles away from Glen Ellyn), Henderson left to found Ginger Creek Community Church. Today the church is attended by close to 700 worshipers on a Sunday morning.

- **Arlington Heights (Illinois) Evangelical Free Church.** In this instance of youth-group-become-church, a mother church did some strategic planning, recognizing that its own growth potential was limited. John Sheaffer, their minister to youth, was asked to create a new church. So he led a church-planting seminar as one of the normal Sunday evening training sessions. Task force leaders were then chosen, and the resulting groups used the church's facilities. Among the core leadership of the new church were students, leaders, and friends Sheaffer had influenced during his five-year tenure in ministry to high school students. Out of this deliberate planning and ground preparation was born Grace Community Church, in September 1992.

> It is time to stop thinking of youth ministry as a lifetime commitment, and begin viewing youth ministry as giving birth to a biblically and culturally relevant church that will, in time, give birth to additional churches in response to the needs of future generations.

- **Hamilton, Ontario, Canada.** Early in 1992 six Baptist pastors here began discussing how they could cooperate in ministry to youth in the area. The largest of the churches was 150 in attendance; most ranged between 60 and 80. David Overholt was asked to create a cooperative outreach ministry, and the plan was to disciple new believers into the churches. In its first year the Hamilton Mountain Youth Mission grew to around 70 kids—large by Canadian standards. By the fall of 1994 over 500 young people were attending the Sunday night gatherings. When they realized that the new believers were not interested in attending unfamiliar churches. Overholt got the blessing of the supporting churches to begin a worship gathering called The Alternative that met one Sunday evening a month.

    Next came the inevitable suggestion: Why not expand the Youth Mission into a church? Overholt, the six pastors, 12 couples, and some of the students spent a year praying about this possibility. In January 1997 another youth ministry genesis church was launched, with over 500 people attending the worship-evangelism service.

- **Brazil.** Young Life in this South American country experienced a similar phenomenon. Hal Merwold, now director of Young Life Canada, reports that after he resigned from a similar post in Brazil, the decision was made to create communities of former Young Lifers who would meet together on a regular basis. Though technically they were like alumni Campaigner Clubs, in effect these were churches—led by people who had no formal theological training, but who had been developed by the informal training process of the parachurch organization. These communities are thriving today. Peruvian Young Life and the Navigator ministry in Brazil have followed a similar strategy, with corresponding success. In effect, the Brazilian strategy is a systematic approach to youth ministry genesis churches.

Compatible with Scripture?

The fact that churches have spawned from youth groups does not mean that the strategy is necessarily a biblical idea or pattern that can be duplicated by other Christian leaders. Though it is tempting to conclude that Christ's disciples were the first youth group and the apostles were the first church planters, youth ministry is a phenomenon that is a product of the late

18th and 19th centuries. Like the Sunday school, faith missions, and church choirs, youth ministry is a response to changes in culture that must be judged by its compatibility with Scripture, rather than by its specific mandate from the pages of holy writ.

Leaders who match the qualifications of elders (1 Timothy 3; Titus 2) and are empowered by appropriate spiritual gifts (1 Corinthians 12-14; Ephesians 4) should be the first consideration of the church-birthing youth ministry concept. If the church plans for the youth minister to become a pastor, the selection of that youth pastor will have to be done with an added degree of seriousness. To have a person with a superficial knowledge of the Bible and a great rapport with young people can no longer be an adequate standard for the selection of youth pastor. It should never have been appropriate in the first place.

To this point, most of the youth ministry genesis pastors are self-taught individuals who have become lifelong learners of God's Word. They read widely and are close to people who have formal theological training. Willow Creek Community Church has even gone so far as to link with some of the leading evangelical seminaries in an attempt to combine the entrepreneurial instincts and theological insights for many of their training events for an emerging generation of pastors.

Intentional, in-ministry theological training for youth pastors will become a key to the long-term effectiveness of youth ministry genesis pastors. One of the benefits of seminary training is the accountability students have for mastering a broad curriculum that provides rootedness in biblical and theological perspectives. If the emerging pastor does not have the benefit of that training, the mother church or campus ministry has the responsibility to provide the opportunity and hold the young pastor accountable for developing the ability to think and act Christianly.

A second concern is the generational issue. Israel in both the Old Testament and the New Testament church gave great honor to the wisdom of elders (1 Kings 12:6-14; 1 Timothy 5:19). The danger of the youth group genesis church is that it may be limited to people who are the

> Like Sunday school, faith missions, and church choirs, youth ministry is a response to changes in culture that must be judged by its compatibility with Scripture, rather than by its specific mandate from the pages of holy writ.

about the same age as the youth pastor and younger. A commitment to eldership may be defined as mentoring functions that take place when a person mellowed by age in his walk with God offers insight and accountability to the creativity of youths.

While Willow Creek's Bill Hybels had his mentor in Dr. Bilezikian, John Sheaffer was accountable to the board of Arlington Heights Evangelical Free Church as the new church was being formed. David Overholt's church in Ontario began with nearly 20 percent of the congregation aged 26 and older, and many of these were in their 40s. Clearly, the youth-group-genesis-church vision needs the exchange of ideas between generations, in order to accurately determine the leading of God.

The youth pastor must choose people of different ages to work as youth sponsors and seek the counsel of spiritually mature parents as he goes about the early stages of ministry so that when the new church emerges, generational diversity will be an established component. When combined with accountability to the leadership of the mother church, the generational factor will become a nonissue.

Strategic thinking

Why create new churches? After all, isn't the future of the church found in larger, full-service churches rather than in a host of smaller ones? Or could the metachurch be the answer to church growth at the beginning of the 21st century? Still more radical is the call for area-wide networks of cell churches that take responsibility for multiplying every six months.

While none of these ideas are necessarily in conflict with the youth-group-genesis-church idea, there is one factor that should provide perspective on church growth. Most of the creativity and dynamic growth of a new movement takes place in the first 15 to 20 years of its existence. This is followed by 20 to 25 years of less spectacular growth while the movement changes leadership or solidifies the model under which it operates before entering a period of redefinition and even decline.

A look at such movements as the Student Volunteer Movement, Society for Christian Endeavor, InterVarsity Christian Fellowship, Campus Crusade for Christ, Young Life, and Youth for Christ suggests this same general pattern in the United States. At the same time, it would appear that new church movements such as Calvary Chapel, Vineyard Fellowship, and possibly Willow Creek Community Church may conform to a similar pattern.

Church growth specialists track an initial eight-year burst of growth for new churches before the growth curve flattens out. If the original growth does not catapult the church past the 250 attendance mark, the church may spend a majority of its lifetime flirting with the same attendance barrier.

Where a new church comes into existence with momentum generated by several years of evangelism and discipleship under a respected leader, the prospects of continued growth and impact are greatly enhanced. Youth pastors who view their youth ministries as strategic opportunities for long-term kingdom influence have the potential for shaping a new generation of culturally relevant and theologically significant churches.

The strategy for the youth group genesis church may be one of the best disciplines for a local church to retain a commitment to local evangelism and church growth from generation to generation. While the philosophy of growth may cause some difficulties for the mother church as groups are periodically hived off, the circumstances under which the church split takes place should create a healthy climate in which numbers will be regenerated.

Objections to Youth Ministry as Church Planting

The very concept of youth ministry as church planting is not without its detractors. Objections frequently assist the discussion to a more realistic and biblically sound set of conclusions. While other reservations might be raised, the following four provide useful clarifications.

Edifice argument/Club argument

If we siphon off the future leadership of our church, who will be around to maintain the edifice or club? While the argument is in part a case for continuity in the local church, it comes laden with subbiblical assumptions.

The faith community in the New Testament was never identified as a physical building or edifice. Christians are described as the building. Cathedrals, while majestic places to worship, were never the "church." Today most serve more as museums than organisms that Scripture calls the church. Protestant church buildings followed in the tradition of the cathedral, shifting the focus of most people to the permanence of architecture rather than on the flexibility of believers. In some ways the Old Testament tabernacle is a better metaphor for the church. It was as mobile as the Bedouin Israelite nation.

The argument could be made that the Lord allowed persecution to befall the first-century church (Acts 8:1) in order to break the church in Jerusalem out of its close identification with the land (in other words her edifice or club mentality). The fellowship (*koinonia*) of the Holy Spirit, by contrast, characterized the clusters of believers as they scattered throughout the world (2 Corinthians 13:14). The Jerusalem club had to be fractured for the Good News to spread.

Another subbiblical assumption presumes a sociological basis for church growth. A successful youth ministry will attract new families to attend church and maintain current members. To lose a generation of emerging leaders is to strike the death knell of the church. Unfortunately, much of their expected church increase finds its base in biological or transfer growth. Evangelism that brings new believers of all ages into the fellowship is not factored into the expectations of the local church.

Parachurch argument

If we begin planting churches, other churches will see us competition and our support base will dry up. Though functioning outside of an ecclesiological structure, paraparochial ministries see themselves as being alongside the local church, and their financial support is drawn from local churches and Christian families.

Most youth ministries aim to bond youths to a local church after winning them to Christ—a goal that churches applaud, though it's more often missed than hit. Yet if a youth ministry wanted to increase their odds of success by themselves spawning a church, some churches would cry foul and financial support for the youth ministry would likely dry up. One wonders if such short-sighted churches would rather have the paraparochial agency fail in their mission of grounding new converts in the faith community than allow what they see as competition with their church's ministry.

Caught in this no-win situation, parachurch ministries have usually taken the path of least resistance. Church partnerships in some communities help complete their mission. For the most part, however, they continue an effective ministry as youth culture specialists and only occasionally attempt to ensure that new converts are adopted by local church families.

Profession argument

By the time youth ministers get to the point where they can be effective professionals, they will begin pulling out of youth ministry and heading into a senior pastor role. It is a new version of the old stepping-stone-to-the-ministry philosophy.

The Strategic approach to youth ministry is a far cry from the stepping-stone approach. Strategic youth pastors are passionate about ministering to youths—so passionate that they want to extend the ministry far beyond adolescence. The youth minister who uses the stepping-stone approach, by contrast, has little passion for young people and merely puts in time with youths until a "real ministry" becomes available.

Statistics gathered from a variety of sources suggest that few youth ministry professionals exceed the proposed amount of time in a local church that is required in this church-birthing proposal. In fact, in many cases a strategic vision might motivate youth ministers who are on the verge of leaving the field to remain in their position with passion and effectiveness for a longer period of time.

The proposal, if commonly adopted, would redefine the youth ministry profession. Colleges and seminaries would need to rethink the career path of youth workers. While there are enough second- and third-decade youth ministers in primary youth ministry to validate the specialization, the vast majority of people who trained as youth ministers have left local church or parachurch club ministry in favor of some other form of livelihood. The absence of a career path in youth ministry leaves many gifted people outside the field at the very time they should be reaching the peak of their effectiveness in their mid-30s. The idea of youth ministry being a church-birthing process provides a career path and may even attract a new type of gifted person to a youth ministry career.

Gender argument

If youth ministry is for people who anticipate becoming preaching pastors, the playing field may be significantly altered for women, particularly in evangelical churches and denominations. It is a subtle way of further restricting the ministry of women in the church.

In churches where the pulpit is a forbidden domain for women, it is true: the church-birthing philosophy will further restrict the availability of youth ministry positions to women. The reality of the situation in those churches is that youth ministry is already out of bounds for women, no matter how gifted they are.

The church-birthing proposal should open more doors for pastoral leadership to women in churches where pastoral polity is less restrictive. In churches where a woman is a youth minister, she has the opportunity to shape a new church with an egalitarian philosophy of ministry. The church leadership of the mother church, by calling her to the role of youth minister, has authorized her to become a church planter and thus shape the ministry in a fashion that honors spiritual giftedness in both men and women.

Women in parachurch ministries have an even greater opportunity. They are already doing the work of an evangelist. Most are already providing the primary spiritual nurture for new converts. From there it is but a small step to become the pastor of an ongoing fellowship of believers. Because many of her parishioners have not been exposed to churches that limit the leadership of women, the traditional bias may not be present.

> The idea of youth ministry being a church-birthing process provides a career path for professional youth ministers, and may even attract a new type of gifted person to a youth ministry career.

Implications for the youth program

A fear that many youth ministers face as they consider the implications of treating youth ministry as a strategy for church planting is the possibility that youth ministry will become boring, predictable, and tradition bound. Worse still, youth ministry might lose its relevance to the young people. The possibility of creativity, flexibility, innovation, and cultural relevance attracts many of the brightest young leaders to the field of youth ministry.

To put it another way, if the church planting idea means conforming youth ministry to the expectations of another generation of church leaders, most of the brightest and best youth leaders would reject the idea immediately. Frankly, that is exactly what they should do. The church planting strategy is not about making youth ministry boring but about making a new church as relevant and vibrant as current approaches to youth ministry.

When Dann Spader gave birth to Sonlife Ministries, he envisioned hundreds of model youth ministries as training centers across the nation. By the end of the first decade of training seminars, Spader discovered that there was a lid on his dream. The vast majority of the churches he was dealing with were not healthy. Their spiritual vital signs of the *churches* were nowhere as healthy as the *youth ministries* they promoted.

Growing a Healthy Church was Spader's initial response to what he considered to be unhealthy patterns of church life.[11] By 1998, seminars based on the book attracted 11,000 church leaders. Spader's intent was not to dumb to down the youth ministry, but to refocus the energies of Christian churches.

The brief history of youth ministry-based church planting draws the same conclusions as Spader. Churches can only be birthed from youth ministries when youth ministries show intense relevance to the needs of local youths and a profound conviction that the answer is found in the Christian gospel, as communicated through the redemptive story line in the Bible. Cutting edge relevance to the spiritual needs experienced by people of all ages provides the basis for an ecclesiology upon which a new church can be built.

Four elements central to youth ministry establish a framework for youth-ministry-genesis-church planting. Before a new church can be birthed, these must be a normal part of a youth ministry.[12]

- **Contact.** Youth ministry begins when a Christian adult finds a comfortable way to enter a student's world.[13] Healthy youth ministries find creative ways to reach beyond the children of the church and establish meaningful relationships with spiritually sensitive youths in their high schools and communities. Youth leaders and students develop a Great Commission mindset. For a church to be planted and thrive as those cited above, the youth minister and the discipled leadership will bring these gifts and resulting skills into the emerging church.

- **Attract.** While the right to be heard by a young person is based on a relationship, time and energy limits even the best of youth ministers from building significant relationships with more than about 30 young people. Some type of ministry activity must be created that appeals to wider circles of young people and within which other Christian connectedness might be built. Some call this a ministry strategy; others call it a pur pose driven program. Either way the ministry vehicle is used to attract and sustain relationships with spiritually seeking youths.

  As a church is birthed from youth ministry, attractiveness to spiritually open adults becomes a key to bringing about conversion growth and not just biological or transfer growth. Public services may be the attraction to seekers. What is more likely in a postmodern age, however, is that people will be attracted to spiritually sensitive people they encounter in settings designed to meet their felt needs.

> As a church is birthed from youth ministry, attractiveness to spiritually open adults becomes a key to bringing about conversion growth and not just biological or transfer growth.

- **Confront.** There may have been a time when young people knew that the love exhibited by youth leaders was the love of Jesus Christ. The general framework of the gospel of Jesus Christ was fairly well known. Yet even then someone needed to explain the four spiritual laws or Romans Road before a repentance and conversion changed the eternal destiny of a young person. Youth ministries that merely attract young people but fail to confront them with the Christian gospel are not candidates for establishing churches. At the heart of most youth ministry genesis churches is a clear pattern of evangelization. Young people have been so steeped in introducing peers and family members to the gospel that the new church merely provides an intergenerational opportunity to do what they are already accustomed to doing.

- *Retain/Train.* The final element essential to youth ministry and required for church planting is a conscious system of shepherding and educating people who have been brought into the ministry. Shepherding is a conscious system of making sure each young person is present or accounted for. When a ministry consists of fewer than 30 students, the shepherding process happens nearly spontaneously. Someone in the group knows when a person is missing. The larger a ministry becomes, the easier it is for a person to slip through the slats without being missed. Youth ministries have learned the value of planned accountability.

  The training aspect of the discipleship process is equally vital. No longer can it be assumed that young people have gained a knowledge of the Bible in their homes. In fact, it is not even a safe assumption that young people have gained much of a grasp of the Christian story line from creation to the final triumph of Christ in their Sunday schools or church education programs. Youth ministries that are potential church plants develop ways of assisting students to grasp the profound implications of the gospel.

Based on successful patterns of discipleship (shepherding and training), youth ministry genesis churches build patterns of spiritual nurture into the philosophy and strategy of the newly formed church. Without such a framework in youth ministry, the newly formed church has every possibility of reverting to older models of discipleship, which may have worked when the community shared a Christian consensus, but fails to have the same impact on a culture in which the Christian gospel is but a distorted memory.

Changes Required in the Church

Church leaders in the 20th century have viewed youth ministry as much for its problems as for its potential. Frank Otis Erb, writing in 1917, cites criticism of youth ministry that saw Christian Endeavor and its denominational counterparts as being "without scriptural authority and usurping the place of the church, which alone had divine authority."

> It was greatly feared that [youth work] would divide the church on the basis of age, and supplant the church in the affection of the young. It was declared by many that it interfered seriously with other church meetings, particularly the Sunday evening preaching service, usually evangelistic, and the midweek prayer-meeting. Many feared that [Christian Endeavor] would divert the young people's money from denominational channels, and would lead to haphazard giving and a lack of interest in the causes to which the church and denomination were pledged.[14]

More visionary pastors viewed youth ministry as mere preparation for future leadership. "In other words, the real tasks of the church [were] being performed by deacons, elders, and such persons, but young people up to, say, 30, [were] engaged in a sort of play by which they [would] be fitted for genuine work later on...[T]he only churches and pastors who have regarded the young people as fit for a great task here and now are those that make much of evangelistic effort."[15]

If there was any changing that needed to be done for young people to be full participants in local churches, it would be the young people who would have to change. Youth societies became holding tanks where youthful zeal could be channeled into harmless activities. Developing skills in churchmanship overshadowed the professed desires of pastors for evangelism, character development, and Christian service. The explosive power of youthful Christian idealism wasted away in a series of youth society meetings and related committee assignments. Churches, both liberal and conservative, settled into an uneasy slide toward religion more defined by a social agenda than by the power of God.[16]

Little changed in the attitude of church leaders during the remainder of the 20th century. While youth societies became youth ministries and evangelism leading to discipleship became the norm for many church-based youth ministries, adults in the church continued to pursue their privatized twin quest of personal peace and affluence.[17] Youth ministry, in many churches, leads the way in attempting to live in harmony with a theological agenda while the adult congregants resist the call of such prophetic voices as C. S. Lewis and Charles Colson to "please God more than the culture and community in which we spend these few, short years."[18]

A premise of the Strategic approach to youth ministry is that the best manner to renew the church is through systematically establishing new churches based in an evangelistic vision, a profound submission to the Word of God, and the power of God's Spirit in the contemporary world. When carefully nurtured and led, youth ministry has the greatest potential for becoming the seed bed for a strategy of church planting.

If the Strategic approach to youth ministry is to be embraced by a local church, it is adult congregants who must change far more than purpose-driven youth ministries wherever they may be found.[19] Four specific changes in adult leadership perspectives are essential.

- **Young people must be seen as people who are shaping the church and being shaped by it.** Change in worship forms will reflect the tastes of all ages in healthy tension. Fellow-ship activities will promote both collective and age group exclusive experiences but neither to the detriment of the other. Issues shaped by compassion and a sacrificial lifestyle will drive the agenda of the entire faith community. The spiritual gifts of young people will be used whenever and wherever appropriate.

- **Youth pastors must be viewed as pastors.** Selection and development of youth pastors will be based on spiritual leadership skills and gifts, rather than personality. Knowledge of biblical and theological content will be expected from youth pastors as they address the issues of the day. A rigorous process leading to licensure or ordination will be expected of youth pastors designated to strategically establish new churches.

- **Young people must lead in mission efforts.** Both local and cross-cultural efforts will find young people in the forefront of vision casting and personal witness. The biblical idealism of youths will be honored as church priorities shape church budgets. Risks will be taken by parents of youths that will ensure that the church reaches beyond its safety zone into the full diversity of communities in which they live.

- **Adult congregations, like parents, must prefer to sacrifice their own lives so that the next generation might live and grow.** The spiritual growth, development, and multiplication of the faith community will take precedence over maintenance of facilities and traditions. Biblical values will balance the needs of the parent church with the autonomy of daughter churches. Strategic decisions, driven by evangelism and Christian discipleship, will govern the priorities of the worshiping community.

Conclusion

Perhaps Roger was right in his conversation with Sheila. When he claimed that more people would remain active if they started a new church (because they would have a greater ownership in what the church is and what it does), he may have identified a central challenge for the faith community. Who owns the church?

The Scripture makes clear that Jesus Christ is the head of the church. Ownership flows from him. The Strategic approach to youth ministry attempts to balance the sense of ownership that flows from the Head to include the church of the future as it emerges today. Rather than fragmenting the church into age group enclaves of *koinonia,* and passing students along to spiritual leaders with whom they have little affinity or relationship, the church should "make every effort to keep the unity of the Spirit through the bond of peace" (Ephesians 4:3). This time, it may be the youths of the church who become the instruments of God, "speaking the truth in love [so that] we will grow up into him who is the Head, that is, Christ. From him the whole body, joined and held together by every supporting ligament grows and builds itself up in love, as each part does its work" (Ephesians 4:15-16).

Notes

1. Pete Ward, *God at the Mall* (Peabody, Massachusetts: Hendrickson, 1999), 137.

2. For this and other reasons, Willow Creek Community Church discontinued the competition-based strategy in the fall of 1998.

3. The community-building benefits of a one-room schoolhouse type of education might be available if the teacher could guide students in utilizing an online curriculum, while older students mentored younger students in a form of mastery learning.

4. This includes only people who had contact with a specific group of adolescents throughout the year. It excludes people employed in such worthy ministries as Christian camping, who by all rights are doing youth ministry.

5. Young Life Field Ministry Staff Statistics, September 30, 1998.

6. Fellowship of Christian Athletes, Data 1992-Present, December 10, 1998.

7. Youth for Christ Web site (www.gospelcom.net/yfc), October 16, 1999.

8. *1998: The Year in Review,* Sonlife Board of Directors Annual Report.

9. Lawrence O. Richards, *A Theology of Children's Ministry* (Grand Rapids: Zondervan, 1983), 18. See also Charles R. Foster, "The Faith Community as a Guiding Image for Christian Education," *Contemporary Approaches to Christian Education* (Nashville: Abingdon Press, 1982), 53-71.

10. Jimmy Long, *Generating Hope* (Downers Grove: InterVarsity Press, 1997), 133.

11. Dann Spader and Gary Mayes, *Growing a Healthy Church* (Chicago: Moody Press, 1991).

12. These are developed more fully in my article, "Emerging Patterns of Youth Ministry at the End of the Twentieth Century," in *Relational Youthwork* (1995): 107-131. See also Richard R. Dunn and Mark H. Senter III, eds., *Reaching a Generation for Christ* (Chicago: Moody Press, 1997), 105-117.

13. Richard R. Dunn and Mark H. Senter III, eds., *Reaching a Generation for Christ* (Chicago: Moody Press, 1997), 123. David R. Veerman, *Youth Evangelism* (Wheaton: Victor, 1988), 61-74. Barry St. Clair and Keith Naylor, *Penetrating the Campus* (Wheaton: Victor, 1993), 101-116.

14. Frank Otis Erb, *The Development of the Young People's Movement* (Chicago: University of Chicago Press, 1917), 59.

15. Erb, 107-108.

16. Mark H. Senter III, "Where We've Come From (and Where We Need to Go)," *Youthworker* (January/February 2000), 48-52.

17. Francis Schaeffer, *How Should We Then Live?* (Grand Rapids: Revell, 1976), 205.

18. Charles Colson, *The Body* (Nashville: Word, 1992), 37. See also C. S. Lewis, *The Screwtape Letters* (New York: Macmillan, 1943), 15-19.

19. "Purpose-driven" is used to include all youth ministries that share an evangelism/discipleship agenda as opposed to an entertainment/program format.

References

Colson, Charles. *The Body*. Nashville: Word, 1992.

Dunn, Richard, and Mark Senter, eds. "Looking Ahead to the Next Millennium," in *Reaching a Generation for Christ*. Chicago: Moody Press, 1997.

Grudem, Wayne. *Systematic Theology*. Grand Rapids: Zondervan, 1994.

Rice, Wayne, and others. *New Directions for Youth Ministry*. Loveland, Colorado: Group Publishing, 1998.

Schaeffer, Francis. *The Church at the End of the Twentieth Century*. Downers Grove, Illinois: InterVarsity Press, 1970.

Senter, Mark H., III. "In Consideration of Youth Churches," *Youthworker* (September/October 1997):28-33.

———. "Where We've Come From (and Where We Need to Go)," *Youthworker* (January/February 2000): 48-52.

Spader, Dann and Gary Mayes. *Growing a Healthy Church*. Chicago: Moody Press, 1991.

Sweet, Leonard. *Aqua Church: Essential Leadership Arts for Piloting Your Church in Today's Fluid Culture*. Loveland, Colorado: Group Publishing, 1999.

Ward, Pete, ed. *The Church and Youth Ministry*. Lynx, 1995.

Ward, Pete. *God at the Mall*. Peabody, Massachusetts: Hendrickson, 1999.

———. *Relational Youthwork*. Lynx, 1995.

Zoba, Wendy Murray. "The Class of '00." *Christianity Today* (3 February 1997), 18.

Response to the Strategic Approach
from an Inclusive Congregational Perspective
by Malan Nel

Yours is a well-articulated and thorough description of the Strategic approach and what it implies when we take this road—a logical road, when one looks at it from the perspective of specialization, as you pointed out in your reference to the situation in schools. You rightfully deduct that "discontinuity of relationships and specialization of content become the normal way of doing education." One tends to perpetuate what one is used to.

In your description of the approach you make the point that this is "the best opportunity to launch a vital Christian witness to shape the faith community for the next generation." In this sense the approach might be called a specific missiological strategy, like church planting in the church-growth philosophy—a valid motivation for the Strategic approach. But, I must admit, it is the *only* motivation I can see for it.

Your explanation of the Strategic approach leaves me with some questions and reservations.

Giving up reforming the church

Isn't it true that this approach has become even popular in some areas because leadership in youth ministry has given up on the reformation of the congregation? I think of your important remark, which to my mind points in that direction: "While the church wanted young people to mature in their Christian faith, maturity was defined in terms that the older generation understood and to which the younger crowd was expected to conform." When and if this is true (and I think it is), the Strategic approach is almost the only way forward. I know there are a number of leaders in my field who just no longer believe that anything good can come out of the church as we know it. The gap between the *defined subject* (the church as portrayed in Scripture) and the *empirical subject* (the local church as we meet it in any given context) is so wide that they rationalize the fact that you cannot poor new wine into old wineskins— although this approach was challenged by Aubrey Malphurs in *Pouring New Wine into Old Wineskins.*[1]

> My question is whether the Strategic approach is not, at least in part, giving up on the possibility that we all can and should reform to make room for each other.

The problem seems to be the adult contingent of congregations. Spiritually speaking, one wonders whether they are that "adult," anyway. After all, openness to change is one of the most obvious characteristics of self-reliant spiritual functioning. My question is whether the Strategic approach is not, at least in part, giving up on the possibility that we all can and should reform to make room for each other. How would you respond to my conviction that behind all of this lies a very low missionary awareness? Normally we are just not compelled by the love of God to reach out to hurting children and adolescents outside the faith community. That's why congregations think they can afford the luxury of being so ingrown that even their own kids become strangers within the church.

Corporate nature of the people of God

My second reservation concerns the ecclesiology behind the approach. I do not think there is one right ecclesiology out there. But there are ecclesiologies that should guide us in our decisions about what is good and what is better. One of them is the corporate nature of the people of God. We all confess *one holy catholic church.* My growing concern is that churches seem to be taking holiness more seriously than unity. Is it possible that the Strategic approach may make it just too easy to start something new? What does this do to unity? When do we really have that freedom?

Viewing the approach as a missionary strategy puts it in a different light: this becomes not splitting congregations, but starting or planting new congregations. Given the strong and ruling youth culture, I am, however, not convinced that mission is the reason for starting new youth congregations. I therefore like your heading: "Youth Ministry as Church-Birthing." But how do we ensure that the approach is not misused for what may be pretty selfish reasons of even a leader or two? ("I want it *my* way.")

Alternative community

Another ecclesiological issue at stake is the fragmentation of community. The youth-group-genesis-church becomes yet another alternative community that draws youths away from the primary community of the congregation. Separating youths from adults, unfortunately, seems to be the norm. I believe that if we take seriously the metaphors about the church, we will hardly find any biblical reasons for arguing the need for specialization, especially to the pointing of youth churches. To name but one: the fact that we are called *children of God* emphasizes the fact that we belong together.

The fact that empirical realities are different almost compels us to confess that we have given in to culture rather than vigorously pursuing our alternative nature. Richard R. Osmer argues a good case for what we might call individuation and individualization of adolescents.[2] We owe adolescents help to become public Christians. A congregation with its normal makeup (representing the good, the bad, and the ugly who are now *in Christ*) and normal struggles (victory, failure, struggle, and so on) is in a sense a laboratory, where adolescents can experiment with Christian life—the life they need to live in public.

I know there may be situations that are almost a Luther moment ("Here I stand—I do not want to go, but have no choice.") I believe that the approach needs this controlling mechanism. Otherwise starting a youth congregation may in some cases be the fad of a leader or group. What kind of control would you suggest to prevent this from happening because it is not the intention of the approach in itself? Maybe you pointed at this when you said: "A nucleus of parents and other adults need to be early adopters of the idea."

> If we take seriously the metaphors about the church, we will hardly find any biblical reasons for arguing the need for specialization, especially to the pointing of youth churches. The fact that we are called children of God emphasizes the fact that we belong together.

Building disciples

Finally is the matter of building disciples. You wrote that "perhaps the most vulnerable point in youth ministry is continuity in discipleship relationships." I agree with this, but fail to see how the Strategic approach will solve the problem.

We all know that the whole biblical discipleship concept comes from the Greek and Jewish world Jesus lived in. The difference was, unlike in those two cultures, the pupils (disciples) did not elect to be in Jesus' school of disciple building. He called them. And because of their calling *by him* to *follow him* they became a unique community. A diverse group, they undoubtedly learned a lot from each other. A true example of what the church as a community of disciples is supposed to be. They were not birds of a feather who flocked together; but they stayed together because they had been called together. They met each other in Christ, not in likemindedness. Would you agree that the Strategic approach carries the tendency to create churches that are not one in Christ, but one in how they feel and on what they agree? To the contrary, don't we need the challenge of the others who are so completely different but share with us in the difference Christ makes in all of us?

Notes

1. Aubrey Malphurs, *Pouring New Wine into Old Wineskins* (Baker Book, 1993).

2. Richard R. Osmer, *Confirmation* (Louisville: Geneva, 1996).

Response to the Strategic Approach
from a Preparatory Perspective
by Wesley Black

Thanks, Mark, for an intriguing view of youth ministry that fascinated me with its possibilities. You almost converted me! For it holds out the hope of youths taking significant roles of leadership and involvement in the movement of God for now and the future.

One of the perpetual concerns of Christians revolves around who will carry on the mission of reaching our world for Christ—a concern that your Strategic approach addresses, albeit untraditionally. Church youth leaders are regularly frustrated to see young people who were once active and involved in the youth group drop out as they move into college and young adulthood. The stereotype says that they return when they reach 30, get married, have children, and get tired of sowing their wild oats.

The pattern today, however, is that those young people are seldom returning to church. So those churches that were once vibrant and filled with youthful energy are now only faint images of dynamic Christian life. There are plenty of reasons to be concerned, and the Strategic approach boldly steps in to solve the problems.

Better alternatives

Your chapter presents better alternatives than some other approaches do to the weaknesses of the past. Let's face it—we have not done a very good job in some critical areas, especially evangelism. "The evangelization of youths was less and less a normal part of church youth ministry," you write. "To put it bluntly, it simply was not happening."

Too often, growth of youth ministry has been biological. That is, the children of adult church members join the youth ministry in greater numbers than those who are not in the church culture. We hoped this latter group would come, planned for them to be a part, and

> Is the Strategic approach realistic and reproducible? I wonder if churches that grow out of such an approach continue parenting new congregations, or settle in to building one growing congregation? Are there any second-generation churches built on a Strategic approach?

strategized creative ways to reach out to them. But still we have not done an adequate job in this area.

Another weakness of the past was the view of youths as the *future* of the church, rather than the church of *today*. As you put it, "In general, young people were not valued for what they brought to the church family as much as for what they would someday become." We wanted them to become mature and step into leadership sometime in the future, when they were grown up and ready to accept more responsibility. But we did not provide adequate places for them to be personally involved at their current levels of maturity and responsibility as adolescents.

This weakness probably grew into the accepted mode of teaching and discipleship that has been practiced in most churches. You mentioned this in your argument about the "factory model of nonformal education which came to dominate formal education in the later part of the 19ᵗʰ century." I agree that we should have been more intentional in developing better teaching or learning models, rather than simply accepting the mode of public school education. As you stated in the opening scenario, "Churches, including Sheila and Roger's, adopted a schooling model of discipleship."

While some forms of this schooling model results in effective transmission of content, it ignores the affective and skills areas in many cases. Even in the cognitive domain, few of us can disagree that many teens who have attended church classes most of their lives are still woefully ignorant of the most basic of Christian teachings.

Cell groups, accountability groups, one-to-one discipling, peer ministry programs, and mentoring strategies have been attempts to creatively approach alternatives to the informal schooling model that we see every Sunday in churches and youth groups.

"Discontinuity of relationships and specialization of content," you write, "become the normal way of doing education." This can result in poor teaching and even weaker emotional ties to the very organism we hope to strengthen. As you said, "A realistic appraisal of youth groups a decade after graduation suggests a disappointingly small number of alumni remain in either their home church or other churches." It often takes an intentional, ongoing effort to maintain contact with youths and young adults after they move away from home and the church to go to college or start their careers.

You made a strong point when you said, "Unless the youth leader maintains a meaningful contact with graduates and encourages them to attend church together, very few establish a lasting relationship with a local church." We can hope that our best efforts with youths will result in active, involved, motivated young adults who step into significant leadership roles.

> It seems to me that your approach opens the door to youth ministers who are not truly motivated to minister to youths today, but rather have their eye on a future church.

But this is seldom the case. One reason lies in the entertainment approach of the past. But even those with more spiritually challenging approaches were guilty of creating a passive, stagnant youth group. "The explosive power of youthful Christian idealism wasted away in a series of youth society meetings and related committee assignments," you pointed out. "Churches, both liberal and conservative, settled into an uneasy slide toward religion more defined by a social agenda than by the power of God."

You particularly indicted the Preparatory approach when you quoted Erb: "In other words, the real tasks of the church [were] being performed by deacons, elders, and such persons, but young people up to, say, 30, [were] engaged in a sort of play by which they [would] be fitted for genuine work later on." We must make the involvement and nurture of youths genuine and significant if we are to truly prepare them for future leadership roles.

Benefits

Another reason the Strategic approach makes sense is found in this approach's benefits, which you articulated convincingly.

I often speak with youth leaders in ethnic churches where the worship services are in their native language. They are concerned with keeping their youths, most of whom speak English, active and involved in the church. Their Bible study classes are normally in English, while their parents' classes may be in their native language. As you said, these churches "use an English-speaking youth service as a means of creating an American style service within the same church." Their parents often face the dilemma of wanting their youths to stay faithful to their heritage and their church, but also wanting them to have a relevant, meaningful experience with their faith community. The solution is often a "church within a church" arrangement.

Another benefit of the Strategic approach deals with the person and ministry of the youth leader, especially female youth ministers. It is true, as you said, that doors may be closed for some women to become pastors of new churches. But other churches that would restrict the pastoral role to men will still allow females to lead their youth ministries. I think the Strategic approach could still allow opportunities for women, even in those churches, to lead the effort and groom male interns to become the pastors of those new churches.

Female or male, the youth minister is moved into a significant position in the overall mission of a church when that church practices the Strategic approach. As you wrote, "Church leadership has treated youth ministers as novice adults rather than permanent parts of the church's strategy of discipleship and world evangelization."

And I liked your emphasis on the motivation behind the Strategic approach. "A premise of the Strategic approach to youth ministry," you wrote, "is that the best manner in which to renew the church is through systematically establishing new churches based in an evangelistic vision, a profound submission to the Word of God, and the power of God's Spirit in the contemporary world."

My criticism of the Strategic approach falls into two categories: the process of the Strategic approach, and issues revolving around generational and family concerns.

Realistic and reproducible?

My first concern deals with the process of the Strategic approach. Is it really realistic and reproducible? You presented some good illustrations of isolated examples in which a new church grew out of an existing youth group. The most visible example of this is Willow Creek Community Church. But does the philosophy continue there? Have other churches sprouted from the existing Willow Creek youth ministry? Is it a Strategic approach now? It is obviously a strong evangelistic ministry, but I wonder if churches that grew out of a Strategic approach continue the pattern or settle in to build a strong growing congregation. Perhaps it would be good if we could see some second-generation churches from a Strategic approach to youth ministry.

Avoid problems of the past?

Another question of process deals with the best way to avoid problems of the past with young leaders who launch new churches. You made a good point that we must view youth ministry "not so much as a means of turning out models of Christian living to perpetuate existing church ministries, but as the best opportunity to launch a vital Christian witness to shape the faith community for the next generation." But if these teens are to assume leadership in a future, separate church, how will they know the existing problems and avoid them in the future? Are they doomed to learn only from their own mistakes and stand the chance of repeating the errors of the past?

How will teens learn the models and leadership skills necessary to organize and carry out the structure of a church? I am not arguing for the perpetuation of an existing, flawed model of the church, but for the organizational and leadership skills needed to function as a group in any effective manner. Is there not the danger of immature, narrowly focused programming that may miss some critical ministry functions due to the lack of mature leadership experiences?

Accountability of the youth minister

Another problem with the process involves the accountability of the youth minister. You mentioned this danger in discussing an emerging pastor who does not have theological training. In that case the mother church or campus ministry is to "hold the young pastor accountable for developing the ability to think and act Christianly." This seems to be a shaky proposition because of the youth minister's split loyalty: on one hand, the youth minister owes allegiance to the mother church, while on the other hand he is creating a separate entity that is different and distinct from the mother church. It seems that the youth minister (a future pastor) could misinterpret any theological correction from the mother church as an attempt to preserve the traditions of the past, which he hopes to correct in the new church.

Stepping stone?

Still another process problem lies in the idea that the youth ministry of the mother church is simply a stepping stone to a new church. You touched on this in the "profession argument" when you wrote that "by the time youth ministers get to the point where they can be effective professionals, they will begin pulling out of youth ministry and head into a senior pastor role." While you acknowledge the difference between the old stepping stone motivation and the Strategic approach, I still think there is a trap here. You went on to say, "The idea of youth ministry being a church-birthing process provides a career path and may even attract a new type of gifted person to a youth ministry career." It seems that this opens the door to those who are not truly motivated to minister to youths today, but rather have their eye on a future church.

Earlier you said that youth ministers should be chosen with the "primary objective...to develop a team of spiritually mature young adults and start a new church." This sounds a lot like someone who has the prime intention of starting a new church with a secondary intention of ministering to the needs of youths in the present. If the new-church genesis takes longer than originally envisioned, the youth minister could become increasingly frustrated with youth ministry and long for his larger pastoral role over a new church.

We have to be careful that the Strategic approach does not become just a manipulation of young people. Youth ministers must be concerned about developmental, cultural, and generational needs of youths, more than simply using them as a process for starting a new church.

Youth ministry of the mother church

And what about the youth ministry of the mother church after a new church starts? Will it continue or move out to the new church? After all, most of the current youth leadership will become the nucleus of the new church. What will become of the rising youths in the mother church?

Parachurch workers building a church

My final objection to the Strategic approach as to process deals with parachurch workers building a church from their youth groups. So many parachurch workers seem to have a bias against "church" in the first place, with its structures, organizations, and traditions (no matter how relevant or effective). Why would they want to create something they perceive as a hindrance? Wouldn't a newly created form of church still hold problems for the free spirited, entrepreneurial approach that drives many parachurch workers?

Generational and family issues

After process concerns, I believe that the Strategic approach has weaknesses in generational and family issues. You acknowledged this when you wrote that "the danger of the youth group genesis church is that it may be limited to people who are the about the same age as the youth pastor and younger." You referenced this earlier: "The Strategic approach to youth ministry creates a community of leaders and youthful Christians." Then you said this "calls upon the youth ministry to be and become a holistic intergenerational church that is relevant to the world in which it lives." It seems to me that the very nature of this approach works against intergenerational interchange.

True, youth leaders may offer some adult role models. But I fear that in most cases these youth leaders will be youthful adults who are disenchanted with the traditions of the past and actually resist contact between their youth members and others of different generations who may potentially sidetrack efforts to create a new vibrant,

> If the youth minister is moving toward the hope of launching a new, separate entity, and the youth group is going to be the nucleus of that effort, what will be the role of parents and younger children in this plan?

untraditional body. You hinted at this again when you wrote that "the youth-group-genesis-church vision needs the exchange of ideas between generations, in order to accurately determine the leading of God." You hit the nail squarely on the head: youths can benefit greatly when they hear the stories of faith from those of different generations. The Bible is filled with examples of those who listened and learned from both the victories and mistakes of other generations.

I also believe that youths need both church and family nurture to grow into Christian maturity. The Strategic approach seems to discount the influence of families on their young. It seems to build on the experiences of peers and church youth leaders only. If the youth minister is moving toward the hope of launching a new, separate entity, and the youth group is going to be the nucleus of that effort, what will be the role of parents and younger children in this plan? Will youths move away from their parents into a new church or will their parents move along with them? You did touch on this briefly, but it still seems unclear how this process plays out. Where will the lines of separation be drawn? Will part of the family (parents, small children, older relatives) be left behind in the mother church while youths and young adults populate the new genesis? If the older and younger members of the family also move, how much does this diminish the possibility that the new genesis will be different from the older mother church?

Finally, when new converts are assimilated, assuming they are youths or older adolescents, what is the hope of reaching their families? Will there be an intensive effort to reach out to them, or will they be left to find their own way without a warm invitation from the new genesis church?

Response to the Strategic Approach from a Missional Perspective
by Chap Clark

I was bombarded by two overwhelming impressions as I read your chapter, Mark: one, this is fascinating, creative, and wild stuff. Two, this is an idea that is so far-fetched and unrealistic for most churches and youth ministry programs that it borders on fantasy.

Yet you have gathered, analyzed, dissected, and codified relevant data in a way that compels the reader to abandon tightly held methodological and programmatic convictions by asking some new questions and being open to creative answers. I commend you for advocating such an approach with both academic and theological support.

I fear that the Strategic approach, however, has some fundamental flaws that, upon closer examination, reveal a strategy that would consistently be the exception rather than the strategic rule of the future of youth ministry.

Compelling aspects

Yet there are several compelling and frankly exciting aspects to your argument. I agree that contemporary youth ministry, especially as it has evolved in middle- and upper-class communities in North America over the past 30 to 40 years, needs to be overhauled. It struck a chord in me when I read how young people often experience the church as foster children (a concept used here and in Malan Nel's article). As dominant cultures around the world segment off and flee from the young, similarly the church loves to resolve what is uncomfortable by pushing it aside.

In many ways, then, youth ministry can be summarized for many adults in the church as a necessary nuisance. In most churches adolescents are a constant reminder of what adults have lost in postmodernity, and how they have lost the sense of control they once had in the good old days, which makes them uncomfortable. But churches that want to survive the coming decades recognize that there must be *something* for the kids. This dichotomy polarizes the contemporary church; for members—especially older ones—do not want young people to influence (or even interrupt) the traditions and modes of the establishment in the church. Yet they also know that the church cannot survive without them eventually assimilating into the mainstream community somehow.

That said, Mark, your Strategic approach is a response to the church's innate discomfort with accommodating adolescent culture in the systemic structures of the church. In other words, this is your chapter's clear premise: the best way to resolve the conflict between elderly (Big Church) and the young (Youth Church) is to take the young and create a church environment one could not have otherwise. Essentially, the emphasis of the article smacked of a "love it or leave it" mentality.

> In most churches adolescents are a constant reminder of what adults have lost in postmodernity—among other things, a sense of control like they once had in the good old days.

Mere euphemism

Many a church has experienced the harrowing and even bloody battles over worship styles, music, dress, liturgy, and even sermon content. Indeed, there comes a time in almost every church when a group senses that the need to leave ("split," or more politically appropriate, "plant") is stronger than the desire to work through issues as a committed fellowship body. In this case the more "appropriate" course of action is to create a *new* environment without the millstone of hassles and pain of the past. I cannot shake the feeling that the Strategic approach is essentially euphemistic.

The question then becomes: Is this a *bad* thing? Is it theologically ill-advised, this strategy of targeted ministry that relies on the breaking up of the young from the old? (I know the article attempted to claim an intergenerational bent and commitment, but it still gave little historical or pragmatic support for this actually occurring in a church that would incorporate such an approach.) In my opinion the only answer to such a question is, "It depends on many complex factors" (which is why, as I stated at the outset, this Strategic approach intrigues me).

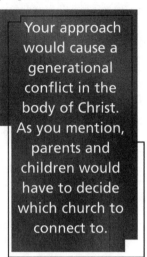

Your approach would cause a generational conflict in the body of Christ. As you mention, parents and children would have to decide which church to connect to.

On the surface I tend to agree that this approach *is* a viable and possibly even desirable course of action for a youth ministry program. As the executive administrator of a large church, I also have felt the temptation to start over. My frustration, fear, and impatience all turn on when it comes to trying to motivate a local church, especially one of any size.

But if I am honest, I do believe that most of the theological and pragmatic scaffolding for the Strategic approach is neither remotely possible for most churches nor ultimately a theologically and developmentally appropriate strategy for the few who could pull it off. In this critique I offer four pragmatic and three theological concerns.

Extremely difficult

First, my pragmatic concerns. The Strategic approach is at best extremely difficult for most churches to pull off. It demands a great many complex factors to come together instantaneously in order to come close to fulfilling your goal. Almost like the "beginning of life" argument, when God decides to intervene in our world, random events *do* occur in such a way that things change. In the examples described in this article, the Creator has seemingly helped to create a few of these types of programs *ex nihilo*.

Willow Creek, Lawndale, and the church in Nepal (a bit of a stretch, that example) are all wonderful examples of movements that experienced the unique stamp of God as complex sociological factors miraculously gelled. However, to try and analyze these (and other) moments in church history and then produce a reproducible model for the church at large is highly questionable. First, the approach requires an almost fully trained and equipped pastor—not *just* a called and gifted person with youths and a few adult leaders, but a highly skilled visionary strategist who is able to teach, disciple, lead, and eventually mobilize. This person must not only be able to maintain what is good for a large youth ministry program, but also able to lead a transitionary team through the maze of tentative newness. There are very few of those folks around.

Some drop through the cracks

Secondly, those who thrive in their involvement with the congregation at large would suffer a huge loss when the youth ministry loyalists moved on. Like the American loyalists during the Revolution, who still loved England, families who embrace their church community would be torn to see the support group for their kids ripped away from them.

Generational conflict

Thirdly, your the approach would cause a generational conflict in the body of Christ. As you mention, parents and children would have to decide which church to connect to. Older, more traditionally minded persons in a congregation may at first enjoy the quiet comfort of knowing there were no kids around to keep asking for drums on Sunday morning, but soon the voices of the young who are passionate for Jesus would be sorely missed. In discussing this approach with author Doug Fields (*Purpose Driven Youth Ministry*), he responded, "What adult wants to go to a youth church?"

Inward focused

Lastly, and perhaps most importantly, the emphasis *continues* to be inward focused. You may offer a nod toward student outreach, but in reality the missional philosophy driving this approach remains very similar to the more traditional models of youth ministry—"Just build it, and they will come." What the youth ministry builds may include cool worship, relevant preaching, and fewer old people around—but it still will not be enough to attract from the dominant culture those who believe the church is irrelevant, arrogant, and antagonistic to their lives. Will the Strategic approach cause the church to be more missionally minded? I seriously doubt it, for the amount of work, effort, and focus required to actualize such an approach would far overwhelm the desire to strategically incarnate the church in the world of the lost.

Theological validity?

I also question the theological validity of your approach, Mark. First, you write that the youth minister is the flag bearer for the Strategic approach. In describing the approach, you begin the first three steps by focusing on the individual ("*youth minister* develops a solid youth ministry," "*youth minister*…begins painting a picture," and "the team the *youth minister* has assembled" [italics mine]).

It is evident throughout this article that there is a key person in the casting and implementation of the approach, and that this person is the one who will lead the group to the Promised Land. But the New Testament church is about body life, body function, and communal leadership. Henri Nouwen claims that Christian leadership must be "mutual and communal." Theologically, your approach has a "forced" feel due to its reliance on a single leader.

Dangerous emphasis on numbers

Secondly, there is an undue and relatively dangerous emphasis on numbers to define a valid methodology. Few theologians would argue that programmatic success (in other words, numbers) is among the most important criterion for evaluating a theologically appropriate course of action. But in the historical defense of the approach, the article equates numerical growth with theological appropriateness in Nepal, Willow Creek, and Lawndale. I am not convinced that these (or any other) programs deserve to be highlighted as theologically desirable methods of ministry simply by the sheer numbers of people they attract. This logic would have to say that the rapid growth of the Black Muslim movement is due to the blessing of God.

Distinct community

Thirdly, you seem to make a subtle assumption that youth ministry is *and should be* a distinct community. I believe you are correct as a diagnosis, but are lacking in your interpretation of that as either a theologically appropriate or sociologically necessary descriptor of youth ministry. I believe that youth ministry must *fight* the tendency to pull back from the rest of the local body of Christ and do all it can to assert itself as an expression of the church at large.

Youth leaders are not registered aliens who hold a green card as a member of a foreign society. They are, instead, representatives and ambassadors of the entire congregation in caring for the unique needs of adolescents. Theologically, young people and old people are members of the same body of Christ. I believe the Scriptures teach that God desires his people to "be one."

The New Testament church was not designed as a factory, a corporation, or a series of disjointed, fragmented programs loosely connected by money and facility. It was, and therefore remains until Christ returns, a body and a family of closely connected, tightly woven, clearly broken, but mercifully reassembled people. Young and old, cool and nerd, organ and electric guitar. Perhaps it was Dennis Guernsey who wrote, "We are the church, and we are family. Let us get on with our business"—and I would add, *together!*

Rejoinder from the Strategic Approach
by Mark H. Senter III

Come on, friends, your criticism is like rearranging furniture on the deck of the *Titanic*. As unsinkable as the church is, we simply cannot stay on board our current cruise liner. If nothing else, youth ministry of the 20th century has taught us that we need to do something fresh. The Strategic approach may not be the new vessel but at least it takes a good shot at grounding youth ministry in continuity with a biblical view of the church.

While I wholeheartedly affirm the biblical concept of inclusiveness, not just with youth ministry but also across racial, economic and gender lines, I see it happening best in a fresh new generation of churches. Similarly, I wholeheartedly advocate the church's mandate for missional activity, especially among those who are spiritually disenfranchised, resulting in inclusive congregations of Christian believers, but I see it happening best where biblical values can be addressed within fresh patterns of relationships, in other words emerging churches. Yes, I affirm the responsibility of the family and faith community to prepare young people for their spiritual journey, but see it most possible where the end goal is a missional, inclusive congregational fellowship. I contend this is most possible through periodic formation of generationally relevant churches.

To paraphrase the words of our Lord, "I have not come to abolish your approaches to youth ministry and the church but to fulfill them." My point is that we simply will not be able to honor the biblical mandate for the church to fulfill its purpose in the world if we keep pursuing our objectives within the existing structures. It is time for new wineskins.

Giving up on the church?

Does this mean the Strategic approach is giving up on the existing church? Is this a move to scrap the old wineskins? Not at all. It is merely suggesting that new wine needs to be put into new wineskins. The metaphor only stretches so far, so let me state it another way. The Strategic approach enables the mother church to become healthier because it forces her to make sacrifices of people and resources to birth a new church. Mission stops being something done with our money somewhere else, it becomes something our children do starting here and continuing close by.

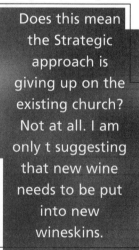

Does this mean the Strategic approach is giving up on the existing church? Not at all. I am only t suggesting that new wine needs to be put into new wineskins.

If framed in a win-lose scenario, where the youth church wins and the mother church loses, then everybody loses. But when viewed as a win-win situation, the mother church becomes healthier when giving birth to a daughter church. The newborn will be healthiest when the mother church pays attention to her own spiritual health. It is my contention that the strategy, when handled as a vital and welcomed part of the mother church's vision and mission, will redirect energies that were formerly squandered in pettiness into a richness of spiritual fruit.

Yet I feel like I need to return to your question, Malan. Am I giving up on the established church? Your question is quite fair. Let me be straightforward with you. I see the greatest hope for accomplishing what you describe as the biblical normal for the church to be found in creation, not in reform. New churches have a far greater possibility of being redemptive than do older, established churches. Obviously there are exceptions, but as a rule the most creative and dynamic ministry occurs within the first 10 to 20 years of a church's existence.

As rich as the Christian heritage is, our traditions sap spiritual vitality. Reform in local churches is energy intensive. I feel the best stewardship of ministry resources is found in church ministry that is entrepreneurial in nature. The absence of a church polity accepted by orthodox and free, Lutheran and Reformed, Brethren and Wesleyan, Catholic and Pentecostal churches suggests to me that God is more interested in the redemption of man worshiping in a faith community than in conforming to an order of service or form of church government. I think this can best be accomplished by a strategy of church planting using the most gifted people available.

So what happens to established churches? Do we just let them die? Even if biological growth was the only means of keeping established churches alive, I am quite confident the mother churches would not close its doors. There will always be a group of young people who choose to remain in the mother church. If a new youth minister is hired prior to the departure of those involved in the church-birthing process, the new person will have the opportunity to begin building a new youth ministry even while the established leadership is moving on to a new and exciting ministry.

Church split?

I agree with you, Chap and Wes, when you warn of the downside effects that could take place if church-birthing is done with a negative attitude. If the Strategic approach is viewed as a euphemism for a church split, the strategy is in trouble. The youth minister, instead of bring-

> This is not a "love it or leave it" mentality. Church-birthing youth ministry, unlike a youth church, is an attempt to capture the spiritual dynamic of a generation of Christian youths that express in fresh forms the biblical modes of God's coming to his people.

ing innovation to a new generation of ministry, will extend the inward focus of self-centered churchmen to succeeding church leadership. Pharisaical youth pastors turned senior pastors may pass along to the new church abnormalities in the spiritual genetic structure. In such cases, the daughter church will not be healthy. In all likelihood, the health of the mother church will be placed at risk as well.

Not a youth church

I was pleased that you did not mistakenly assume the Strategic approach to be synonymous with the current Youth Church fad. Youth Churches are just another form of the ghettoization of a generation of young people. The idea, while attractive to many, appears to me to be nothing more than an in-house, worship-based, missional approach. While I applaud all efforts at missional ministries and encourage any missional efforts that are tied to worshiping the Lord of heaven, I feel the idea does not overcome the need for continuity of discipleship or assimilation into a broader faith community that I addressed in my article.

Church-birthing youth ministry, unlike a youth church, is an attempt to capture the spiritual dynamic of a generation of Christian youths in order to bless other generations by expressing in fresh forms the biblical modes of God's coming to His people. No, Chap, this is not a "love it or leave it" mentality. If it becomes a "my way or the highway" mindset, then the efforts will self-destruct. The unity of the body of Christ will be scandalized. Church birthing requires loving and responsible care similar to that required for bringing a healthy child into the world.

Evangelism

All of us have acknowledged that evangelism, especially for the disenfranchised, is a weak spot for youth ministry. I would contend that even a missional approach has a tendency to settle in and go native after a while. By that I mean a "go oriented" youth evangelist finds her niche and then invests the majority of her energy in evangelistic ministry within that niche. In a very limited fashion the "go" ministry becomes a "come" ministry for a specific population of disenfranchised youths. Is that a problem? Absolutely not, unless that sub-population of the youth society has been substantially evangelized (whatever that means). Then it is time for the "go" to start all over again.

The Strategic approach to youth ministry is merely an attempt to replicate that go or come strategy in a more holistic fashion. In addition to evangelism, the church-birthing ministry grows young people and the adult believers associated with them into a lasting faith community nourished by the other seven modes of God's coming that you developed so well, Malan.

Is there not a vulnerability to losing the missional vision in the Strategic approach? Absolutely! That is why the emerging leadership is key. Mission must remain a priority of the church-birthing pastor.

Training of pastors

But mission is not the only manner in which God comes to His people. The experience of the youth ministry genesis churches I cited and many more suggests a gifted youth minister turned senior pastor is the key to balanced effectiveness. After all, it was gifted people that Christ gave to the church (Ephesians 4:7-13), not committees, strategies, or boards. In none of the youth ministry genesis churches I have researched, however, does this mean a one-man show. Gifted leaders attract other gifted people. The eight-fold coming of God is experienced in the strength of a multitude of gifted Christian leaders.

What does this mean for the training of church-birthing pastors? Is there a set of ministry skills needed before assuming the role of pastor/leader in a new church? Are youth pastors equipped to lead churches? The answer is complex. Many youth pastors

> The Strategic approach is the best and highest form of stepping stones—especially for a person who is passionate and effective as a youth minister and thereby qualifies to continue serving as a midwife for a new church.

would make awful pastor/leaders. They are still novice adults, passionate about young people, but still experimenting with the responsibilities associated with the world in which they will live for the rest of their lives. No training, formal or informal, will transform these people into effective pastors.

Church-birthing pastors fit no set of leadership traits, except effectiveness in communication skills. They share no single approach to ministry training, except a deep desire to maintain integrity with God and his Word. Most are lifelong students (at least so far). Some have formal training, others do not. Leadership styles differ from the very outset of their ministries. Theological and biblical concerns tie church-birthing pastors firmly to the issues of the day, yet these issues drive church-birthing pastors back to the same Scriptures that sustained Augustine, Luther, Calvin, Wesley, Spurgeon, Barth, and the theologians of our day.

With all this discussion about where youth ministers could be in their late 30s, the idea of youth ministry seems to have disappeared. What will happen to contact work on the high school campus, small group Bible studies, worship songs, concerts, retreats, mission trips, and lock-ins? Most of these will go on just the way they did before, except now they will have both a long- and short-range objective. The youth minister must be effective in evangelizing and discipling young people or else there is little reason to think they could lead in giving birth to a church.

Stepping stone revisited

I know what you are saying, Wes—it is just a sophisticated way of bringing back the stepping stone philosophy of youth work. You commented that "it seems that this opens the door to those who are not truly motivated to minister to youths today, but rather have their eye on a future church." Two comments seem appropriate. In the first place, many youth ministers view youth ministry as a stepping stone to a larger, more influential youth ministry in another church. The net result is a revolving door of youth ministers. In my opinion, the Strategic approach would dismantle this status-driven motivation and refocus the energy on a more biblical ecclesiology.

My second comment has to do with the fact that a de facto stepping-stone philosophy already exists. Except, the stepping stone is *out of ministry*. Because there is no clear career path for youth ministers (except into larger churches or some administrative role in parachurch agencies, such as area director) or because growing families place increased financial demands on youth workers, many of the most gifted ministry people find it necessary to leave ministry, rather than burn themselves out.

I guess what I am saying, Wes, is that the Strategic approach is the best and highest form of stepping stones. I am not talking about the recent seminary graduate who cannot land a senior pastorate and so takes an associate pastor position where most of the responsibility rests with youths, until such time that a "real" pastoral position opens up. I am talking about the person who is passionate and effective as a youth minister and thereby qualifies to continue serving as a midwife for a new church.

One size fits all?

If I counted correctly, you raised 17 or 18 criticisms or questions about the Strategic approach. Most of these, to my surprise, were process questions focusing on how this rather novel idea might become a reality rather than on its theological viability. I tried to address these questions in my comments above. Still, situations will differ. The only way these questions can be answered is in the local situation. This simply cannot be a "one size fits all" proposal.

Conclusion

As I end my rejoinder, I would suggest the following questions, drawn in part from your responses and your chapters. These could serve as wonderful tools for the youth ministry to prevent serious flaws from being built into the church-birthing process.

- To what extent are the eight modes for God's coming to the church mentioned in Malan Nel's chapter (preaching, worship, teaching, pastoral care, mutuality, service, witness, and administration) active parts of the current youth ministry?
- In what ways is the current youth ministry effective in reaching disenfranchised people?
- To what extent is the current youth ministry a laboratory for becoming an effective expression of the faith community?
- In what ways is the youth pastor accountable to biblically defined elders while becoming a church-birthing pastor?
- To what extent does the mother church bless, support, and pray for the church-birthing concept for the youth ministry?
- Where will people come from who are gifted in leading all aspects of the daughter church? How will their giftedness be developed?

Thanks for all of your wonderful interactions as we examined the Strategic approach to youth ministry.

Epilogue
An Open Letter to the Church

Epilogue
An Open Letter to the Church

Dear church leaders in the 21st century,

May the grace of the Lord Jesus Christ, the love of God, and the fellowship of the Holy Spirit be with you all. As I view our churches at the beginning of the 21st century through the lens of youth ministry, I find much in which to rejoice, but more that brings heaviness to my heart.

Rejoicing in progress

The last two decades of the 20th century witnessed more effective ministry to youths than ever before in the history of the church. Many of our local churches have been directly or indirectly on the cutting edge. Evangelism and discipleship have replaced program committees and social activities as the primary youth ministry focus for many of our churches. Movements like Challenge 2000, National Network of Youth Ministries, and First Priority, when coupled with traditional parachurch youth ministries and local church-based outreach ministries, have made possible the establishment of witnessing Christian groups on or near every one of the 56,000 U.S. high schools and middle schools early in the new century.

Admittedly, we could be doing a better job of ministering to disenfranchised youths through our church-based efforts (but at least we aren't as self-absorbed as previous generations of youth work). Nor has discipleship translated effectively into the holiness of life or fellowship with the broader faith community sought by many youth ministers. But the progress that high school youths have made toward becoming kingdom people in their generation has been at least encouraging and in some places dramatic.

As church leaders, you must be commended for your role in enabling youth ministry to move from activity expectations to spiritually focused outcomes. You have chosen leaders gifted in discipleship and evangelism to head the high school and middle school ministries. You invested in their development as disciple-makers and defended them from tradition-bound critics. You joked with them when they failed to wear socks to worship services, coached them as they learned life-management skills, and prayed for them as they took ministry risks the rest of the congregation was not ready to assume.

Not all of our efforts are success stories. You know that as well as I. We've had our share of failed marriages, theological aberrations, personality conflicts, sexual abuse, and dysfunctional social systems. But by God's grace, these have been a small minority of the total youth ministry picture.

Our churches indirectly promoted youth ministry by supporting entrepreneurial, parachurch activities in our communities to build loving relationships with young people who have not yet discovered the amazing grace of God shown in Jesus Christ. Despite the horror stories of resistance by a few overly zealous or insecure church leaders, these missional efforts to youths, disassociated from our churches, have been carried on primarily by people from our churches, both lay and professional.

A veritable army of nonprofessional adult youth workers, over 25,000 strong in the United States, touched the lives of young people outside the church. Most of these are people from our churches who are finding a niche to do youth ministry that is consistent with their God-given passions. Add to this the thousands of high schoolers and middle schoolers from our churches who lead Bible studies and prayer groups on public school campuses, and the number of nonprofessional leaders may double.

Another chord sounded in youth ministry of the 1990s: worship and spiritual journey, perhaps more than anything else, began laying to rest the entertainment orientation of previous youth ministry generations. For some observers, the pendulum may have swung too far from cognitive approaches to more contemplative expressions of worship, yet the change is a breath of fresh air, influencing many of our churches in a positive manner. At the heart of the new expressions of worship, music seeks to discover the special presence of God in a gathering of Christian believers. Its repetitive pleas to know, feel, see, and hear God express in a new genre the classic pleas of contemplative theologians.

Heaviness because of the church

The heaviness that comes to my heart as I view the church through the lens of youth ministry reminds me of the title of David Elkind's book *All Grown Up and No Place to Go*. The faith community has not yet figured out what to do with young people. For the past several months Wes Black, Chap Clark, Malan Nel, and I have wrestled with the question, *How does God want youth ministry to relate to our churches in our postmodern world?* Each answered the question differently; yet as we did so, we discovered a shared concern. There is a distinct possibility that after youth ministry has made all the adjustments required by theologians and sociologists, church leaders and parents, pastors and youth ministry trainers, the church would remain a foreign, even unsafe place for young people to gather. *No place to go.* Perhaps Chap said it best as he concluded his rejoinder: "By the way, did any of you notice that we *all* agreed the church *must* change, but we all felt very little power to make it happen? That God would cause the church to have the heart of Jesus for those that he came to seek and save!"

It seems to me that adults in the West have come to understand the church to be an adult place where parents get a little help with their kids. Rather than a faith community, we have become a collection of individual adults governed by a lowest common denominator set of spiritual norms. It is quite possible that the church is no longer a "God place." Like other human institutions, our churches have focused more on status and social norms than on our collective progress toward the Celestial City.

Please don't misunderstand me. Young people and their leaders are not perfect. For years I have suffered under reports that youth ministry has fallen short of what it could be. Illustrations abound of the trivial youth activities that are sponsored and apparently blessed by the church. I've also wondered what lock-ins, "the world's largest" events, American gladiator competitions, or killer basketball games have to do with the Christian gospel. Some of my colleagues act as if they are more interested in recapturing a squandered adolescence than in building up the church of Jesus Christ. Some stories are even worse. For this I am deeply sorry.

Many of us at some point have bowed to the pressure to entertain kids. Some gifted personalities did so on the strength of charisma and communication skills. Others used their creativity and organizational ability to generate an environment to which young people responded. Many times any kind of Christian witness was buried so deeply in the fabric of what we did that it was virtually invisible. For this I am sorry.

While there are some sour apples among us, most youth ministers have a genuine love for young people and for God. As the support systems for young people fragment around them, we are often the last adult friend they have. A cacophony of voices call out to children and youths, but the forms of communication have become so distorted, even in the church, that we want to stand up and yell, "FIRE!" just to gain someone's attention. Then when no one seems to respond, we give up, gather in our own conventions and networks, and lick our wounds. For this retreat from you, I am sorry.

Mr. Holland's church

A potent scene from *Mr. Holland's Opus* might help you understand our dilemma. In this movie Glenn Holland teaches music at John F. Kennedy High School during the mid-1960s where he finds students apathetic toward the music curriculum. One day, in desperation, Mr. Holland scraps the curriculum and begins using rock and roll music to illustrate what classical music is all about. For the first time the students respond—and learn. Unfortunately, not everyone is as happy with the students' newfound interest in music. Gene Walters, the uptight vice principal, reports Mr. Holland's curricular departures to the principal, Helen Jacobs, and the music teacher is called on the carpet.

Mrs. Jacobs has a dilemma on her hands. Next week she must face the school board with the full realization that in the community there are people who are convinced that rock and roll is straight from the pit of hell. "What should I tell them?" asks the principal.

"Tell them," says the music teacher, "I am teaching music and I will use anything from Beethoven to Billy Holiday to rock and roll if I think it will help a student to love music."[1]

"That is a reasonable answer," says Mrs. Jacobs. "I can tell them that."

Youth ministry finds itself faced with a similar question, but in the pastor's office instead of the principal's.

"What should I tell the board and the parents about the methods you are using with the young people?"

For the vast majority of youth ministers, the answer rings with the spirit of Glenn Holland.

"Tell them I am teaching them to love God, and I will use anything from John Calvin to Jars of Clay to 'The Simpsons' if I think it will help a student to love God."

The decision rests with the pastor. Will he respond fearfully and narrowly like VP Gene Walters, or with the visionary kindness of Helen Jacobs? The very nature of the local church lies with the leadership of the pastor. Though the board may have the right to fire the pastor and youth pastor for methods deemed inappropriate, the chances are quite good that godly leadership will create a community of faith that will take the necessary risks to become people of faith.

Church as apologetic

The Christian apologetic for young people and adults of the 21st century may be the church itself. While apologetic arguments remain appropriate in many situations, the emerging generation needs a more holistic apologetic. Narratives (individually and collectively), explanations of a Christian worldview, expressions of that worldview seen in real life (such as prayer), symbolism and ritual, and moral behavior combine to provide a compelling apologetic to postmodern youths.[2] Postmoderns need to see a group of people living in a fashion prescribed by our Lord. The church must live as the church. The community of faith must exemplify integrity.

If the church is the apologetic of the 21st century, what church are we talking about? Is it your church or ours? Old or young? Anthems or worship choruses? Theology or practice? Exposition or need responsive? Liturgy or freedom of the Spirit? Evangelism or edification? Rich or poor?

To ask these questions in this manner is to do a disservice to the church. The church should never be divided into such simplistic categories. The answer to each of the questions above should be "yes." If the church is to be a witness before a watching world, it must be your church and ours, old and young, anthems and choruses, theology and practice, exposition and need responsive, liturgy and freedom of the Spirit, evangelism and edification, rich and poor.

Weaknesses in the church

So what changes does the church have to make if youth ministry is to be fully integrated into the life of the faith community? Before suggesting changes, I would remind you of some weaknesses in local church ministry that might justify the suggestions that follow. Some may be unique to the church of the 20th and 21st centuries. Others appeared in biblical times.

The most evident deficiency in the nurture of children and youths is the dropout rate that compounds as youths move from grade school to middle school, then to high school, and finally on to college or the workplace. At the heart of the problem may be the sinful nature and the fragmenting structure of families, but the faith community must recognize its contribution to the problem. Current structures, which make continuity of spiritually mentoring relationships impossible, are totally out of step with the biblical ideals of discipleship through the extended Christian family—the church.

Adults have disregarded and resisted the spiritual leadership of children since the days of Samuel, David, the servant girl of Naaman's wife, Daniel and his friends, Jesus' mother Mary, Phillip's unmarried daughters, and even the children metaphor in Matthew 18. Yet today, in most churches, the situation is much more pronounced. If the servant girl in the house of Mary (John Mark's mother) rushed into our prayer meeting proclaiming answered prayer, as she did following the release of Peter from prison, no doubt we would conclude she was out of her mind, as did the prayer warriors of Acts 12.

Why is it that so many of the spiritual revivals and evangelistic movements begin with young people, yet the church finds so few places for them to exercise their giftedness and leadership in local assemblies of believers? This is by no means a call for young people to be the only ones overseeing the affairs of the church, nor a call for young people who are not above reproach in their lifestyles to shepherd the flock of God. It is a call for superficial age restrictions to be removed from opportunities for spiritual leadership.

What about evangelism and works of service in the broader community? Who are the people most actively emulating our Lord in this fashion? In most churches the answer is young people, coached by a handful of young adults. While adults have done a wonderful job of meeting the needs of people already associated with the church, younger people are far more likely to be the ones who venture outside the congregation and declare their faith before their peers. While middle and high school youths pray for their campuses (three million strong gather annually around the flag poles on their campuses), where is the parallel movement for adult Christians in the market place? Why is there no See You at the Copier campaign?

Changes in forms of worship, especially music, often come from young people and those in tune with them and are later embraced by local churches. In *Growing Up Evangelical*, Pete Ward describes the pattern in England in the chapter "Songs for each Generation."[3] The music of Youth for Christ, the Jesus Movement captured and promoted by Maranatha Music, Jesus marches and Christian festivals in England, and more recently Vineyard style worship music have their strongest supporters among young people and their greatest resistance among the church choir and Christian college conservatory crowd. By no means do I want to see worship music of one generation summarily discarded because of new tastes and styles, but I do call for a more active blending and expansion of worship styles.

Suggested changes for the church

Every worship service must be shaped for and with young people. Yet this must not exclude the other generations in the congregation. The pastor must find ways to address the spiritual needs of youths as well as adults in each message. Music should aid the spiritual journey of young people as well as their grandparents. Young people need to realize that older people may not find protracted periods of standing to sing very worshipful, while older believers will have to yield on hymnology that employs metaphors reflecting an agrarian society. Appropriate expressions of art, drama, media, and dance will take their place beside the pipe organ and anthem.

Every new person—young or old—must be bonded to people of their age group and two other generations. In many of our congregations, new attenders are fortunate to be bonded to anyone in the church. Basis assimilation has to be a starting place, but it cannot be the final goal. While young people who have started on their faith journey through a parachurch ministry must be welcomed with open arms by the youths of the church, an equally great need for these new believers is to observe models of Christian living in older and perhaps younger people. Many will have no idea what faith means to people of their parents' age or what it means to live as a Christian parent. The church must alter its social structures (including that safe haven called youth ministry) in order to link the journeys of Christians of all ages.

Every Christian witness effort must rely upon the evangelistic giftedness in young people. The involvement must be from beginning to end. It is not a matter of setting up a witnessing program for youths and then calling upon them to participate. Relying upon gifted young people means learning from them about how evangelism might be done. For me this is very uncomfortable because I have used so many bad methods of evangelization that I prefer not to see repeated. Ironically, the uninhibited boldness of some young people may be the exact prescription the church needs for evangelism in the community. By no means does this mean that people of other ages are exempt from evangelistic efforts. In fact the leadership of youths may be the greatest catalysts for evangelism of all ages that the church has ever had.

Every service opportunity must be equally available to young people. When middle schoolers ask if they can teach Sunday school rather than go to the morning worship service, the answer will be "Of course!" When a young person demonstrates spiritual maturity, they should be given the same consideration for leadership offices as persons three times their age. In fact, the presence of a young person on a board may cause other board members to give additional attention to their conduct during discussions. At the same time, a youthful conscience contributing to the decision-making process might be extremely valuable to the church. Mature leadership must not be sacrificed for the sake of including youths in leadership positions, so the church may need to find new ways of establishing a succession of godly leaders in the church.

Every refinement in ministry vision must draw upon the insights of youths. If the church of tomorrow is to become the church of today, the vision for what we are all about must be forged and maintained together. The church is not yours or mine, it is ours—or more correctly, the Lord's—with all of us as the beneficiaries. Vision building can be very boring work for young people, so our responsibility is to make the process unboring. The fact that young people find the slow-moving process of envisioning future ministry directions dreary is our problem, not theirs. If they do not participate, the church loses more than the young person. Though young people live in our houses and in our neighborhoods, we may not live in the same communities. Vision is only effective if it is adequate.

Every resource for spiritual growth must be accessible to youths. Biblical teaching, models of the spiritual disciplines, intentional mentoring, materials designed for a variety of learning styles, training in spiritual disciplines and ministry skills, accountability groups, coaching, and even corrective counseling must be available to people of all ages—especially youths. As leadership gifts and spiritual maturity become apparent, special funding for seminars or educational programs may be appropriate. Our pattern has been to provide "separate but equal" spiritual-growth resources, split along developmental lines. As pointed out in the earlier chapters, this may be wise. But if the developmental breakouts inhibit intergenerational nurturing, then changes must be made.

Spiritual readiness

The idea of making young people full participants in your churches may be a bit unsettling. It should be. It represents change.

In the introduction to this book, I defined spiritual readiness as *passion for God*. As a leader of your church, you have the responsibility to evaluate all of these ideas in light of the chief end of man—to glorify God and fully enjoy him forever. Two perspectives are necessary. To what extent will these functions of the church contribute to a passion for God within the congregation as a whole? And to what extent is a passion for God preparing the congregation to function in this manner? The two questions are inseparable.

My fear is that the young people in many of our churches may be more passionate for God than their parents were at that same age or currently. I may be wrong. I hope I am. But if I am correct, the heaviest burden for bringing about a passion for God in the congregation lies not with the youth ministry, but with the adults of the church. If properly shepherded in an environment of full participation by you and the youth ministry leaders (paid or volunteer), young people may be your greatest ally in discovering a passion for God throughout the congregation. Most young people have survived their early doubts and find comfort in God's grace. They still take the scripture at face value. They are not surprised when prayer is answered.

To not include young people as full participants in every aspect of church life may be far more detrimental to the spiritual welfare of the entire congregation than it is to the young people themselves. They have been raised in a generation where lowering their expectations of others has become the norm. I, and many like me, still hope the church will be different—set apart, and inclusive.

What becomes of the four approaches?

The four approaches described in this book came about not because the church was healthy, but because it had failed to live up to its own mandate. If the church begins to experience wholeness and a biblical inclusiveness, will the four approaches remain valid? I suspect so. In fact because of a variety of emphases in the purposes of local churches, I feel that each of the approaches may find its niche better supported and more effectively accomplished than ever before. Each approach will be effectively integrated with the vision of the entire church. Until then, the four approaches will serve as a vehicle for assisting young people to live as Christians in a non-Christian world.

Notes

1. "Mr. Holland's Opus" (Hollywood Pictures, 1995).

2. Dennis Hollinger, "The Church as Apologetic," *Christian Apologetics in the Postmodern World* (Downers Grove, Illinois: InterVarsity Press, 1995), 188-191.

3. Pete Ward, *Growing Up Evangelical* (1996), 107-142.

Index

Resources from Youth Specialties

Youth Ministry Programming

Camps, Retreats, Missions, & Service Ideas
(Ideas Library)

Compassionate Kids: Practical Ways to Involve Your
Students in Mission and Service

Creative Bible Lessons from the Old Testament

Creative Bible Lessons in 1 & 2 Corinthians

Creative Bible Lessons in John: Encounters with Jesus

Creative Bible Lessons in Romans: Faith on Fire!

Creative Bible Lessons on the Life of Christ

Creative Bible Lessons in Psalms

Creative Junior High Programs from A to Z,
Vol. 1 (A-M)

Creative Junior High Programs from A to Z,
Vol. 2 (N-Z)

Creative Meetings, Bible Lessons, & Worship Ideas
(Ideas Library)

Crowd Breakers & Mixers (Ideas Library)

Downloading the Bible Leader's Guide

Drama, Skits, & Sketches (Ideas Library)

Drama, Skits, & Sketches 2 (Ideas Library)

Dramatic Pauses

Everyday Object Lessons

Games (Ideas Library)

Games 2 (Ideas Library)

Good Sex: A Whole-Person Approach to Teenage
Sexuality & God

Great Fundraising Ideas for Youth Groups

More Great Fundraising Ideas for Youth Groups

Great Retreats for Youth Groups

Holiday Ideas (Ideas Library)

Hot Illustrations for Youth Talks

More Hot Illustrations for Youth Talks

Still More Hot Illustrations for Youth Talks

Ideas Library on CD-ROM

Incredible Questionnaires for Youth Ministry

Junior High Game Nights

More Junior High Game Nights

Kickstarters: 101 Ingenious Intros to Just about Any
Bible Lesson

Live the Life! Student Evangelism Training Kit

Memory Makers

The Next Level Leader's Guide

Play It! Over 150 Great Games for Youth Groups

Roaring Lambs

So What Am I Gonna Do with My Life? Leader's Guide

Special Events (Ideas Library)

Spontaneous Melodramas

Spontaneous Melodramas 2

Student Leadership Training Manual

Student Underground: An Event Curriculum on the
Persecuted Church

Super Sketches for Youth Ministry

Talking the Walk

Videos That Teach

What Would Jesus Do? Youth Leader's Kit

Wild Truth Bible Lessons

Wild Truth Bible Lessons 2

Wild Truth Bible Lessons—Pictures of God

Wild Truth Bible Lessons—Pictures of God 2

Worship Services for Youth Groups

Professional Resources

Administration, Publicity, & Fundraising (Ideas Library)

Dynamic Communicators Workshop for Youth Workers

Equipped to Serve: Volunteer Youth Worker
Training Course

Help! I'm a Junior High Youth Worker!

Help! I'm a Small-Group Leader!

Help! I'm a Sunday School Teacher!

Help! I'm a Volunteer Youth Worker!

How to Expand Your Youth Ministry

How to Speak to Youth...and Keep Them Awake at the
Same Time

Junior High Ministry (Updated & Expanded)

The Ministry of Nurture: A Youth Worker's Guide to
Discipling Teenagers

Purpose-Driven Youth Ministry

Purpose-Driven Youth Ministry Training Kit

So That's Why I Keep Doing This! 52 Devotional Stories
for Youth Workers

Teaching the Bible Creatively

A Youth Ministry Crash Course

Youth Ministry Management Tools

The Youth Worker's Handbook to Family Ministry

Academic Resources

Four Views of Youth Ministry and the Church

Starting Right: Thinking Theologically about
Youth Ministry

Discussion Starters

Discussion & Lesson Starters (Ideas Library)

Discussion & Lesson Starters 2 (Ideas Library)

EdgeTV

Get 'Em Talking

Keep 'Em Talking!

Good Sex: A Whole-Person Approach to Teenage Sexuality & God

High School TalkSheets

More High School TalkSheets

High School TalkSheets from Psalms and Proverbs

Junior High TalkSheets

More Junior High TalkSheets

Junior High TalkSheets from Psalms and Proverbs

Real Kids: Short Cuts

Real Kids: The Real Deal—on Friendship, Loneliness, Racism, & Suicide

Real Kids: The Real Deal—on Sexual Choices, Family Matters, & Loss

Real Kids: The Real Deal—on Stressing Out, Addictive Behavior, Great Comebacks, & Violence

Real Kids: Word on the Street

Unfinished Sentences: 450 Tantalizing Statement Starters to Get Teenagers Talking & Thinking

What If...? 450 Thought-Provoking Questions to Get Teenagers Talking, Laughing, and Thinking

Would You Rather...? 465 Provocative Questions to Get Teenagers Talking

Have You Ever...? 450 Intriguing Questions Guaranteed to Get Teenagers Talking

Art Source Clip Art

Stark Raving Clip Art (print)

Youth Group Activities (print)

Clip Art Library Version 2.0 (CD-ROM)

Digital Resources

Clip Art Library Version 2.0 (CD-ROM)

Ideas Library on CD-ROM

Youth Ministry Management Tools (CD-ROM)

Videos & Video Curricula

Dynamic Communicators Workshop for Youth Workers

EdgeTV

Equipped to Serve: Volunteer Youth Worker Training Course

Good Sex: A Whole Person Approach to Teenage Sexuality and God

The Heart of Youth Ministry: A Morning with Mike Yaconelli

Live the Life! Student Evangelism Training Kit

Purpose-Driven Youth Ministry Training Kit

Real Kids: Short Cuts

Real Kids: The Real Deal—on Friendship, Loneliness, Racism, & Suicide

Real Kids: The Real Deal—on Sexual Choices, Family Matters, & Loss

Real Kids: The Real Deal—on Stressing Out, Addictive Behavior, Great Comebacks, & Violence

Real Kids: Word on the Street

Student Underground: An Event Curriculum on the Persecuted Church

Understanding Your Teenager Video Curriculum

Student Resources

Downloading the Bible: A Rough Guide to the New Testament

Downloading the Bible: A Rough Guide to the Old Testament

Grow For It Journal

Grow For It Journal through the Scriptures

So What Am I Gonna Do with My Life? Journaling Workbook for Students

Spiritual Challenge Journal: The Next Level

Teen Devotional Bible

What (Almost) Nobody Will Tell You about Sex

What Would Jesus Do? Spiritual Challenge Journal

Wild Truth Journal for Junior Highers

Wild Truth Journal—Pictures of God